SHIFTING GEARS

SHIFTING
GEARS

*Planning a New
Strategy for Midlife*

ANDREA GROSS

Crown Publishers, Inc.
New York

Published by Crown Publishers, Inc., 201 East 50th Street, New York, New York 10022. Member of the Crown Publishing Group.

CROWN is a trademark of Crown Publishers, Inc.

Manufactured in the United States of America

Library of Congress Cataloging-in-Publication Data

Gross, Andrea.
    Shifting gears : planning a new strategy for midlife / Andrea
Gross.
        p.   cm.
    1. Middle age—United States.   2. Retirement—United States—
Planning.   3. Life style—United States—Case studies.   4. Quality
of life—United States.   I. Title.
HQ1059.5.U5G76   1992
305.24′4—dc20   91-24049
                                                            CIP

ISBN 0-517-57768-2

10 9 8 7 6 5 4 3 2 1

First Edition

To Irv

CONTENTS

Exercises: My-Time Goal • Are You Sure? • All in a
Night's Sleep • Tomorrow's Résumé • Mind-
Mapping • A Master Plan • Integration

Resources

ACKNOWLEDGMENTS

My thanks . . .

To Susan Pollock, whose enthusiasm for the idea of shifting gears bolstered me from the very beginning; to Bob Shomer, who forced me to crystalize my thinking; and to Sandy Martin, who encouraged me when I needed it most.

To the people profiled in this book, who answered questions that must have occasionally seemed intrusive if not downright rude, and who revealed details of their dreams as well as their bank accounts.

To the many restylers who, although not included in these pages, helped me understand more about lifestyle changes.

To John Tucker, Vice President of Merrill Lynch, Pierce, Fenner & Smith, Inc., whose help on the financial aspects of shifting gears was invaluable.

To the scores of other experts who willingly gave of their time and knowledge.

To members of my writing group who reviewed numerous drafts and listened to countless wails: Marge Best, Henci Goer, Chris Gove, Carol Maibach, Theodora Nelson, and Ruth Priest.

To my parents, Pearl and Jerry Gross, who, as always, knew when to encourage, when to suggest, and when to critique.

To my agent, Jane Dystel, who believed in the concept of restyling from the start; and to my editor, Erica Marcus, who tactfully pointed out my blind spots and helped illuminate them.

To the numerous friends who went out of their way to find subjects for me to profile: Gene Ulansky, Sandra Cortright, Roselle Pizer, Shirley Desser, Jane Levy, Cheryl Cooper, Mirielle Grovier, Matthew Gibson, Diana Bennett, Barry Johnson, Danielle Freeman, Bob Gross, and Laurel Bolin.

Finally, to my sons: Michael, who supplied me with an eclectic stockpile of articles, quotes, and ideas; Peter, who served as my on-call computer consultant; and Douglas, who designed the graphs and charts.

To my daughter, Lindy, who politely hid her boredom as her parents let this book dominate dinner-table conversations.

And most of all to my husband, Irv Green, who in so very many ways coauthored this book.

SHIFTING GEARS

There is no reason why the same man should like the same book at eighteen and at forty-eight.

EZRA POUND

INTRODUCTION

I was nine when Uncle Harry quit his job. The whole family whispered about him behind his back. "But he's only forty-seven. How can he do this?" "What about his family?" "What will he do?"

What Uncle Harry did was begin making wooden toys. "Ever so much more pleasant than selling insurance," he said. Trucks, airplanes, doll cribs; they were stacked everywhere in his small workshop in the garage. Once a month he visited some of the stores in town and left items on consignment, and as word got around people began coming to his house to buy toys for their children and grandchildren. Every December he dressed up like Santa Claus and took a big bag of gifts to the kids in the hospital. I thought he was absolutely wonderful.

As for his wife and children, they thought he was wonderful, too. My aunt moaned about having him home all the time, but you could tell she was delighted. After about six months she started helping him out, mostly by painting the toddler toys in bright primary colors. When Uncle Harry died five years after becoming a toy maker, his son Hap confided that "at least Dad had a few years to do what he always wanted to do." Six years ago Hap, then forty-nine, quit his job, too. Last time I heard from him he and his wife were in Turkey living on about $600 a month.

Over the years I kept noticing other stories about people who

1

made radical midlife changes in their workaday world. Were they all, I wondered, as happy as Uncle Harry had been? Why did they decide to make such a drastic move? Weren't they afraid? Didn't they know that only rich people can afford to take such risks? And finally, how did they go about doing what most people only talk about?

On my husband's fiftieth birthday, I vowed to find out. We might want to follow their examples, and if so we'd better get started. After all, the majority of working Americans leave their career jobs before the traditional retirement age of sixty-five. If we wanted to "retire early," we didn't have much time.

I started my research, as I always do, by reading everything I could find about the subject. There wasn't much. To begin with, no one even knows what to call these people. Yes, they retire from one career, but not all of them stay retired. While some pursue their hobbies full-time and never make another cent, many become involved in all-encompassing work that can only be called a second career. And others, like Uncle Harry, engage themselves with part-time work that, whether accidentally or otherwise, brings in a bit of income.

What was the common thread? The people I admired, I realized, were those who made an adventure rather than a crisis out of middle age. They left the security of a longtime profession to strike out on a different path and, whether or not they continued to produce income, they were doing what they wanted to do. They were living their dreams. I decided to call these people *restylers*.

Along with my husband, Irv Green, I resolved to interview some restylers. First though, we had to settle on some parameters. We agreed to interview only those people who met four criteria:

- They were well established in a primary career at the time they made their change. Their jobs were secure and had earned them the respect of their colleagues.
- The change was voluntary. They did not have to leave their primary careers because of layoffs or illness. They had not yet reached a point of complete burn-out. They didn't run *from* their jobs as much as they moved *to* something else.

- The change was planned. These people were prepared, both financially and psychologically, for their transformation. They acted out of conviction, not whim.
- They were middle-aged, roughly between forty and fifty-five years old, at the time they made their change.

During the following year, Irv and I spoke with restylers from all over the country. What did we learn from these interviews? First of all, we found that restylers are, except for the single act of restyling, just ordinary people. Until they made their midlife change, they led very traditional lives—waking up in the morning and going to work, coming home at night and playing with their kids. "I don't think I did an unusual thing in my life before I quit my job," says Rich Henke, formerly employed by a large aerospace company, now a full-time mountain climber and amateur photographer.

We interviewed restylers of both sexes and most marital situations. Many were still married to their first spouse; some were enjoying second marriages; others had divorced and not remarried; one had never married. We found that the pleasures and problems of restyling are much the same whether the person is male or female, married or single.

In about half of the cases where the restylers were married, both spouses left equally thriving careers in order to work together on something new. In three cases that are profiled in this book the wives moved from supporting roles at home to equal roles in restyling, and in two instances the wives encouraged their husbands' lifestyle changes but chose to remain on their own career paths. We did not meet any women who restyled while their husbands remained in longtime positions; but as labor patterns change for both sexes, this may become more prevalent.

The restylers we met are financially comfortable but not overwhelmingly wealthy. Ken and Shelley Cassie were both schoolteachers earning combined salaries of about $80,000 a year when they restyled to produce and sell pottery at East Coast craft fairs. Kinney Thiele was a research analyst making about $26,000 annually when she left for two years to be a Peace Corps worker in Sierra Leone. And although Gene Estess was making a healthy six-figure salary as a Wall Street broker, he hadn't finished paying college tuition for his eight children when he restyled to become the director of a New York City project for the homeless.

None of the people we spoke with had abandoned their responsibilities in order to change lifestyles. They hadn't neglected their children; they hadn't ignored their parents who, in some cases, were beginning to need care themselves. They merely factored these obligations into their plans. Fran and Dick Easton, for example, don't travel overseas as much as they would like to because Dick wants to be on call for his aged father in Kansas. Tom Christensen postponed his new venture for a few years until he had enough money to provide security for his wife and daughter even if his new undertaking proves to be financially unrewarding. And David and Laura Rausch interrupted their sailing adventure when it became clear that their son, Michael, needed to complete his high school education in a stateside school. Says Laura, "Traveling with Michael was wonderful, but it was time for a pause. As soon as he graduates and is on his own, David and I will go off again with the winds!"

Finally, not one of the restylers regrets his or her decision. Despite interruptions, despite setbacks, they are pleased with their new lifestyles. Even when problems crop up, they remain convinced that change is its own reward; and with the confidence engendered by their first move, they simply adjust their plans a bit and go on. "Security is a relative perception," says David Thimgan, an architect turned ice cream store owner.

Meeting these people was both a treat and a revelation. A treat because they are, for the most part, relaxed and at peace with themselves, a real pleasure to be with. A revelation because they were, until they restyled, so much like us. They were people we could relate to because of their very ordinariness.

Yet, we still had doubts. Could we *really* do what these people had done? Could we actually prepare in advance for a midlife workaday change: decide what we wanted to do with our middle years, adapt these plans to fit our reality, map out a strategy, and then put the plan into action? Could we control our lives instead of letting events control us? In short, could we restyle, too?

We went to career counselors, psychologists, and financial consultants for advice. We told them about the people we'd met, and they helped us to see the commonalities in the different tales. Then together we devised an organized program for successful restyling, one that codifies what many of the restylers did instinctively.

Hence, this book. In it you'll find stories of the restylers we interviewed as well as the step-by-step advice we gathered from professionals. At the end of each chapter are exercises that will help you to explore your own feelings about your workaday activities and to formulate your own plans. And, if you want to investigate a specific topic further, there's a list of resources to point you on your way.

While the book is organized in a "how-to" fashion, the life stories of the restylers cross all boundaries. The Eastons, for example, are discussed at length in the chapter on "A Sense of Self." Yet they also have valuable things to say about money matters and an awareness of mortality. Kinney Thiele is profiled in the chapter entitled "Discovering Your Dreams," but she also speaks eloquently on the difficulties of restyling for single women.

For this reason I've included at the back of the book a list, Who Did What, that categorizes the restylers in a variety of ways. It shows, among other things, that Tom Christensen, Marian Gibson, Megan and Bob Harris, Rich Henke, Laura and David Rausch, and Melanie Thimgan all made radical changes while they still had responsibility for minor children. It indicates that Carolyn and Bruce Bade, Terrence Grace, Megan and Bob Harris, Carlene and Jim Pasin, Laura and David Rausch, and Melanie and David Thimgan all moved to new locations; and it reveals that seven restylers have valuable comments on the transferability of skills. After you read the book, this chart will help you refer back to those restylers who speak most directly to your own interests.

As Irv and I spoke with the men and women who shared their lives with us, we found that we reacted differently to their stories. In hundreds of little ways our own personalities came into play, and we found ourselves listening more closely to restylers who had interests similar to our own or who in some way seemed like us. Irv, for example, found that Rich Henke's systematic approach to finances meshed well with his own orderly nature; and he gained confidence from Dave and Melanie Thimgan, who consider their adventure a grand success despite some unpleasant surprises. On the other hand, I found myself drawn to the stories of Kinney Thiele and Laura and David Rausch; their tales of wanderlust struck a responsive chord.

During the year and a half that it took me to write this book, Irv and I had continual discussions; and gradually—very gradually—we began to draft our own plans. We agreed that we have a few years to go before we can significantly change our workaday ways, but that's okay. We'll still be in our early fifties. Meanwhile, the process of restyling has prompted us to re-examine our present, imagine a variety of futures, and discover ways to, as an anonymous wag once said, "hitch our wagon to a star while keeping our feet on the ground."

As you progress through this book and meet the restylers, who tell their own stories in their own words, I hope you too will find people with whom you can identify. In this way, you'll have roadmaps from the experts but, much more important, you'll gain confidence from people who have already traveled the road before you.

Helen Keller once said, "Security is mostly a superstition. It does not exist in nature, nor do the children of men as a whole experience it. Avoiding danger is no safer in the long run than outright exposure. Life is either a daring adventure or nothing."

It is my hope that reading *Shifting Gears* will help you plan your own daring adventure, one that will make your midlife sparkle with satisfaction and gleam with zest.

We cannot live the afternoon of life according to the programme of life's morning—for what was great in the morning will be little at evening, and what in the morning was true will at evening have become a lie.

CARL JUNG

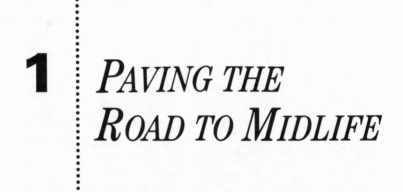

1   *PAVING THE ROAD TO MIDLIFE*

No matter how much we like our jobs, most of us want to quit them . . . someday. We want time for ourselves, to do what *we* want to do. Hang the bosses! Hang the insurance payments, the benefits, the stifling security! A few years of freedom while we're still young enough to enjoy it—it's the American dream!

> *ITEM* A television reporter approaches a group of young adults outside a Wall Street health club. "Would you continue working if you suddenly got rich and didn't need the money?" he asks. Nearly all vote for quitting.

But at the same time, most of us are afraid to leave our jobs. It's not only a matter of money, though that's a considerable worry; it's also a matter of identity. Who are we if we're not our professional selves? If we retire, won't we cease to be?

7

ITEM Talk show host Larry King is interviewing former First Lady Nancy Reagan about her post–White House years. He takes a call from a listener. "Would you return to the movies?" asks the caller. Nancy hesitates for a moment, and King seems worried. "Why not?" he says anxiously. "You're still living. You're not *retired*, are you?" His voice reflects a common fear: If we retire, won't we cease to be?

The problem, quite succinctly, is how do we shift gears without stalling the motor? Can it be done? Of course it can. The people you'll meet in this book all stopped doing what they were *expected* to do and began doing what they *wanted* to do. They left jobs that had dominated their young adult years and found new paths that were more in keeping with the opportunities and realities of midlife.

They took risks, yes, but they took only carefully calculated risks. Their actions were always the result of careful planning and deliberate forethought. In short, they restyled their lives. As a result, their midlife years are full of new experiences and new challenges along with greater freedom and greater flexibility. And they've never been happier.

What's Midlife All About?

One thing's for sure: midlife isn't what it used to be. To begin with, it lasts a long time. People used to simply grow up, reproduce themselves and raise their young, and die. But now we have time to do a lot more. That's both the pleasure and the problem.

Statistics tell us we are living longer than ever before. The U.S. Census Bureau reports that since the turn of the century Americans have added twenty-six years to their average life expectancy, and we add more every year. A man born in 1945 can expect to reach age seventy-five; a woman has an additional two or more years. What's more, life expectancy increases with age. Those of us who make it to sixty-five are likely to live on to nearly eighty.

And for most of these years we'll probably enjoy reasonably good health. When Erdman Palmore, a Duke University gerontologist, looked at the health of Americans over sixty-five, he found that fewer seniors, proportionate to the population, were infirm in 1980 than in 1970, and fewer in 1970 than in 1960. Never before in history have so many of us been alive and well for so long.

Sound reassuring? Of course it does—except most of us don't believe it. Not for a minute! We look in the mirror and panic. Despite a dietary regimen of whole grains and alfalfa sprouts and a rigorous exercise program of aerobics and isometrics, we're aging and we know it.

ITEM For Lindy McFarling* middle age sneaked up with all the subtlety of a masked monster with a sledge hammer. It was on a Tuesday morning. She was working at her customary job as a library researcher when she realized she could no longer see the small print at the bottom of the page. Panicked, she pleaded with the optometrist to see her that afternoon. He examined her briefly and smiled—sadly, she thought. "You're growing up," he said gently. And thus, Lindy became a member of the Bifocal Generation. She was forty years old. According to the U.S. National Center for Health Statistics, she was right at the midpoint of her life. I've reached the peak, she remembers thinking; from now on, it's downhill.

Psychologists call this realization an "awareness of mortality." At twenty-one people see death, if they see it at all, as something that happens to someone else. By middle age most people realize that, although the odds say they're likely to live on for quite a while, someday they actually could—they really will—die!

ITEM For Bob Harris, the death of a colleague was a mind-shattering event. "I attended my own funeral when I was forty-two," he says. "It was actually the funeral of a much older architect, one I'd known since I was a kid. He was one of the best architects in the state of Texas; he'd designed the church in which we were standing. I closed my eyes and suddenly it

---

*Name and other identifying characteristics have been changed to protect the individual's privacy.

was me in that casket—lying in a building that had seen better days, surrounded by colleagues who wished they were elsewhere. Is this all there is? I thought. Is this what all this effort is for?"

Hank Walfesh, president of Retirement Advisors, a New York–based counseling firm, calls this "the Peggy Lee syndrome." He explains: "People . . . are affected by the Peggy Lee syndrome that asks, 'Hey, is that all there is?' Many of them wake up one day and realize that they're tired of the daily work grind and of the three-hour commute from Connecticut."

That's exactly what happened to Bob and his wife, Megan. The voice of middle age began playing on the turntables of their minds, and they decided to change the record. With their two youngest sons in tow, they traveled around Europe, finally settling for a while in Greece, where they lived in a small hut and danced with the local Zorbas.

As middle age approaches, most of us feel the tug of opposing beliefs. While statistics tell us to prepare for a long, healthy old age, secretly we're sure we're going to die tomorrow—or at least slide into physical or mental incompetence. We sense an urgency, a desire to enjoy ourselves *now*, while we can. For a good many of us, that means we want to quit our jobs. But, heaven forbid, we don't want to *retire*.

What It Means to Retire

Retirement is one of those words that has two opposite meanings. On the one hand, like Larry King, we associate retirement with death. Retirement means "to withdraw," says the dictionary. "It means to become worn out, to grow obsolete," says an elderly man who is fighting it with every bit of energy at his disposal. For a few people, retirement is virtually a fast slide into the grave. (The statistics that indicate recent retirees have extraordinarily high rates of death and suicide are misleading. According to Jacqueline Kelley, board member of the International Society of Retirement Planning, "Many people retire because they are in ill health, and that affects these figures.")

ITEM When George Eastman, age seventy, was forced to retire from the presidency of Eastman Kodak in 1925, he was miserable. For seven years he haunted the corporate offices; then he committed suicide. The note he left behind stands as a testament to the life-giving power of work. "To my friends," he wrote. "My work is done, why wait?"

We read about retirees who, unhappy with their new life, return to work. Some, it's true, become consultants to younger members of their professions. Consulting brings an abundance of prestige and independence, but for most of us it is not a realistic goal. According to the Conference Board, an independent business research firm, the majority of retired folks who appear in the statistical charts as "returned to work" are employed in the retail, fast-food, and hospitality industries. For those of us who don't want to spend our golden years beneath the golden arches, that's a depressing thought.

Still, in our ambivalent way most of us, while fearing retirement, also think of it as liberation. Even though the mandatory retirement age went from sixty-five to seventy in 1979, the average age of retirement in the United States keeps spiraling downward. Twenty years ago 83 percent of men aged fifty-five to sixty-four were still working; today only 68 percent are. And of those people between the ages of forty-five and fifty-five, nearly 100,000 say they're retired. "Most people still seem to want to retire early," says Carolyn E. Paul, director of the Business Institute on Aging at the University of Southern California's Andrus Center.

So what, exactly, is going on? Is there a way to be liberated from work and yet avoid the agonies of retirement? The people profiled in this book have found a way. By leaving their primary careers at an early age, they had the energy and vitality to start something new. They've found lifestyles that will give them freedom while they can still enjoy it and provide meaning to their lives when they are beyond the traditional retirement age.

"Mainly, [when you retire early] you have better health and more energy than you would at a later age," says Ann Smith, president of Smith Goodwin Associates, a New Jersey consulting firm that runs retirement seminars. Simply put, a new route in midlife is different from the traditional path that dead-ends in an age sixty-five retirement.

The Four Quarters of Life

Perhaps it's time to rethink the life cycle, dividing it not into three stages (childhood, adulthood, old age) as we used to, but rather into four. Nowadays a combination of longer life and changing values invites the insertion of a second-phase adult-hood, one during which midlifers can relax from the pressures of the younger years. When people are in their twenties and thirties, they are busy establishing careers, beginning families, and buying homes. Later they have time to pursue the dreams they were forced to defer.

"I rather like the suggestion that we think of life in four parts instead of three," says Dr. Wilma Donahue, dean emeri-tus of the School of Gerontology, University of Michigan, Ann Arbor. "The third quarter of life should be a time of choice. Some people might want to continue with their regular career, but others might rethink what they're doing and take on a new role. To me that's an exciting idea."

It's an idea that originally was put forth by Alan Pifer, presi-dent emeritus of the Carnegie Corporation of New York and former chairman of the Carnegie Corporation Project on the Aging Society. Although Pifer was concerned with the societal rather than individual aspects of aging, his "third-quarter con-cept" recognizes the need for midlife change. "Since," he says, "the majority of Americans at age fifty today still have a third to a half of their life spans ahead of them, [the concept assumes that] these years should constitute a period of rebirth, with the awakening of new interests and enthusiasm for life."

Ken and Shelley Cassie couldn't agree more.

• •

Profile: Ken and Shelley Cassie—Teachers to Artisans

People don't choose their careers: they are engulfed by them.
                                                            JOHN DOS PASSOS

Ken and Shelley Cassie resigned their high school teaching positions in June 1988. He was fifty-one and had been teaching Russian language and culture for twenty-six years; she was fifty-two and had been unlocking the mysteries of English literature and grammar for twenty-eight years. Now Ken is a potter and Shelley a businesswoman. Working together, they sell Ken's pottery at craft fairs up and down the East Coast. Although they're making much less money than they did before, they have more control over their time and commitments. The Cassies have one daughter, Elise, who was twenty-five when her parents made their move.

"You won't have any trouble finding our house," says Shelley Cassie when I call her for directions. "It's the one that's different from all the others."

My husband and I drive quickly through the quiet streets of Brielle, New Jersey. Located on the Atlantic shore, the town is full of vacationers in the summer; on this early morning in late October, it seems deserted. Jack-o-lanterns adorn the porches of clapboard homes, most of which are painted in rustic hues of ochre or blue. We drive past a yacht club and along the river's edge, following Shelley's directions. Sure enough, as soon as we round the designated corner, we spot the house. Tall, narrow, and starkly modern, the natural-wood structure appears to soar into the sky, offering a dignified contrast to the traditional homes that surround it.

As we climb out of our car, Shelley zooms into the driveway in her 1987 Mazda. (Later we learn the car was purchased at an auction, a new money-saving strategy she and Ken have perfected since they left their teaching positions.) She jumps out, a short, pert, casually dressed woman in her early fifties. "I got lunch for us," she calls with a merry wave. "An East Coast deli

spread—rye bread, turkey, pickles. . . . Come on in. Ken's in the
studio. He'll join us in a few minutes.

"*Ken's sort of a Renaissance man,*" *she continues, barely*
pausing to catch her breath. "*He designed this house himself.*"
Evidence of Ken's many interests is everywhere: a classical gui-
tar in the upstairs study, books in Russian and English, draw-
ings and etchings from his days as an art student and, of
course, pottery. Mugs, bowls, casserole dishes are perched on all
available shelves and countertops.

One of Shelley's several cats brushes against my leg as Ken
walks in. He's wearing gray sweats and a T-shirt emblazoned
with the slogan No More Books. "*Sorry I'm late,*" *he says with*
a disarming grin. "*We have another craft fair next weekend,*
and I have to produce the goods. Shelley's my slave-driver. She
entered us in twenty shows this year."

A tall, lanky man with dark, wavy hair, he settles himself
comfortably on a long sofa covered with throw blankets. "*He*
made that, too," *Shelley whispers. I nod admiringly and sink*
into a chair by the fireplace.

KEN: Leaving teaching was a big step for me. Teaching is very
secure. You know each day what's going to happen; you know
about the size of the paycheck; you belong to a paternalistic
structure. Now I'm out on my own. I make pottery and then,
with Shelley's help, I sell it. We arrange it on a display stand
and it's right there for people to judge. I can reap failure, and
I dread personal failure even more than financial failure.

As long as pottery was just a hobby, I was safe. But trying
to sell it means I have to look the world straight in the eyes
and say "This is who I am, and this work is the best I can do."

I liked being a teacher for the first ten or fifteen years. But
then it got tiring. I always prided myself on having a great
deal of energy in teaching—running around, never sitting
down, getting kids motivated. But still, it's Sisyphean, the
same thing over and over, year after year. I feel there's a cloud
that covers you as a longtime employee, a certain attrition of
energy and initiative. I didn't want to stay around and collect
a paycheck till they swept me out of the institution.

I had a concept of myself as being my own person, my own
boss. Being part of a bureaucracy leaned on me a little too

much. In a sense I'm realizing a self-image by being on my own, and it's exciting. I feel as if I'm growing, building, as if I'm slowly improving. There's a sense of growth. I want that to be my goal—growth. I think of it as a fluid thing, not moving from point B to point C but constantly working toward being the best person I can be. I feel I'm on the threshold of doing interesting and exciting things as far as creative work is concerned. Does that sound corny? Maybe, but that's the type of fellow I am.

SHELLEY: I always felt that being a teacher was good. It was a basic equation: teacher equals good. So it was very difficult for me when, after I resigned, people asked me, "What do you do?" For the longest time, I said, "I'm a retired teacher." After all, if I wasn't a teacher, who was I? My identity was all wrapped up in my profession. It took me nearly a year and a half to build a new one. Finally, one evening at a friend's Christmas party, I heard myself say, "I'm the co-owner of a pottery studio. My husband is the craftsman and I am the business manager."

I love doing the business part. I do all the selling in shows, all the pricing. Ken goes to the shows, but he wanders off or he goes jogging or he sleeps. I think it's hard for a person to sell his own work. It's really easier for me. People are very complimentary. I can talk about the pottery because it's not my work. I like to be a partner with Ken in this way. I'm not creative at all so this is my contribution.

Ken and Shelley, like so many young people, fell into their first careers. For both of them it was, as Ken says, a "happy accident." They were both good teachers and, for the most part, they enjoyed their work.

KEN: I didn't know what I wanted to do when I got out of high school. I was only seventeen and at first I prepared to go into the service. Then I got an art school scholarship. I figured, well, why not? But after I graduated from art school, I couldn't find an art-related job that I liked. I came home and said, "My life is a shambles." I thought I was finished at twenty-one.

The one thing that really intrigued me was learning. I wanted to learn as much as I could about as many things as possible. I applied for, and got, a scholarship to a New Jersey state teachers' college. Everything was free as long as I agreed to teach when I got out. While I was at this college I became friendly with an elderly professor who had lived in Russia. She introduced me to the Russian language and culture. I was fascinated; there was a touch of exotica about it. When I graduated, I began teaching Russian to high school students.

SHELLEY: I knew exactly what I wanted to be when I was a teenager. I wanted to be the person Barbara Walters is today. I tried to major in drama, but my parents said "No. That's not a proper profession for a nice Jewish girl." So I majored in education instead. After I graduated my father drove me to this teaching interview in Lakewood, New Jersey, and I got the job immediately. To my surprise, I found I really enjoyed teaching. I loved the kids, loved the challenge, and loved the preparation involved in teaching English literature. For a long time I thought teaching was the most wonderful thing a person could do.

Ken and I met while he was still at the teachers' college. We were married in June 1960. My parents were not happy at the thought of a Catholic son-in-law, but I was too much in love to care. Anyway, I had this dream. Ken was going to be a big college professor, and I was going to be a big college professor's wife. The ivy was going to be climbing up the sides of the house; I was going to have lovely little cocktail parties and nice little teas. Then I was going to say to my Jewish parents, "See, he's not just a penniless Catholic; he's a well-known professor." In my mind I had him writing a book and appearing on TV . . ." [She laughs and looks at Ken affectionately.]

All during the early years of our marriage Ken was teaching high school during the day and taking graduate courses at night. But about the time he graduated [with a Ph.D. in Russian in 1975] the colleges were starting to cut back on staff. The Vietnam War was over and people weren't hiding out in the universities anymore.

KEN: I loved going to school; I was thirty-nine when I finally got that doctorate. Then when I couldn't get a job as a college professor, I thought, My God, here's my career. I'll be a high school teacher forever. This is it for me.

Like many midlifers, Ken had reality thrown in his face. "This is it for me." Overeducated and underutilized, he realized he wouldn't climb any further on the educational ladder. His response? "This is fine for now, but one of these days I'm gonna get out." It was 1976. Ken "got out," with Shelley, in 1988.

KEN: I decided I wasn't going to groan for the rest of my life. As soon as it was feasible to leave, I would. Some people say, "Boy, you're really courageous," but I say, "No way. Don't even use that word with me." They say, "You just walked away," and I said, "Of course I didn't. I planned for twelve years."

Shelley and I had to make a decision about what we *wanted* to do and then make a feasibility study about what we *could* do. I'd always been interested in art and doing creative things, and I'd been locked off from that for so many years. Then a friend offered to lend me a potters wheel and I started experimenting, teaching myself the craft. It took three or four years until I began to turn out some pretty good things. Then partly because it was overflowing the house, we said, "Okay, we've got all this pottery. Let's see if it'll sell."

SHELLEY: There's a lot of complexity involved in running even a small business; but gradually I began to develop expertise as a merchandiser, as a market expert, in dealing with people. Along with Ken I developed criteria for evaluating a show. How far away was it? We didn't want to drive more than 100 miles each way. What were the logistics for loading and unloading? How much would it cost us to eat and sleep? How much did it cost to enter the show? How much did we think we could earn? Were the promoters of the show doing a good job advertising it?

We did shows for nine years while we were still teaching. We came home Friday afternoons and packed and drove. Saturdays and Sundays we were at the show. I used to grade papers while I manned the booth. Even though we only did twelve or thirteen fairs a year, it was rough.

KEN: Oh, the Monday mornings. . . . *[He laughs and groans.]* It was a big investment, not only in time and energy but also in money. The kiln cost money, the wheel, the material, building the studio in the backyard. We set ourselves up as a business, so at least the costs were tax deductible. We were able to gradually build up our show itinerary, hone our skills, and learn the business aspect. So many small businesses fail, but we were able to make our mistakes on a small scale.

It wasn't until about four years before we left teaching that we really began to think we could make a living selling pottery. When we realized we could make this pay us a small but decent wage, we knew it was our key to freedom.

Making "a small but decent wage" doesn't in any way mean replacing their former salaries. The Cassies gave up combined annual wages exceeding $80,000. The pottery grosses about $20,000; they net only $12,000. Their pensions bring in about $32,000; two small rental properties yield a bit more. All told, they figure their yearly income is around $56,000.

SHELLEY: I'd always been very insecure about money, but now it's not important in the same way. I'm so happy and so content with my life that money just doesn't seem to be a big deal anymore. It used to be a big deal. When I'd come home from school on Fridays, I'd be tired and frustrated so I'd go buy a new dress to give me a lift. Or sometimes we'd go out to a wonderful, beautiful restaurant and spend $100 for dinner. We don't need to do that anymore.

I used to need money to compensate for the frustrations and unhappiness of my job. I was spending it on clothes and possessions; now I'm using it for time and freedom. What I do want, we can afford; and I want much less than I used to.

KEN: Money was never the most important thing in my life, but a person does need a certain amount. If money is the most important thing in your life, you just keep plugging away at whatever it is you do that makes you the most money. I think we're okay financially. We'll never have a yacht, but that's not a problem for me. I'm a doer, not a collector.

We've never lived beyond our means. Just thinking about that always terrified me. I could not bear the thought of car payments, finance charges, huge mortgages. That was never the way I wanted to live, and I think it's paid off for us. All we have is a small mortgage, and we'll be done with that pretty soon. We have no other debts at all; we never did.

About three years before we left teaching, I took a sabbatical. It was a trial period. We lived on Shelley's salary. We wanted to see what the unseen expenses were. After that little experiment, we pretty much decided we could make it.

We set a target date. I had to teach two more years to honor the agreement for the sabbatical, so we planned to leave after those two years, in June 1988. We only got diminished pensions because we left before we were fifty-five. My colleagues refer to this as a penalty. I say that's an abstract term; a penalty is staying for four more years!

Although they'd planned well financially, it wasn't until after they left teaching that Ken and Shelley realized how the formality of the classroom had structured their lives. Their work week had bookended their play, and now they had to create their own time structures. Otherwise, as Shelley said, "There was always tomorrow and tomorrow and tomorrow. Nothing ever got done."

SHELLEY: I never expected to miss the routine of going to work; but when I first realized I didn't have to be anywhere at a certain time or didn't have to get papers graded by the next day, I felt adrift. Now I'm on more of a schedule, but it took me over a year. Every morning I either exercise at home or run about three miles, then I spend between two and four hours on the business. I do all the banking and bookwork, the pricing and special orders. We have business licenses in three states. Then I get slides made and applications filled out so we can enter juried shows and do a lot of promotional stuff. On Thursdays or Fridays, depending on whether we're going to a two- or three-day show, we have to load up the van and travel. The weekends are spent at the shows—we did twenty this year— and Mondays are spent coming home and unpacking. It's a full week.

KEN: I had no problems setting routines. I like to get up early; otherwise my whole day collapses. I jog or swim and then work at least four to six hours on pottery. During the summer and fall when we're doing a lot of shows, I may have to do even a little more. Once I've accomplished at least that much, I can relax. Doing all the shows helps with self-discipline. We have to be ready for them; we have to be prepared.

But even though I like to structure my day, it doesn't have to be structured the same way all the time. For example, in the summer I get up and swim at sunrise; in the fall I wait until around 10 or 11 A.M. because the water is so cold. We do try to get out every day for at least a little bit. Now our place of employment is where we live. We have to go somewhere, take a walk somewhere, to freshen our thoughts. Otherwise there's a danger we'll slip into a slovenly cycle.

It helped that this wasn't a complete break for me. I left teaching but the studio was there waiting for me the next morning. The pottery had been going on before; it was a continuation of something I knew. I knew what I wanted to do and where I was going. And I felt confident that I could get there.

My dad used to say, "Son, whatever you do, make sure you're the best." I'd answer, "Dad, I'll *do* the best I can, but I can't guarantee I'll *be* the best." I know there's always going to be artists who are better than I am, but now I can accept that fact. I'm happy with who I am.

Despite the fact that an outside observer might call the Cassies retired, they vehemently reject that label. "We're not retired," says Shelley emphatically. "I think a retired person gets a chance to sit down and read. I haven't had time for that since last summer! We're too busy working our own business."

Next year the Cassies are going to Russia for six months. Ken will be working for the United States Information Agency (USIA) as a Russian-speaking guide for an exhibit on American architecture and design. The USIA promised Shelley a job too, but they haven't told her exactly what she'll be doing. "Passing out brochures, I imagine," she laughs, "and smiling my American smile. It's about all I can do. My Russian is limited to three phrases: hello, good-bye, and chocolate ice cream."

After their stay in Russia, they'll probably travel for a while before coming home to resume their pottery business. They haven't decided for sure. But then, they don't have to make plans anymore. The ones they made before have paid off.

Gee, I Wish I Could But I Can't

The Cassies are having a wonderful time. No doubt about it. But is it really that easy? Most of us read stories like this and get a funny feeling in the pit of the stomach. It's so tempting, so inviting. No rigid schedules or ornery bosses, no rush hour commutes or late night meetings. Instead, time to jog and swim—every day, not just on weekends. Time to be carefree and young.

ITEM In 1954 theatrical wizards outfitted Mary Martin with the elfin costume of Peter Pan, strapped her into a harness and sent her soaring over the stage, much to the delight of audiences full of cheering children and their smiling parents. "I'll never grow up, I'll never grow up," she boomed merrily, and for hundreds of thousands of us this became a goal.

"Youth," as Peter Pan says, "is joy." Middle age? It's traffic jams and overtime, mortgage payments and Saturday chores. Who needs it? We'll quit the job and follow the dream!

But no! Impossible! We have responsibilities and obligations. We can't just walk away from the security and safety of our jobs. It's silly to even think about such a thing! Not only silly, but selfish. Brush those thoughts away!

And so, good little Puritans that we are, we continue to abide by the work ethic that's been instilled in us. Nine to five—or six or seven. Monday to Friday—or Saturday or Sunday. An occasional day at the beach, an annual trip to the mountains, but the rest of the time? Keep working!

"Most of us react exactly this way," says Robert Shomer, Ph.D., a Los Angeles psychologist. "Thoughts of voluntarily making a major lifestyle change are scary. They activate all sorts of anxieties and guilt."

As a result, we repress these thoughts. We listen to stories of restylers and, after allowing ourselves a moment of envy, we begin listing reasons why similar actions are impossible for us. The tales awaken desires for freedom and excitement, but we shove these longings into the back recesses of our mind. Then, a few weeks or months later something else happens that activates our dreams. The death of a friend maybe, or even a bright sunny day. Again, freedom calls, but we refuse to admit we hear her voice. It's a game we play with ourselves: "Gee-I-wish-I-could-but-I-can't."

And so it goes. Our regular job, the one that we once wanted so badly and that, most of the time, we actually do enjoy, begins to seem like a prison. "We want to follow the dream impulse," says Shomer, "but we feel trapped. Eventually we try to spring the trap doors and sometimes, oftentimes, we do so in inappropriate ways."

The Midlife Crisis

Springing the trap door frequently causes a full-fledged explosion. While only a few laymen have studied the works of Else Frenkel-Brunswik, Carl Jung, Erik Erikson, and Daniel Levinson, millions have read Gail Sheehy's 1976 bestseller *Passages*. Sheehy, who freely acknowledges the contributions of the aforementioned experts, made "midlife crisis" a household term. Most of us decided it was nothing to look forward to.

During the midlife passage, she says, "demons may lead us into private hells of depression, sexual promiscuity, power chasing, hypochondria, self-destructive acts (alcoholism, drug taking, car accidents, suicide), and violent swings of mood." If, she continues, we hold these demons in abeyance and refuse to succumb to the age 40 reevaluation, "the crisis will probably emerge again around 50." Or, another possibility: "The person who arrives at 50 having ignored the opportunities for reassessment in midlife passage may take the familiar, mulish stance of protector of the status quo. It is no mistake that such people are called 'diehards.'"

While Sheehy and others assure us that by surviving this crucible we will emerge stronger, wiser, and happier, who, in heaven's name, wants to spend a few years in a pit of demons?

ITEM When Jay Carsey, college president, was forty-seven years old, he simply disappeared from his home in southern Maryland. He walked out on his wife, his friends, his job, and his community. "I could see that in twenty or thirty years I was going to tumble into a dark hole. You start thinking about—as everybody used to try to tell me—what a fantastic life you have had up till then, about all the things you've done. But once you start adding up what you *haven't* done, then you say, 'Well, the things I've done, I've done. I don't necessarily want to keep doing them—or do them again,' " he explained when he resurfaced in Texas many months later.

Carsey is surprised that his story, retold by Jonathan Coleman in the 1989 book *Exit the Rainmaker*, interested so many people. The *Washington Post* carried it on the front page; *People* magazine covered it; so did *USA Today* and CBS Morning News. But, he supposes, there must be "a lot of people who sit around and fantasize about just getting up and chucking it."

Among those he left at home, that is certainly the case. "If only Jay had chartered a plane, we all could have gone," muttered Mike Sprague, discussing his friend's flight with a group of mutual acquaintances, mostly males in their forties and fifties. And psychologist Herbert J. Freudenberger, who appeared on the CBS show, stated that the "fantasy of wanting out" is very common.

Would restyling help those who, like Jay Carsey, are caught in the throes of midlife crisis? Can it help prevent such a crisis? It's certainly possible. Because restyling is a *process*, not an *act*, it provides an escape valve for battling emotions. Drastic resolutions become less necessary; smooth transitions become more likely.

Ken and Shelley Cassie didn't restyle the day they left their classrooms, not even the day they handed in their resignations. Their restyling was a process that began as soon as Ken realized he wanted his tombstone to say something more than "high school teacher." From that moment on, he and Shelley began planning. He built a studio; she researched craft fairs. He practiced pottery; she got a business license. Together they found out how much money they could earn selling Ken's creations, and together they proved they could live on a reduced income. For nearly twelve years they planned and prepared; for nearly twelve years they restyled.

They didn't need a midlife crisis. The building dissatisfactions and frustrations with their teaching jobs were relieved by a sense of future escape. Weekend craft shows were hard but rejuvenating. They had something specific to look forward to; they had new challenges ahead of them. It was just like being young again!

In an attempt to identify those skills and strategies that contribute to a person's success, Charlie Garfield, an Oakland, California psychologist has spent most of his professional life speaking with more than 1,500 high achievers. "In every case I've studied," he says, "successful people were too busy reinventing themselves and striving for new goals to be waylaid by something as arbitrary as 'midlife crisis.'"

So Why Are We So Afraid?

But reinventing ourselves is scary. "The only sense that is common in the long run, is the sense of change—and we all instinctively avoid it," wrote E. B. White. Of course we do. Most of us find change of any sort downright terrrifying.

> *ITEM* A group of college sophomores at Kent State University was asked to write down what words or images came to mind when they thought about change. Seventy-five percent of the students wrote the word "death." Furthermore, they agreed that change was something that happened to them; it was almost never something they chose. Rather than planning for change, they adapted to it—and only because they had no choice.

Change implies risk. In order to change, we have to risk the unknown. We may not like trudging our particular path, but at least the scenery is familiar. Another road? Who knows where it will lead?

Our imaginations run wild. What if we try something new and we're a complete failure? We won't be able to get our old job back, we'll end up in the poorhouse, our kids will have to drop out of college, our friends will laugh, we'll suffer public humiliation. The mortifying list goes on and on.

Yet do we really have a choice? In the world of careers if we do not choose to leave, we'll eventually be forced to leave. Whether by a mandate from our boss, by disability, or by death, our primary career will end. The only real control we have, if we're gutsy enough to take it, is deciding when. "If you do not risk changing when the time is right," says psychiatrist David Viscott, "you will probably be forced to change when you are least prepared for it."

Each of us has to decide when the time is right. Restyling helps us make that decision. It is a way of conquering fears through slow, deliberate planning. As we convert our fears into reasonable cautions and concerns, we can devise ways to circumvent them. As proper preparation begins to turn our dreams into reality, these concerns drop away.

And in the meantime, the planning is safe. Until the day we hand in our resignation, nothing is final. All we've risked is the hours we've spent pursuing our dream.

Mileposts on the Road to Restyling

In order to shift gears we have to take action. We can't put our lives on cruise control and expect events to provide us with an enjoyable journey through midlife. We not only have to steer our own course, we have to draw the map as well. (See page 27.)

My goal in writing this book is to help you do just that. In the following chapters you will gain knowledge and skills that will enable you to make the most of the third quarter of your life. By the time you finish this book, you should

- know the various paths restyling can take
- understand what money means to you and how this understanding can help you restyle
- recognize how you can work with your partner, whether or not he or she wants to restyle
- feel confident that restyling need not interfere with your obligations to your children and parents
- understand the importance of separating your job identity from your personal identity
- be able to assess your aptitudes and skills to learn what types of work are possible for your middle years
- be able to assess your values, personality, and interests in order to find a lifestyle that is appropriate for your middle years

- know how to devise a plan for getting from where you are now to where you want to be in midlife
- learn how to put that plan into action

It's time to begin.

E X E R C I S E S

Is It Time for You to Restyle?

Read the following scenarios. Do any of them ring true for you? If so, it's time to begin restyling.

- It's Monday morning. "Traffic is backed up over a mile on Interstate 101. If possible, take an alternate route to work," says the radio announcer. "I'll be late tonight. Can you drive by the cleaner's and pick up my jacket?" asks your spouse. "I need a ride home from soccer practice. Will you pick me up?" wails your twelve-year-old. Life should be simpler, you think.
- It's Tuesday morning. Traffic isn't as bad today, and as you drive to work, you take a few minutes to reflect on your current job situation. I really am lucky, you muse. I'm making a good salary, have a fair amount of responsibility, and actually like my job. Things could be a lot worse. You slide into the left lane so you can pass the slow car ahead of you. But do I want to keep doing this same thing for twenty more years?
- You get to the office and it's abuzz with gossip. Len, a fellow who works on the next floor, has just handed in his resignation. He's forty-five years old. You meet Len in the elevator as you're going to lunch. "What's the story?" you ask. "My wife and I are going to travel," he says. "See the world, that kind of thing. But we're also going to import some fabrics, *songket* from Malaysia, batik from Indonesia, silk from Hong Kong. It's a way of making a few bucks and deducting the travel expenses. I think it's going to work out real well." You wish him luck but feel a pang of envy.
- That night your mother phones to tell you that an old college friend has died. "The funeral's Sunday," she says. You haven't seen Bob for years, but surprisingly tears

Mileposts on the Road to Restyling

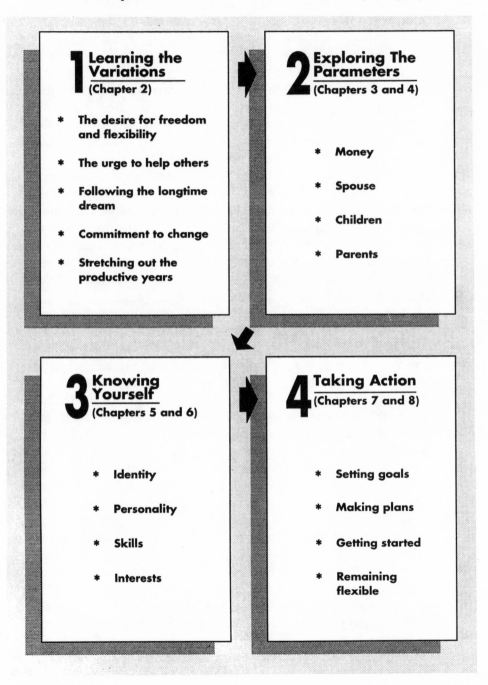

1 Learning the Variations
(Chapter 2)

* The desire for freedom and flexibility

* The urge to help others

* Following the longtime dream

* Commitment to change

* Stretching out the productive years

2 Exploring The Parameters
(Chapters 3 and 4)

* Money

* Spouse

* Children

* Parents

3 Knowing Yourself
(Chapters 5 and 6)

* Identity

* Personality

* Skills

* Interests

4 Taking Action
(Chapters 7 and 8)

* Setting goals

* Making plans

* Getting started

* Remaining flexible

spring to your eyes. That poor sucker, you say to yourself, he was only fifty-one years old. He died before he had a chance to live.

- The "Style" section of the Sunday paper announces a watercolor exhibition by someone you used to sit next to in art class. "I was as good as she was." "What's that?" asks your spouse. "Oh, nothing," you say. The next day you go up to the attic to see if you can find your old watercolors. The place is a mess. And anyway, you're being silly. You really don't have time to paint. You have to get to that pile of bills on your desk.

- That night you go out to dinner with friends. "Did you hear about Libby and Stu?" says the wife of the other couple. "They're getting a divorce. Libby says that now with the kids gone, they just don't have any interests in common." You look covertly at your spouse. Right now, you think, most of our conversation does center on the kids. We each move in our own spheres at work. I wonder what we'll talk about after the kids move on.

- A project you've been working on for months reaches completion. It went well and you know the boss will be pleased. It might even mean a raise at the next salary review. Funny, you think, I really don't care all that much. It's not that you don't need the money; of course you do. It's just that lately you've been thinking things over and wondering if it's really fair. You have so much and other people . . . well, other people are hurting. Maybe it's time for you to give something back to society. I wish, you muse, I were Tom Monaghan [the fifty-two-year-old founder of Domino's Pizza who talks about selling his company so he can build churches in Central America].

- Your dad, age sixty-six, wants to know if you can play golf with him on Saturday. Gently you explain that you have a bunch of chores that you simply must get done. As you hang up, you feel guilty. "Dad can't seem to find himself since he retired," you say to your spouse. "He always seems to be at loose ends." You pause for a minute and then say softly, "Do you suppose it's possible to reach a proper balance, one where you're not stressed with too much work or bored with no work?" Your spouse shrugs.

The Two Main Routes

As you approach midlife, you must make a choice to (1) continue your present job until you are either forced out or choose to retire, or (2) plan an early retirement and new path for the third quarter of your life. Listing the pros and cons of each path can help you choose your direction. The chart below will give you a start; but as you read this book, you may want to add or subtract factors that make the lists more specific to your own situation. Use a pencil because your ideas are likely to change as you read along.

Pros	*Cons*
REMAIN IN SAME JOB, RETIRE AS LATE AS POSSIBLE	
financial security	boredom
companionship of colleagues	stress
power, prestige, status of present job	time constraints
	less energy upon eventual retirement
_____	_____
_____	_____
_____	_____
_____	_____

RESTYLING	
freedom to try something new	financial risk
energy to try something new	identity risk
flexible time	loss of work friends
feeling of rejuvenation	_____
_____	_____
_____	_____
_____	

Two roads diverged in a wood, and I—
I took the one less traveled by,
And that has made all the difference.

ROBERT FROST

2 | *MY-TIME: VARIATIONS ON A THEME*

Speed down the fast lane. Make big bucks *now*. These were the goals of the eighties. But the rules of the road are changing. For many of us, time—simple time to do what we want to do— is even more valuable than money.

ITEM In 1973 the average American worked less than forty-one hours a week, including commuting time. Over the past fifteen years the average worker's leisure time has shrunk by 37 percent. Today he or she works nearly forty-seven hours, and for many people eighty-hour work weeks are the norm. "Time," concludes pollster Louis Harris, "may have become the most precious commodity in the land."

It seems that Ben Franklin's adage "Time is money" is being rethought for the nineties. Rather than spending time to earn money, we're beginning to forego money to buy time. Given the choice between spending time on family and friends or spending time pursuing a career and making money, more of us choose the former.

ITEM American adults don't consider a successful career or a good income as important as a happy family life and close friends. According to a 1990 Louis Harris poll, when asked which of these things were essential or very important, people replied as follows:

Happy family life	97%
Clean environment	95%
Close friends	85%
Successful career	80%
Satisfying sex life	71%
Good income	60%

"Simple 'givens' from our past—time off, time together, time enough—have now become part of the luxury we will find ourselves striving for in the nineties," forecasts Lou Weiss of Yankelovich Clancy Shulman surveys. We're reminded of the words of Will Durant: "No man who is in a hurry is quite civilized."

And so it goes. Having swung too far in the direction of materialism, the pendulum in now returning to the values of the sixties. Psychic income is becoming as important as dollar income: How do we want to live? Where do we want to live? What activities are important to us?

For younger people, the desire for time translates into a few hours for a picnic, a few weeks on the beach. But for midlifers, it joins with the awareness of mortality to produce an overwhelming desire for "My-Time."

Marilyn Kennedy, a consultant with Career Strategies in Chicago, sees this every day. "My clients say, 'I went for security; I went for health insurance. Now, by god, I'm going to throw off the constraints and fly.' They're like Superman emerging from the phone booth. They're determined to do what *they* want to do. They've earned it, they feel. They've earned some 'My-Time.' " A few years to fulfill our own dreams doesn't seem like so much to ask.

The meaning of "My-Time" varies with each individual. For most it involves a downscaling, a coupling of part-time work with a goodly amount of freedom to pursue other interests. For some it means a chance to help others, to repay society for the good fortune they feel has been bestowed upon them. For others it's a chance to pursue the "always-wants," the longtime dreams that have been deferred during the young adult years. And for a few it's an opportunity to do something different, to escape anticipated boredom or to pursue an occupation that may intrigue them well past the traditional retirement age.

The restylers in this book cross all lines when it comes to their specific motivations. Like Ken Cassie, who wanted more freedom as well as more time to pursue an interest from his past, most people restyle for more than one reason. But whatever the particulars, they have one thing in common: a desire for My-Time.

Downscaling for Freedom

George Washington taught us not to tell lies. Abraham Lincoln showed us about fairness and equality. And Horatio Alger gave us the work ethic. Written in the last half of the nineteenth century, his books taught generations of children to believe life was a matter of *Luck and Pluck* and *Sink or Swim*. Our grandparents believed him; so did our parents. Like H. L. Mencken, they all kept "on working for the same reason that a hen goes on laying eggs."

But, says Nancy Mayer, author of *The Male Mid-Life Crisis*, "Horatio Alger lied." Scrambling up the ladder of success doesn't always bring personal happiness; sometimes it brings at least an equal dose of frustration.

ITEM "Stress used to be noticeable around age fifty-five, but now we find it at earlier and earlier ages," says Dr. Robert Hodges, senior vice president of Sampson, Neill & Wilkins Inc., a management recruiting firm in Upper Montclair, New Jersey.

"There appears to be a lot more pressure on employees today by employers."

And a lot of us say, "To hell with it!" We're tired of the grind, and we want to find something else. "It used to be that people said the purpose of leisure time was to recharge so they could do better at work," says pollster Bickley Townsend of the Roper Organization. "Now they're saying the purpose of work is to give them more leisure time."

Of course, most of us can't afford to quit working completely. And anyway, it isn't work we dislike. It's stress. It's drudgery. It's routine and regimentation and confinement. It's getting out of bed at 6 A.M. every single Monday morning!

When can we read a book? When can we visit our kids? How can we get out of the rat race? Bruce and Carolyn Bade found a way.

· ·

Profile: **Bruce and Carolyn Bade—Business Owners to Vagabond Writers**

Take this job and shove it.
   SONG BY COUNTRY-AND-WESTERN STAR JOHNNY PAYCHECK

Bruce and Carolyn Bade, now fifty and fify-nine, used to have one of the biggest recreational vehicle rental operations in Southern California. Then in December 1988 they became nomads, living full time in their own rig, a 38-foot home pulled by a three-quarter-ton Ford pickup. Now they meet their expenses through a combination of lecturing and writing on RV-related topics. Carolyn has four children and Bruce has three from early first marriages; all are grown. The Bades have been married to each other for twenty-two years.

"Stress? I was a walking definition of the word three years ago," says Bruce Bade. Today he's the very picture of tranquility. In fact, it's hard to imagine that this genial, low-key, slightly overweight man could ever feel pressured or tense. He just doesn't seem the type. "And Carolyn was so overwrought *she was hospitalized for chest pains. We thought she'd had a heart attack."*

Carolyn, comfortably clad in turquoise pants, a blue sweatshirt, and moccasins, smiles from her easy chair. She smooths back her short, blond hair. "I'm healthy as can be now," she affirms.

We're all relaxing in the living room of the Bades' custom-designed recreational vehicle, a blue-carpeted, wood-panelled "room" with all the amenities: console television, two VCRs, stereo and compact disk player, computer and printer. A few feet away there's a stove, refrigerator/freezer with ice-maker, dishwasher, washer and dryer, garbage disposal, and large round oak table. My preconceived notions of "roughing it" are fast disappearing.

A quick tour past the thousand-plus coaches parked at the fairgrounds in Los Banos, California, had introduced me to the basics of the Bades' vagabond lifestyle. "We're meeting here for an RV convention," Bruce told me. "Regular campgrounds aren't this crowded." I was surrounded by rigs of every description: converted buses, trailers where the coach can be disconnected from the tow vehicle, slide-on campers and chassis-mounts on trucks, motor homes that are combined driving and living units. Although I knew that RVing was popular—more than 100,000 Americans live full-time in recreational vehicles, and hundreds of thousands more use them part-time—I was still overwhelmed by the variety.

"Why did you choose a trailer instead of a motor home?" I asked.

"We've had them all, at one time or another," Bruce said with a shrug. "Finally we decided we don't like having a steering wheel in our only living room."

As the Bades talk, the conversation skitters back and forth; one begins a thought and the other finishes it. Both seem to enjoy their demonstration of mutual mind reading.

CAROLYN: Sure, there's apprehension when you change careers or something like that, but there's never been any great turmoil. Change for Bruce and me is water off a duck's back. If there's something else out there, we say "Let's find it." But whenever we've made a major change, we've had the background for it. Our previous experience always prepared us for the next step.

BRUCE: When I met Carolyn, my background was in construction. I'd started as a stonemason. When I was fourteen, I watched a guy build a wall next door to my mom's new tract home. Mom wanted a wall too, and I said, "Hey, Mom, you don't need to spend the money. I can do it." So I did. That's how I got into it.

After high school I went into the Navy for four years. I was a jet mechanic. Since I worked nights, during the day I'd do odd construction jobs. After the service, I started supervising tract construction and got my contractor's license.

CAROLYN: I come from a background of stodgy midwesterners. My father, my brother, my brother-in-law ... they all worked for one company for forty, forty-five years and then retired. They all live in the same house they bought the year they got married. Not one of them would consider selling their home; that's security. They think I'm sort of a maverick.

But I started off real ordinary. When I was married to my first husband, I was a homemaker and a tech writer for a valve manufacturing company. Then Bruce and I got married, and we started a construction business.

After a few years of running the construction company—Bruce did the field work and Carolyn managed the office—the Bades opened a real estate company along with Bruce's mother and sister. They did well, but Bruce had a different dream: "My goal," he says, "was to open a series of RV campgrounds all around the United States, every 300 miles or so, under the banner of Camp America Corporation."

BRUCE: It seemed as if it would be perfect for us. We'd been RVing for about five years then, and we really knew the business.

CAROLYN: We started RVing because we wanted to go back to Chicago. We wanted to see my mother and she was desperately lonesome for us and our kids. At that time we had four of them living with us, three of mine and one of his. So, we had to find a way to economically transport a family of six from California to Illinois.

Planes, trains . . . they were all more than we could afford at the time. Then we looked into renting an RV. The prices were right and it sounded real good. But Bruce said, "Heck, we've got a pickup truck. Why don't we just go ahead and buy a slide-on camper? Then we'll have it for next time."

We shopped around and finally found a floor plan we liked. When we got home, Bruce said, "I can build that sucker." It took him about three months. Then we piled the kids in and went back to Chicago to see Gramma. We had a great time, just a great time.

BRUCE: We kept that camper for a couple of years, and then I mounted it permanently on a ton-and-a-half chassis. After about a year we sold that and bought a mini-motor home, then a fifth wheel . . .

CAROLYN: And we've never been without an RV since. We've had, let's see, we've had nine rigs in twenty years. So when Bruce wanted to start these campgrounds, we thought we knew all about RVing. And it was a perfect time for us. The kids were gone. My youngest had graduated high school and was on her own. Bruce still had two in high school, but at that time they were living with their mother. So we sold our home and decided to full-time it . . . looking into sites, trying to buy property.

BRUCE: But it didn't work out. There was a gas crunch, so it was impossible to find financing. And Carolyn didn't like full-time RVing. She still needed a home base.

CAROLYN: You have to remember this unit contains all our worldly possessions. I could have stored all the silver and crystal and china and keepsakes, but that seemed kind of ridiculous to me. Why store it? But I wasn't ready to get rid of them. I couldn't consider an RV a home back then. We moved back to a house in Southern California.

"Down but not out," is the way Carolyn describes them at that period of their lives. "We weren't quite sure what we were

going to do. Something to do with recreational vehicles, but what?" The answer was born more of necessity than of inspiration.

BRUCE: One afternoon Carolyn said to me very casually, "Bruce, you know we could use some extra money. Why don't we rent the motor home?" And that was it! We rented our home and then we offered to rent someone else's. Within three years we had a rental fleet of forty-five coaches. We took them on consignment; they were all privately owned and people wanted to earn money off them. We stored them, scheduled the rentals, advertised them, took care of all paperwork, kept them clean and repaired. The owners got a percentage of the rental.

CAROLYN: We went from a small lot to a larger lot to a larger lot . . .

BRUCE: Then one day I couldn't find anyone to fix up one of the coaches. Rental units get shabby just like anything else. So I did the repairs—helped by that construction background, I guess. After all, an RV is just a home on wheels. Pretty soon we had a second line in the same company: remodeling and refurbishing. We were one of the first remodelers in the industry.

CAROLYN: It just kept getting bigger and bigger. We had a tiger by the tail, and we didn't know what to do with it.

BRUCE: We were working ten to twelve hours a day, seven days a week. Sometimes sixteen hours . . .

CAROLYN: In 1986 we finally sold our house and began living in a motor home on the lot. It was like full-timing it but without the freedom to travel or relax. Finally I said, "Bruce, this isn't the way we want to live. What do you want to do for the rest of your life? Make a list. You're too young—and too poor— to retire, and you've got background in all sorts of things: construction, real estate, the RV industry . . ."

BRUCE: When Carolyn asked me to list ten things, the first thing that came to mind was giving RV seminars. I knew I could rep for a company, but that would mean a schedule. I knew I didn't want a desk job. And for certain I didn't want anything to do with another big business! The day we closed down I wrote a note: "I will never again open another business and employ people." I signed it and gave it to Carolyn . . .

CAROLYN: . . . and I called in a friend to witness it! *[She laughs merrily.]*

BRUCE: I knew I could give seminars. Years before, I'd been so awful talking in front of people—Oh God, I used to stammer and stutter—that I'd decided I had to do something to become more at ease. So I'd joined Toastmasters *[an organization that promotes public speaking]*. Public speaking is like anything else, like riding a bicycle. The more you do it the better you get. I got pretty good at it, and over the past six or eight years I'd developed a seminar on RVing to promote the business. So giving seminars was on the top of my list.

CAROLYN: Then we saw a small ad in *Trailer Life*. They wanted someone to write technical articles for them. We called up, and everything began to fall into place.

BRUCE: Of course we didn't know if we could write!

CAROLYN: But Bruce knew the information, and I figured I'd once been a tech writer so I could learn what else I needed to know about writing. We went out and got a couple of books and studied like crazy.

BRUCE: Once the editor accepted a few articles, we figured we could close the business.

By this time, Carolyn was emotionally prepared for full-time RVing. She decided to distribute her prized possessions (the china, the silver, the photographs) to her children.

CAROLYN: All this stuff had been in storage since we'd sold the house. But now, I said "Why are we keeping these things? The children would love them. The grandkids could enjoy them while they are growing up." So we gave it all to the kids, distributed it the way we wanted. *[She laughs.]* Now for Thanksgiving we get to go to one of *their* homes. Mother did it many, many, many years; now it's their turn.

BRUCE: We went through all the photos that we'd been collecting for years. It took us six months. Then at Christmas of 1987, when we knew we really were going to close the business and RV full-time, we gave each kid his or her own photo album. We spent the whole day sitting there looking at pictures together.

CAROLYN: When the kids heard our plans, my oldest son thought his mother had flipped her lid. He could not conceive that his mother would be happy living in an RV. He never came right out and said, "You're crazy," but you could tell what he thought by his body language. I told him I'd much rather have this to clean than a four-bedroom, three-bath home! As for the rest of the kids, some thought it would be pretty neat and the rest had a wait-and-see attitude. We have a good rapport with all our kids.

With this accomplished, the Bades began their new life. As always, they worked together—he using his technical know-how, she using her office skills.

CAROLYN: We've a system now. Bruce sits and writes, just the way he talks. He rambles about a particular subject. Then I put it into readable form. I pay attention to the continuity, sentence structure, spelling, that sort of thing. We write three or four articles a month. Each one takes each of us ... oh, about three days. And remember, our work days are only four or five hours long!

BRUCE: Then I do the seminars. I want to do twenty-two this year, all in the western part of the United States. Next year we'll do the East.

CAROLYN: We're just learning about all of this. Last year we didn't do the lecture circuit. Last year we just had fun. We wrote and visited relatives from Seattle to Niagara Falls and then down to Atlanta. I wanted to see the antebellum mansions. Then we visited his family in St. Louis and mine in Chicago.

BRUCE: We had a great time. And, we wrote our first travel article. It was on Niagara Falls. But that was last year; this year we're working more on developing and giving seminars.

CAROLYN: But see, in this lifestyle you can pick and choose how much you want to work. It's an easy pace, and we're not responsible to anybody except the editors. Really we're only responsible to ourselves because if we want to do five articles a month, that's fine; and if we want to only do three, that's fine too.

BRUCE: During the winter months we spend a lot of time in an RV camp in Southern California. It's quiet, about twenty-five acres. During the week there aren't more than about fifteen other coaches up there. It's near a lake, and I carry a little outboard with us so I can fish a lot. I just got a new set of golf clubs. I'm going to get back into golf. Carolyn's going to try it a bit, too.

CAROLYN: I like to read, and I like puzzles. I'm a cryptogram nut. Sometimes I crochet. I have all my painting equipment with me, but I really have to be motivated to paint. I do it in spurts. This is a nice life!

But financially, as both admit, it's tight—tight, but not scary.

BRUCE: We didn't have a lot of money when we closed down the business. Pretty much all we had was a couple of IRAs, our truck, and this rig.

This is an '83 rig, worth about $9,000. Then I put in $40,000, probably closer to $50,000, and that's my cost, which is low because I was in the business. Also, I did a lot of the work myself. So we have about $60,000 in it, but we could never sell it for that because it's still an '83 body. You design something like this to live in, not to resell. Still, it's cheaper than most houses.

And our cost of living is low, real low. Carolyn and I calculated that last year our total "house" expenses—utilities and rental fees—averaged two dollars and fifty cents a day. That's less than $1,000 for the year. There's no mortgage, no property taxes.

CAROLYN: But that doesn't include food, telephone *[cellular]* and gas. Gas is a major expense. We average six-and-a-half miles per gallon. But usually we can work it so we don't have to pay for the gas. If an organization is sponsoring Bruce's seminar, they pay the traveling expenses.

BRUCE: About 50 percent of our income is a tax write-off because all of our expenses involve going to and from rallies; and our home is our office.

CAROLYN: So we're working about half-time and making enough to cover our expenses. We're not touching our savings. This is a pay-as-you-go operation. Right now that's what we strive for.

BRUCE: So far so good. We'll probably keep on doing what we're doing. We have no plans to move into a house, and there are some things in the works with the magazines that will make our life a little more secure, let us put a little bit away for retirement. I don't foresee major changes. But then, life is change.

CAROLYN: Bruce and I do what we want; we change ... together.

BRUCE: When the business started to be such a burden that it was affecting our marriage, we knew we had to change. Our marriage is too important to us. If seven kids didn't break us up, we're damn sure not going to let anything else do so!

CAROLYN: We know we'd have burned out in the business. This lifestyle looks like it can last a lot longer. That's what makes it so exciting.

She pauses, then grins. "You know what I want on my headstone?" she asks. " 'Yeah, but she was a good sport!' "

• •

Making a Difference

As delightful as the Bades' existence may sound to some, many of us need roots. Not just a house with a sturdy foundation but a full-fledged, well-earned membership in a community. For some folks, the third quarter of life is a chance to give back a little, to say thank you to a world that has been kind to them.

According to Erik Erikson, whose theory outlines the eight stages of life, "adult man is so constituted as to *need to be needed* lest he suffer the mental deformation of self-absorption, in which he becomes his own infant and pet." At midlife mature people strive for "generativity," a psychosocial state in which their primary concern is "establishing and guiding the next generation. In addition to procreativity, [generativity] includes productivity and creativity." In other words, these folks want to leave the world a little better than they found it.

We read about Joseph Kordick, a former high executive of Ford Motor Company, who is ministering to the needs of the dying at Hospice in Stuart, Florida; and Frank Reilly, once a senior vice president for Chase Manhattan Bank in New York, who is now assistant director of the Baltimore Zoo.

We hear about an increasing number of midlifers who start new careers as teachers. Some companies offer their pre-retirees an educational program if they will commit to future service in the public schools, and some school districts offer special incentives to men and women who choose teaching as a second career.

Terrence Grace, former lawyer, felt that teaching was a perfect way to make a contribution. He found his students in one of the most impoverished regions of the world.

· ·

Profile: Terrence Grace—L.A. Attorney to Honduran Teacher

We make a living by what we get, but we make a life by what we give.

WINSTON CHURCHILL

Terrence Grace is forty-seven years old. Until recently he lived in Los Angeles and worked as an attorney for the police department of a nearby community. He was earning $70,000 a year. Now he's a school teacher in Honduras, making an annual salary of just over $1,000. Grace is not married and has no children.

A friend phoned me from Los Angeles. "There was a human interest piece in the paper this morning—about some lawyer who's going to teach in Central America. If you call him right

*away, you might be able to reach him before he heads south."
As soon as I hung up the phone, I dialed information.*

Terrence laughed when I told him what I wanted. "I'm surprised that people find this so interesting," he said, "but sure, I'll be glad to talk with you. Let's do it now, because I'm leaving next week."

I plunged right in. "Why?" I asked. He thought for a minute. "Well, I guess when it comes right down to it, I admire Mother Teresa more than Donald Trump."

Right now I'm living a good life. I'm advisor to the chief of police of Santa Ana. It's really a multifaceted job. I review documents and procedures to see that they're in compliance with the law, write ordinances, review requests for subpoenas, defend officers when necessary, work with the chief if he wants to discipline an officer for misconduct—all kinds of things. The work is interesting, and the people I work with are high-quality professionals. It's a good job, a very good job.

And, when I go home after work, I also have it nice. You know, I have a comfortable condo with wall-to-wall carpeting, a color TV, a CD player, all that.

It's sort of hard to give this up, but I think sometimes you just have to move on; you just have to do what you have to do. While I'm not expecting to go through a whole lot of culture shock—I've been to Central America before—I'm sure it will be an adjustment. El Progreso, where I'll be teaching, is big by Honduran standards, about fifty thousand people; but there are only two paved roads—one going north-south, the other going east-west. There's running water, sometimes. The same with electricity. And the garbage . . . well, let's put it this way: it's illegal to kill vultures because they eat the garbage—they sort of make up the sanitation system. But it's a nice little town— a lot of stores up and down the street leading to the central plaza, cantinas and quaint little restaurants, houses built up to the sidewalks. I pretty much know what I'm getting into.

My friends are skeptical, though. I'm getting kind of a mixed reaction from them. The initial reaction is usually, "He must be crazy," followed by, "I wish I could do something like that." It's kind of like "there must be a touch of insanity here" mixed with a bit of envy.

Of course, I've never been married, and I realize I'm in a position that a lot of people are not in. I have some financial security from money I've saved and I don't have a spouse or kids, so it's easier for me to make this kind of move than it would be for some people.

[He takes a deep breath.] But it still wasn't an easy decision. There was a good possibility that if I had stayed at my job, I could have been appointed to the bench. The person who had this job before me was appointed to the Municipal Court and then went on to Superior Court. The idea of becoming a judge was tempting. That is something I struggled with a lot.

And then I was quite serious about a very lovely woman; and I knew if I decided to go to Central America, it would mean the end of our relationship. She made it very clear to me that if I wasn't going to be around, she wasn't going to be around—and she wasn't going to live in Honduras.

I've been through a lot of soul-searching. Do I want to do this, do I not want to do this? Is it the right thing for me, is it not the right thing for me? Do I care that I will probably never be a judge? Can I accept the consequences of my decision?

Terrence had enjoyed teaching while he was in graduate school, but somehow he never thought of it as a career. Instead he became a lawyer because he wanted to please his dad, a Chicago cop whose eyes gleamed at the thought of a lawyer son. Then too, law seemed like a profession that would pay pretty well.

I come from a real traditional Irish-Catholic family. I grew up in Chicago but went to high school in St. Louis at a seminary run by a Catholic religious order. In St. Louis I spent a lot of time going down to the ghetto to tutor kids. That was a big thing in the sixties, going into ghettos and tutoring.

Then later, after I finished college at Loyola University in Chicago *[where he majored in psychology]*, I went back to St. Louis for a masters in psychology at Washington University. During my last semester—this was in 1966—I was writing my thesis, and I decided I could do that nights and weekends. So during the day I got a job as a schoolteacher in that same tough area of St. Louis. It was in a high-rise public housing project that was so horrible it was dynamited a few years later. I taught remedial reading and English to seventh graders. It was a Catholic school so it was okay that I didn't have a teaching credential.

Even today I think that this teaching experience helped me become a successful trial attorney. It's the same skill. You go into the courtroom, and you have information to present to the jury. You can't go too fast or you'll leave them behind; you can't go too slow or they'll get bored. So you have to look at them and be aware of where they're at, if you're making your point, whether or not they're understanding it. It's just like presenting information to a roomful of kids. I think I'm pretty good at the attorney business because I had great preparation for it by being a teacher.

Anyway, psychology just wasn't what I wanted. It's sort of funny: on the night that the civil rights march on Selma took place, I was studying patients in a locked ward in the V.A. hospital. I thought to myself, Now look at me. I'm locked up in a mental hospital, the world is moving in front of my eyes, and I'm not part of it. That was sort of symbolic for me, like psychology was locking me away from the world or something. Although I got my degree, I never really worked in the field.

Also, that was a time in my life when my goals were to get rich and to make tons of money and to have fancy cars and stuff like that. In fact, I remember thinking to myself that I'd like to go to Las Vegas and gamble. I thought, If I could just get to be a lawyer, I'd have more money and I could afford to go to Las Vegas and gamble.

Terrence accomplished his goal: he became an attorney and, sure enough, he could afford a fling in Vegas whenever he wanted one. But he found this was no longer important to him. Instead, he preferred to use his weekends ladling out food for the homeless. Gradually, his values were changing.

In November of '86 I started volunteering in a soup kitchen. Every Saturday morning we served a hot meal to homeless people. I got very involved with these people and I came to ask myself, What are my basic values? What are the really important things in life? Is it making big bucks, driving big cars, living in big houses?

Then I got to know one of the women who volunteered at the soup kitchen. She was the director of an organization that sends volunteers—doctors, nurses, nutritionists, teachers—to Third World countries. She was going to Central America to visit some of the volunteers and check on the projects. She gave a general invitation that if any of the soup kitchen volunteers wanted to come along, it would be fine.

I had vacation coming up, and I thought a trip like that would be interesting, so in July of 1987 I traveled along with her group to El Salvador, Honduras, Nicaragua, Costa Rica, and Guatemala. In Honduras, in this little town called El Progreso, I visited a nutrition project where they feed malnourished kids and care for them until their legs become stronger. A lot of these kids are so malnourished they can't even walk. *[He swallows hard.]* And in El Salvador I saw violence and bloodshed and poverty—desperate poverty—and horrible injustice. It just has an effect on you. I decided I wanted to try to live a life that is a little more meaningful than just making money.

I really just made a conscious decision that I'm not going to fall into this life of quiet desperation where you spend your whole life getting up in the morning, running off to work, waiting for the next paycheck to arrive so you can pay off your bills because you have to live in a bigger house and you need a bigger car or a fancier car and you have to buy more stuff.

I see that all around me, and I don't want to live like that. One of my goals, going off to the Third World like this, is to try to live a little more simply, a little poorer, a little slower. I don't want to be caught up in this tremendous concern for material things.

When Terrence visited the nutrition project in Honduras, he was housed in a Catholic retreat next to a school. He had some free time, and he wandered over to talk with the nuns who taught there.

The first time I visited that school it was one of those feelings where you go somewhere and you say, You know, I really like it here. It's like walking into a house that's for sale and saying, This is it; this is the one I like. I just felt really comfortable there; and I said to myself, You know, I'd like to be able to come here someday and teach.

I didn't do anything about it, though. I came back to the States, and by coincidence a few months later I was contacted by some people in Washington, D.C., who wanted me to go to Honduras. They needed an attorney with a background in local government and who spoke Spanish.

I'm reasonably fluent in Spanish—for an Irishman. I learned it years ago when I went on a summer program to study law in Mexico City. After I finished law school, I worked for a law firm in Mexico City for about eight months, dealing with national investments and big corporations. I thought about making a career there, but . . .

Anyway, when these people asked me if I'd be willing to go to Honduras to work on a project on local government, I was delighted. It would give me a chance to visit that school again. So I got a leave of absence from my job with the police department, and I spent two more months in Honduras. Most of the time I was in the capital city of Tegucigalpa, but I did get to go to El Progreso, too. And again, I liked it.

About fifteen months later I got still another opportunity to go to Latin America, this time to study Spanish in Bolivia. I was gone for three months, and on the plane ride home I started filling out the application to teach in Honduras. That was in June, but I didn't actually make the final decision until late October. All in all, it took me more than two years to mentally prepare myself.

Now that I've notified the school that I'm coming, and given notice at my job, I'm very excited. I'm sort of like a little kid getting ready to go to Disneyland. I'll be teaching about ten hours a week down there, which is fine with me. I'm looking forward to the chance to do some reading and writing.

I leave here January 15, and I'm driving down. I bought a four-wheel drive vehicle, sold my car, and made arrangements for a guy to rent my condominium while I'm gone. *[He laughs as if anticipating my next question.]* No, I have not become a Franciscan overnight; I haven't sold all I have and given it to the poor!

• •

Pursuing the Always-Wants

Terrence might have been happier if he'd decided to be a teacher the first time 'round. "I think teaching is really my true calling," he says. But he didn't know that at the time. When he graduated from Washington University, he simply took what seemed to be the path of least resistance.

Most of us did exactly the same thing. When we were asked to make career decisions in our late teens or early twenties, we had no idea what we wanted. "Select a college. Choose a major. Find a job," said our parents, much as they'd once told us to brush our teeth. We were asked to make important decisions, pivotal decisions, the kind of choices that would affect the rest of our lives. And all we wanted to think about was Saturday night!

Some of us simply fall into our first careers. Like Ken Cassie, we're offered a scholarship to a certain college. Like Bruce Bade, we rent our own RV and find ourselves swept up by the excitement of a new business. Maybe there's an opening in a certain department, an opportunity at a certain company. Without thinking, we say yes. Twenty years later we're still saying yes, only this time to a boss we never really wanted to serve.

Others of us don't fall; we're pushed. Our parents, recognizing our indecision, make the decision for us. "It starts the day the poor kid's delivered," says John Holland, professor emeritus of social relations at Johns Hopkins University and author of *Making Vocational Choices: A Theory of Careers*. "If you're the son of a lawyer or the son of a doctor, you have a very good chance of being a doctor or lawyer."

Now, having spent twenty or so years in jobs we got into more by default than by choice, we'd like to do something else. Who can blame us?

For some, grabbing the "always-wants" means enjoying full-time leisure. David and Laura Rausch, for example, always dreamed of living on a sailboat, free to explore the world according to wind and whim. But others, agreeing with George Bernard Shaw, who once said that a "perpetual holiday is a good working definition of hell," choose to take on added responsibility, often by starting their own businesses. They don't want the freedom to play golf as much as the freedom to make their own mistakes. No more orders. No more pleasing the boss. It's time to *be* the boss. Now or never!

> *ITEM* A survey by Challenger, Gray and Christmas revealed that two out of three executives at least consider starting their own businesses. It means, says David Birch, an M.I.T. research director who has studied entrepreneurship, that they are "controlling their own destiny."

> *ITEM* According to studies at the University of Minnesota and the University of Pennsylvania, the prime age for starting a business is midlife. "A great many business owners do not start their business until they have a wealth of experience," says Thomas A. Gray, director of the Office of Economic Research at the Small Business Administration.

It's not an easy road—almost 25 percent of new small businesses cease to exist for one reason or another within two years—but while some folks dream of ease, others dream of challenge. "My-Time can be busier than before, but it doesn't feel busier because the people are finally doing what they like," says career counselor Marilyn Kennedy.

And, the difference between captain of a ship and owner of a company isn't all that great—as long as it fulfills the dream.

A Thirst for Change

A few of us have change built into our jobs. Most of us don't. Most of us do the same thing over and over again. Oh, we may move to a different company, work on different projects, advance to different positions. But we're still occupied with the same basic set of problems: how to design a computer, cure a patient, or sell a product.

The years pass, and we get very good at what we do. But what was once a challenge is now a routine. We've climbed the mountain before, and we already know what's on the other side: another damn mountain. The hike is getting routine; the backpack seems increasingly heavy. In short, we're bored.

But there's another reason we may want change: frustration,

coupled with a tinge of fear. We feel young. We look young. But as we look around us, we see all these kids, young enough to be our children, being promoted to positions of responsibility. If they're grown-up enough to be young adults does that make us, heaven forbid, *old* adults? Does that mean that soon we'll be, oh no, *unnecessary?*

Quite likely. While we can't be forced to retire till we reach seventy, we can be forced to stand still. And most of us will be. In 1980, says Judith Bardwick, a professor of clinical psychiatry at the University of California at San Diego, white male managers peaked in their careers at forty-seven; now they hit the top between forty and forty-two. Because of racism and sexism, women and minorities plateau by age thirty-eight. But at that age we've got almost half a life left to live!

This stagnation is perfectly understandable from the company's point of view. When we were hired, fresh from college with sparkling résumés, our employers needed a lot of eager beavers. But, says Bardwick, "of a hundred people who are hired because they have all the right qualities and look outstanding, only ten will reach any level of middle management and only one will reach the executive level. . . . It's the reason promotions end long before retirement for essentially everyone." It is, she adds, "a numbers game."

And it's going to get worse.

ITEM Today there are ten people vying for every middle-management spot. By 1995 there will be thirty, says Ron Zemke, president of Performance Research Associates in Minneapolis.

Can our egos withstand the blow? "In our society," says A. J. Jafee of the Bureau of Applied Social Research at Columbia University, "the lack of continued progress is tantamount to failure." Maybe, just maybe, we decide, it's better to quit while we're ahead. Maybe we should walk out before we're thrown out. That way we can find something else to do while we've still the energy to make a go of it.

This was the idea that motivated Jim and Carlene Pasin.

• •

Profile: Jim and Carlene Pasin—Midlevel Manager and Full-Time Homemaker to Direct Mail Gurus

Change is one form of hope; to risk change is to believe in tomorrow.

LINDA ELLERBEE

Jim Pasin, now forty-nine, worked for Chevron U.S.A. Inc. for twenty-five years, beginning as a gas station attendant and ending up as a senior training specialist. During those years his wife, Carlene, now fifty, took charge of raising their two children and supervising the family's frequent moves. Since Jim's retirement in 1986 the entire family has joined together to run Money Mailers℠, a direct mail marketing firm that both serves the Seattle-Tacoma area and sells franchises throughout the Pacific Northwest. Their daughter Selena, who graduated from college with a degree in international marketing, is twenty-seven; their son Tony is twenty-two.

"Haven't you ever wished you could have another lifetime so you could be a farmer, or so you could lie on a beach, or so you could do whatever?" Carlene Pasin, a small woman with short gray hair and a trim figure, usually speaks softly and lets her husband dominate the conversation, but now her voice rings with conviction. "Well, Jim's early retirement gave us another life. You don't say no when you get the opportunity to go on and do something else."

Jim looks at her affectionately and nods his agreement. We are in the Money Mailer conference room, seated around a large wood table. Soft music is playing over the speaker, and on the walls are some nicely framed displays of successful mail packets.

The Pasins had asked us to meet them at their office in Gig Harbor, Washington, a small village on the southern shore of Puget Sound. Although it was 6:30 P.M. when we arrived, several people—including all four Pasins—were still busily at work. Jim, a rather large man dressed in the conservative executive's uniform of gray suit, white shirt, and dark red tie, greeted us enthusiastically; and as he led us through the office, *he gave us a rapid-fire introduction to the vagaries of direct mail and to the workings of Money Mailers in particular. It was obvious that in the two and a half years since he officially opened the company, things have started to boom.*

"It's strange," he says. "When Carlene and I discussed leaving Chevron, we talked about retiring. I never looked at it as a change of career, although I guess that's what I ended up doing. We just saw an opportunity that seemed challenging and we said, 'Let's give it a try.' "

"But why did you leave?" I ask. "You had a pretty good job, didn't you?" Jim leans forward and rests his arms on the table.

JIM: I had a *very* good job. A lot of people couldn't visualize why I'd want to give that up to do something else. A lot of people would like to be at the level I was at. I got to a point, I guess, where I just had to look at what my values are.

Because of where I was in the organization, I was privy to a lot of information about people and numbers of people. I knew how many jobs were above me and what my probability was for going much higher in the organization. Just to kind of share with you: out of eighty-six thousand people, there were only three thousand jobs in the whole organization worldwide that were higher than my job classification. In my area there were just a hundred and forty-six jobs above mine. So I just said, "I'm forty-five now. Do I want to stay where I am or maybe just advance a step or two more for the next ten or fifteen years, or do I want to move on?"

A few years earlier, Chevron had purchased Gulf. The two companies had, like I said, somewhere around eighty-six thousand employees, and their goal was to get it down to about sixty thousand. Now that's quite a drop. Some of it would be through attrition, but they also started offering early retirement packages to people who'd been in the system a long time. I saw this as an opportunity.

Carlene and I had already decided I was going to leave the organization at around age fifty-five. This just moved it up a few years. Carlene lost her father at a fairly early age; he was fifty-two when he died. And I had to talk like mad to get my father to retire from Seattle First National Bank when he was sixty-four. He and my mom enjoyed maybe five or seven years of good health when they were able to travel and do their thing, and then Dad got sick, Mom got sick, and it was . . . *[His voice trails off.]*

There were other things, too. A few years earlier I'd gone into work on Monday and found one of my friends had died over the weekend while he was working in his garden. He was the same age as I was. And maybe six months after that a fellow from my home town—I'd known him for such a long time—he died. I think he was about fifty-three at the time.

I said, "You know, life's too short to not enjoy it." *[He smiles at Carlene.]* We did some crazy things then. Like I'd always wanted a big boat and we'd always said, "No, we can't afford it." Then the first friend of mine died, and I said, "To hell with that," and we went and bought a boat the next weekend.

What good does it do to have a lot of money and time when you're too old to enjoy it or you're not around to see it? I just took a look at what was going on in the world with my friends, and I said, "I'm not going to let that happen to me. Hopefully."

And there's one more thing that really began to hit me in the face around the time I decided to leave Chevron. I'll qualify some of this because in no way could I ever be derogatory about that company. I was fortunate in my career beyond what most people ever expect; but when I walked out the front door after twenty-five years, everything I had done and accomplished was left behind. I had some money and some stock, but I had nothing else to give to her *[he nods toward Carlene]*, to my kids, to anybody. All of my ideas and programs were owned by the company; some of them are even copyrighted, so I can't use them at all.

Now I look at this crazy business, Money Mailers, and I think that I'm building something that's mine. Four or five years from now, I hope I'll have a little office that I just come to once in a while and Tony and Selena can run the business. They'll have something here and, if they take care of it, they'll never have to worry about anything. I'm helping build something for my kids.

So when the early retirement offers were announced, I knew I had to look at them closely. I turned the first one down; it just wasn't right for me. But then about eighteen months later they modified the program, and it was something I really had to consider.

A lot of my friends are still trapped in the system, as I put it, because now the early retirement offers are gone and they can't get out. There's this one fellow . . . he and I used to go to lunch together, and I tried like mad to talk him into leaving the company when I did. But he could still see this little carrot out in front of himself, so he stayed. *[Jim shakes his head sadly.]* Since that time his wife has died of cancer. Now he's retired, but he's all alone. It's that kind of thing that drove me to do what I did.

But when I told my boss, the vice president of finance, that I was going to leave, he started to laugh. "Come on, you're kidding," he said. "You're too young."

CARLENE: That was a lot of people's reaction. The word "retire" is like a cane; people associate it with old age. Jim just didn't fit people's image of a retired person.

When Jim retired, he wasn't exactly sure what he was going to do. But because of his philosophical belief in early retirement, he and Carlene were both psychologically and financially prepared to cut the corporate ties. Jim left Chevron with a lump sum of $200,000 from his pension and savings funds, and the couple owned three condominiums plus their house in the San Francisco area. They knew that money wasn't an immediate concern.

JIM: We figured we could always move back to the little town where we grew up, Cle Elum, Washington. You can buy a fairly nice house there for $50,000, and you could live on $1,000 a month if you wanted to. We could have moved there and kicked back and not worked at all.

But I wasn't sure that's what I wanted to do. I was fortunate, because all the positions I had held at Chevron gave me an education, a lot of marketable skills, whether I wanted to work for somebody else or do my own thing.

We just cleared off the table and said, "What do we want to do, where do we want to be, how are we going to do it?" We really started having fun exploring things.

CARLENE: Jim has such an energy level that I don't know if he could ever do just nothing. His mind just works too fast.

JIM: We spent about seven months looking around. We looked at all kinds of businesses, up and down the West Coast, like 7-Eleven stores, galleries, Hallmark stores. For a while we thought of starting a consulting business. Then we came across this direct mail thing. It just looked good.

I looked at my skills to see if I had the ones needed to make it work. I took all the information they gave me and phoned other regional owners to check things out. Then I looked at the competition and went over my financial calculations. I suppose I was a little nervous about the capital investment required to buy rights to the northwestern states. But because of some of the evaluations I did, I knew that if I sold x number of franchises, I could get my initial investment back fairly easily.

Before I bought the business, I made up the first year's budget. I did a lot of figuring. The first year's budget almost hit it on the nailhead, and the second year was about right, too. Like I said, I was pretty familiar with this kind of planning and budgeting from my experience at Chevron. I use the things I learned there every day.

Oh, I suppose there are a few little things I miss by not being with a big company. I don't know what you call it exactly, maybe "recognition." If you tell someone you work for Chevron, they know what you're talking about; tell them you work for your own company, and they've never heard of you. And there were some exciting things I was always involved in, sales meetings and that kind of stuff.

But I guess the only part I really mind is losing track of some of the people. When you leave a big company, your friends are all over the place; and you don't stay in touch with them anymore. You try to, but you can't keep up the network like when you actually work in an organization.

The Pasins lived near San Francisco during Jim's last years at Chevron; Money Mailers allowed them to move back to the Northwest. Their current home in Gig Harbor is not too far from where Carlene and Jim, high school sweethearts, grew up.

JIM: My father still lives up here in Cle Elum. Since he was a banker, I think he always expected me to be one, too. But here I was, pumping gas at a part-time job to put myself

through college, and I was making more money than some of
the bank people.

After I finished college—I went to Central Washington University and majored in economics—I went to my boss at the
gas station and said, "Hey, I've graduated now; you oughta
give me a good job." My boss said, "Just relax and pump gas."
[Jim flashes a wry smile.] So I did, but within two or three
months they transferred me to another small town and made
me assistant manager of a gas station. I was still pumping gas,
but I got to supervise a couple of people. Then they called me
one Friday and said, "Be in Spokane on Monday." I'd been
promoted to the regional office, and I got to wear a suit. Things
just kept going along like that.

We got transferred all over, ending up down near San Francisco. It's good to be back up here, closer to my father. He's
eighty-one years old now, and I'm not too sure he understands
why I retired. All he says is, "Boy, I hope you know what you're
doing." I think I do.

Am I working as hard as I did at Chevron? I don't know. It's
hard to measure, but I like it better. I can make things happen
here. I don't have to go through a bunch of committees and wait
around for decisions. If we want to do something, we do it. If it
works, great; and if it doesn't, we change it. I enjoy that. And
working together with Carlene and the kids is good, too.

My son, Tony, came in right at the beginning. He and I kind
of laughed because we just had one little section of office space
and we had to remodel and we didn't even have a desk or
chair. We sat on the floor in there trying to figure out what we
were going to do. We didn't have any place to live at first—
Carlene was back in California selling the house—so we bought
a boat, which we were planning to do anyway, and he and I
lived there together for a while.

CARLENE: This has been good for all of us as a family. We've
always been close, even with Jim traveling as much as he used
to, but this has really given us each other again.

Tony and Selena live with us in our house. We're lucky
because moving up here from California, where houses are
more expensive, we were able to afford a fairly good-sized
home. So we're not tumbling over each other all the time. And

when we come in the front door of the office in the morning, we all have our own separate duties that we need to do. We're not really together all that much during the day.

[Carlene hesitates for a second, and then a rush of words pours forth.] I've always been a follower, and Jim's always been very good at putting down a path for me to follow. I liked being a homemaker but, well, I guess maybe you do get to a point where you want a lot more. Now, of course, my learning scale has been almost vertical. I've been very sheltered, and this has been quite a growth experience for me, quite a learning curve. I love it; I absolutely love it.

JIM: It's true; we've had a lot of good times working together. *[He smiles.]* We can all laugh about some of the good things, and we can all laugh about some of the bad things that have happened.

I'm pretty sure I know the answer, but I ask the question anyway. "If you had it to do over again, would you still choose early retirement?" Jim's answer is instantaneous. "You bet!" he says with a broad grin.

• •

Like so many other midlifers Jim recognized the fact that, as Jacqueline Kelley, board member of the International Society of Retirement Planning, puts it, he was "no longer a 'going-to-be' but an 'I am.'" And, she continues, "There's a point when you know you don't have that much time left, so if there's something else you want to do, you'd better get on with it."

About this time, most of us begin counting our money.

EXERCISE

The Years to Come

Imagine your life stretched before you like a long road that vanishes somewhere on the horizon. When you turn and look over your shoulder to see the distance you've already traveled, you see years filled with events, activities, and, yes, work. What do you see when you look ahead?

Take a piece of narrow-ruled paper, and cut off the wide space at the top. Now cut the paper vertically into three equal parts. Tape these parts together so that you have one long strip of paper. The lines divide your strip into ninety-nine equal parts—one for each possible year of your life.

Using a pen, mark the year of your birth in the space on the far left of your life-strip. Then, count up the years until you reach your present age; mark this space as well. Along the way, fill in some of the highlights of your past: the interests that have filled your life, the activities you have participated in, the awards you have won, the personal milestones you have experienced.

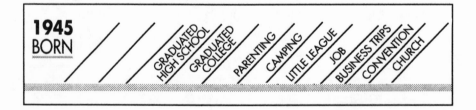

Finally, on the far right of the paper in about the eightieth space, put a big question mark. As the chart below shows, most of us can expect to live until approximately eighty years old. (Remember, in most cases a person's life expectancy increases as he gets older.)

DATE OF BIRTH	LIFE EXPECTANCY/ MEN	LIFE EXPECTANCY/ WOMEN
1965	73.3	79.5
1945	75.1	77.4
1925	79.2	83.1

The future stretches out on the right, the years still empty of activities. How do you want to fill these years? What things would you like to accomplish? What activities would you like to pursue? What subjects would you like to explore? Write the

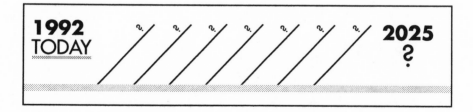

answers in the blank spaces of your future. Use a pencil (so you can easily change your mind), and write down the first things that come to your mind. This is just a preliminary look at some of the possibilities that lie ahead of you; as you progress through this book, you'll undoubtedly change and refine your ideas.

If you don't want to work, you have to work to earn enough money so that you won't have to work.

OGDEN NASH

3 | *MONEY MATTERS*

Money's importance can hardly be overestimated. When pollsters asked a group of Americans if they spent more time thinking about money or about sex, the answer was money, by a margin of 13 percent. If we think about it that much under ordinary circumstances, you can imagine how money-obsessed we become when we consider retiring or changing jobs. In fact, most retirement and career planning seminars are concerned with little else.

On the surface financial management should be relatively easy. Money, after all, follows certain relatively immutable rules: If we work more, we'll earn more. If we save now, we'll have later. And if we live modestly, we won't need that much, ever. Why then is money so complicated? And why do so many of us manage it so poorly?

Experts say it's because money is an emotional currency as well as a financial one. Dollars we can cope with, but our psyches are another story! Money, they explain, buys much more than cars and clothes; it also buys psychological satisfaction. We can spend it wildly—fancy cars, glitzy jewels, expensive gifts—in order to bolster our self-esteem, demonstrate our power, or try to purchase love. Or we can do the opposite, squirrel it away in order to build a greenback wall between ourselves and an uncertain world.

Few of us are totally rational about money. "Amazingly, the psychological and financial arenas have never joined forces," says Kathleen Gurney, President of Financial Psychology Corporation in Cincinnati. "None of the advice givers get to the root of the dilemma—making your emotional self work in harmony with your money self." And Henry Clay Lindgren, professor emeritus of psychology at San Francisco State University, says, "If the history of the human race were reduced to the span of a single week, money would have appeared on the scene only fifteen minutes ago. It has nevertheless penetrated and permeated the human psyche more than any other intervention except language."

Even those who have money, plenty of money, act a little crazy about it.

ITEM Howard Hughes had a financial empire worth over $2.5 billion dollars. If he had spent $2 million a month, twelve months a year, it would have taken him over 100 years to get rid of this much money—and that's not counting the compounding effect of interest! Yet he died a recluse, interested only in amassing more and more wealth.

ITEM J. Paul Getty was another of the richest men in the world. He made his first million when he was only twenty-three years old, and he continued to multiply it throughout his life. Yet he asked his guests to use pay telephones which he installed throughout his seventy-two-room home.

ITEM Hetty Green inherited her father's estate of $6 million. By the time she died, her shrewd investments had increased it to approximately $100 million, a tidy sum in 1916. Yet she spent little on herself; and when her son injured his knee, she refused to take him to a private doctor. Instead, she disguised him as a pauper and tried to get him treated as a charity case. Because the leg was not treated promptly, it had to be amputated.

Those of us with less money may squander it more, but regardless of how much or how little we have, we keep the details a secret. A study by psychologist James A. Knight revealed that "[People] show far less resistance in relating hatred for their parents or in disclosing sexual perversities than in discussing their money status or transactions. It is as if they equate money with their inmost being."

Money Mystique

Few of us see money for what it really is: a medium of exchange. In and of itself, it has no value. It's a piece of paper, a disk of metal, a rectangle of plastic. "It's just a figment of our collective imagination, really. A symbol for what it represents," says Maria Nemeth, an associate professor in the Department of Psychiatry, University of California at Davis.

Not all countries and cultures use the same symbols. Woodpecker scalps, pig jawbones, salt, animal skins, and beads have all served as money in various parts of the world. Today the people of Yap, one of the four island-states of the Federated States of Micronesia, exchange huge calcium-carbonate disks that are sometimes 12 feet in diameter. And in much of the world, checks and credit cards are used nearly as often as coins and bills.

But unless you have an unlimited number of these papers of green and coins of silver, restyling will force you to make some choices. You'll have to ask yourself some hard questions: How much is a new lifestyle worth? Do you prefer it to an annual trip to Hawaii? To a new car every few years? To an Ivy League education for your kids?

Even if you don't need a regular paycheck in order to survive, do you need one in order to sleep? How will you feel if the Dow drops fifty points? If inflation runs rampant? How big a safety net do you need in order to be comfortable?

The first step to planning your financial future is to understand your present money attitudes. "Positive and negative experiences during infancy and childhood, cultural impact, and early training all help to define attitudes and behavior toward money," says Herb Goldberg, professor of psychology at California State University at Los Angeles. "If those attitudes and behavior now prove troublesome or inappropriate, they can be unlearned."

It's not easy to be totally pragmatic about money. But Rich Henke rarely forgets that money is, after all, no more than our society's version of 12-foot rocks.

....

Profile: Rich Henke—High Tech to High Altitudes

Money often costs too much.

RALPH WALDO EMERSON

Rich Henke, forty-seven, worked in both engineering and finance for a large aerospace company, first in Northern California and then, after a promotion, in Southern California. He quit right before his forty-fifth birthday. Now he spends his time climbing mountains, taking photographs, and traveling to remote corners of the world. He got divorced long before restyling entered his mind; but he keeps in close touch with his two daughters, Andrea and Marla, who were seventeen and thirteen when their father left his job.

For Rich Henke there was no single incident that sparked his urge to retire. He just counted. "If you wait till fifty-five or sixty or sixty-five to retire, you just don't have that much time remaining to do all the things you want to do," he says simply.

He agreed to meet with us at our home near San Francisco, since he was driving up from Los Angeles to see his daughters. He rings the bell right at the appointed hour, and although he speaks softly, the air around him seems charged with vitality. He's a small man with thinning blond hair and sharp, chiseled features. Bounding in, he sets his briefcase on the floor and smiles. "Let's go," he says. The words—punctuated with self-deprecating chuckles—tumble out.

It all started in 1982, February I think it was. I went up to Sequoia National Park with my girlfriend on a weekend ski trip. For some reason we started talking about all the things I like to do and about how I'd really like to stop work early and have time to do them. That was when I said, "Hey, I'm going to put together a plan and see if I can really do this."

Before that it was just kind of a dream. You know, Well, gee, it'd be nice to not have to work and have more time. But I never really thought about it seriously. That weekend for the first time it became, Hey, maybe this isn't just a wild dream. Maybe it's something that is really possible.

It was this realization that got me to sit down when I got home and start writing things down on a piece of paper. I asked myself how much money would it take, and what type of style of living would I want, and what would I really want to do. The end result was I ended up with a plan that said, Yeah, this makes sense. In five or six or seven years I can quit work. After that initial planning, life just kind of went on; but I had something to look forward to.

I was working in the finance department at TRW, a very high technology kind of place that does work for the government. But I always had a lot of outside activities and never enough time to do them. I was—still am—into a lot of mountain climbing, sports, photography, everything.

I used to leave work Friday night, drive all night to go someplace, then ski or climb all weekend, get back at midnight on Sunday and go back to work the next day. I also had some "comp time" arrangements so a lot of times I'd put in forty hours Monday through Thursday, not work on Friday, and then the next week not show up till Tuesday and put in forty hours Tuesday through Friday. Since I'm a high-energy person, I was able to do all that. Every so often though, I'd get kind of tired . . . *[He laughs heartily.]*

Finally sometime in the late seventies I decided I was going to start taking future raises in time off without pay. If I got a ten percent raise, I'd just take time off without pay and have the same money as before. But about that time I had a promotion opportunity. I figured, Well, I'll just make more money and postpone all this. So I started working three times as hard. Then came that weekend at Sequoia, and I realized I really didn't have to do all this.

He rummages in his briefcase for a few seconds. "Here are some of the forms I used," he says, handing me several sheets of paper. I comment that they look very similar to the standard forms that many financial planners use. "They are," he answers, "except a lot of forms want to find out how to use your money to make more money; mine want to see how to take your money and live off it." He occasionally lapses into a professorial manner as he explains his approach to retirement.

This isn't very sophisticated stuff; it's not like you need a degree in finance to do it. You just sit down and do some calculations like how much money do you have in the bank, how much is your house worth, what about inflation, how long do you think you are going to live, and—the key thing—how much money do you need per year to do the type of things you want to do. You think about all those things, not in a vague sense but in a more analytical sense. First you say, What am I really putting away toward quitting work? You see what your salary is, how much is really going into savings, and how much is being spent and how it's being spent. You come up with your total annual savings.

Then you look at your assets and say, What's my net worth? You recompute this every six months or so. It's supposedly getting bigger.

The third part is to figure for the future. In the future what would you like to spend, in today's dollars. Remember money is your standard of living. If you like to do expensive things, take luxurious cruises, it's a tough trade-off. Hopefully, in the future your monthly expenses are going to be somewhat less than they are now because you'll cut back on your lifestyle. If they're not going to be any less, you just need more money before you quit your job.

In my case, I felt comfortable quitting work with maybe a lower level of assets than many people would because I'm not a heavy consumer of the latest gadgets—with a few exceptions here and there!

I did the calculations pretty carefully. I didn't actually get out my last year's bills, but I thought everything through month by month: house payments, mortgage, gas and electric, food—all the things I pay by check. Then I put a couple hundred dollars into miscellaneous expenses per month, and I added in the annual expenses: property tax, income tax—those things. I have a fairly good feeling of how much money I'm spending. Of course I also had to factor in my obligations to the kids. This is something I had to project into the future, factor in getting them through college.

Inflation really complicates things. You tend to say, Gee, I can't do this because who knows what inflation is going to be. So I decided that in order to make my plan work, I just couldn't get caught up in all these details. Then I'd just say, It's too complicated. I can't figure it out; therefore, I'm going to keep going to the office every day. I made the decision way up front to keep it simple and worry about the details later.

In planning how much money I'll have, I use a real simple formula. If you have $500,000 and invest it at ten percent, that's going to give you $50,000 a year as income flow. You don't get caught up in how you're going to invest that money; that's something you can work on later. If $50,000 is what you need to live comfortably, then at that point you're not bringing down your assets; you're just living off the interest. The real simple assumption I made was to assume that as inflation goes up, I'll start drawing down my assets, use them to cover inflation. It may or may not work out exactly right; but otherwise it gets so complicated, you just give up. I figure if it ever looks like I have a little less money than I thought I would, I'll figure out a way to earn a little bit more. But since I quit work, my assets have been building up, so I feel very comfortable. Hey, they're going the right way!

Once you have these three pieces of data—how much you're saving now, what your assets are, and how much you need to spend in the future to be happy—then you can start to plan.

Over a period of time, my plans got more definite. In the spring of 1986 I told my boss I was going to quit work that summer. All I had to do was sell my house because that was the last step in the process.

Rich devised a scheme whereby he would carry the financing on his home in Los Altos, an upscale community in the San Francisco Bay Area. It made financial sense, but putting it into action was more difficult than he anticipated.

I planned to carry the financing when I sold my house so I'd have money coming in every month instead of getting it all at once. I didn't want that one big tax hit when I sold the house. I knew I'd still be paying taxes on the money as I received it each year; but after I left work, I'd be in a fairly low tax bracket.

This plan takes a little more work because you have to make sure you get the right buyer and the right deal. You have to work with someone who's willing to have you carry the financing, but if you give them a better interest rate than they can get somewhere else, you can usually talk them into it. I'm not taking any risk. I'm just acting as a bank. If the buyer doesn't pay, I just repossess the house.

I tried to put in a prepayment penalty, but I wasn't able to negotiate that part. So if the buyer sells the house, there's no guarantee the new buyers will pick up my note. If they refinance the thing, the bank would pay me off and I'd have big taxes that year. I have that risk.

It took me a long time to find the right buyer. I had the house on the market, and I just couldn't sell it. I was very frustrated because I had this whole summer planned—travel, doing stuff with my kids, and so forth. But the real estate market was dead. I really couldn't quit work unless I sold the house because it was the difference between $2,000 coming in per month or $2,000 going out. So I went back and told my boss, "Well, I'm going to hang in here for a while yet." *[He runs his hand through his hair and grimaces.]* It took another year and a half before I managed to get the house thing settled.

I was nervous up to this point because everything wasn't cut and dried yet. Until I sold the house, I didn't know how much I was going to get for it, whether I was going to carry the financing, what the tax liabilities would be. These were a bunch of things that could vary a lot. But now the plan is all set up and working.

This isn't necessarily risky. Not working is probably less risky than the person with a high standard of living who's making $100,000 a year and goes off to start a new venture. If it doesn't work and he wants to keep living the way he is, he's in trouble. But I know exactly how much is coming in and how much is going out. It's pretty secure once you do it.

I mean, assuming you don't think your assets will disappear, the only uncertainty tends to be, Are you really happy with how much you think you're going to be spending? Did you set that right, or did you say, Yeah, I'll never eat out again?

Well, sure, at the time I actually had my going-away party at work, I felt a hesitancy. Not a lot, but I had a few funny feelings, like Gee, I'm really doing this. I'm not going back! What if I made a mistake? Maybe I should have looked more at inflation!

Rich left work in February 1987, five years after initiating his plan at the ski cabin in Sequoia National Park. Not working was, he says, "no adjustment at all."

I just didn't miss it a bit. I continued working part-time for a few months on a consulting basis, finishing up a job, but then I left and didn't come back. I hadn't worked at all for about two years when my boss called and said, "We've got something we could use you to do for a month or so." There was really some trepidation then because I wondered if I would remember any of this stuff. Would I be able to do anything useful or would I be twiddling my thumbs while they were paying me a consultant's salary? That was a bigger transition—coming back—than when I left initially. It worked out all right, but I doubt if I will go back again unless for some reason I need the money. Anyway, if I stay away very long, I'll be obsolete technically.

Until I quit work I was a very traditional person: college, job, family. I was a good student in high school and then I majored in physics in college. I ended up getting my masters in applied math and did engineering for ten years. Then I realized I was more interested in the management and organizational aspects of the company so I eventually got my MBA and moved over to the financial side of the same company.

Now I have absolutely no trouble finding things to do. I almost laugh when people say, "What do you do to keep busy?" That's just never been an issue for me in my entire life. I've always had more things to do than I had time to do them in.

Where should I start? I've always been very active in sports. In school I played basketball, baseball, and track. I still play basketball—now I'm in an over-forty league—and I try to run almost everyday. I started skiing when I was twenty-seven or twenty-eight, started mountaineering and rock climbing in my mid-thirties. For the last eight years that's really been my main emphasis, mountaineering. But I'm still picking up new sports. Mountain biking has been a hobby for the last four or five years, and in the last two years I've been river kayaking and sea kayaking.

Then I love to travel. I do budget travel rather than luxury travel. It's an interesting way to see the world because it gets you closer to the people you're there to see. The more money you spend, the more you isolate yourself from what you came to see.

When I first left work, Rena *[his companion]* and I went to Nepal, Tibet, Singapore, Bali, Java, Hong Kong, and China. We were gone four months in all. The whole trip cost us about $5,000 each; about half of that was airfare. Then we were in Africa for five weeks. I did a Mt. Kenya climb. Now I want to go to Indonesia . . .

I thought I would have more time than I really do. I've gotten involved in too many new things, which is predictable for me, I guess. I've been taking photographs for a long time, ever since I got out of college. I've been doing it fairly seriously for the last fifteen years in terms of really trying to take good pictures. I don't do any developing, just work on composition and try to be in interesting places, which is one of the things that makes pictures look good.

I could clearly make some money with photography if I ever got around to spending some time doing it. I have twenty-five thousand cataloged slides. Well, half of them are cataloged, the others aren't. But like I said, I never have enough time!

In 1988 Rich combined his three main interests—sports, travel, and photography—by leading a group of people on a trek in Nepal. It was so successful, he formed a small company, Adventure Plus.

I've come up with treks that are a little different from what other companies do. I specialize in areas that are least influenced by Western visitors. I just market to friends and friends of friends. So far I've been doing one trip a year. I'm sure I could do more trips, but then I'd be so busy running them that

I wouldn't have time to do other things. There's a lot of work involved in setting it all up.

If I make some money from this, fine; but if I don't make money from it, that's okay, too. In 1988 I got all my expenses paid for and I made $10,000, but that's not part of the plan. Anything I get from it is a plus.

Right now I like doing this—it's fun and I get a kick out of it—but I may or may not continue. It's not like I quit my job in order to form this company. I haven't just traded one job for another. I want to be very careful about that.

Clasping his hands behind his head, Rich sits back and reflects for a minute.

I guess I've been lucky. I've had a lot of support. I didn't get any negative response at all when I told people I was retiring. Not even at work, where people think quitting early is unbelievable. TRW is a fairly conservative place where people don't do very different things, and just the fact that I liked mountain climbing made me kind of weird. My boss just shook his head, but he supported me.

Many people can't even comprehend not working until they're fifty-five or sixty. They think, It'd be nice not to have to work, but it's just purely a dream. It couldn't possibly happen for me. I say just the opposite. Many, many people could leave their jobs if they were willing to make some of the trade-offs. Just live a little simpler.

It's really a trade of money for time, and I wanted the time more than I wanted the money. It all seems pretty straightforward to me.

• •

Most of us make it a lot more complicated. Like King Midas, who wanted everything he touched to turn to gold, we *love* money. We seem to forget the end of the Midas tale: the old fellow nearly died because he could not eat or drink the gold.

It's true that having money is nice. No doubt about it. In 1976 researchers for the Gallup/Kettering Global Survey on Human Needs and Satisfactions debunked the myth of the poor but happy native. After interviewing 10,000 individuals of all economic levels living in seventy countries, they announced, "In the planning stages of this global survey it was hoped that somewhere in the world a nation would be found whose people are poor but happy. We didn't find such a place."

Yet how much money do we really need? The 1960s, when human concerns replaced monetary ones for a large segment of the population, were but a bleep on the graph of materialistic yearnings of Americans. One hundred fifty years ago French traveler Alexis de Tocqueville noted that "the love of wealth is at the bottom of everything that the Americans do."

As restylers we have to reevaluate our quest for money. Why do we want money? What needs does it fulfill for us? And are there other ways of fulfilling these needs? Then we can move on to the number-crunching stage of preparing a financial plan for restyling. But until the psychological ground is firm, the bottom line keeps shifting.

Emotional Currency

Respect. Power. Love. Security. Freedom. Worthy goals, all of them. Deep-seated needs. And desires that many of us try to fulfill with money. Consider:

- People who dress tastefully but expensively feel important. Their self-esteem is bolstered through costly props.
- People who influence legislators, have underlings do their work for them, or use money to control their children are buying power. They may be less interested in the results of their actions than in the fact that they can force others to do their bidding.
- People who give glittery gifts may not be able to buy love, but they are rarely without companions.
- People who accumulate money so that, if necessary, they can afford the best medical care, repair their houses in case of an earthquake, and survive even if the government goes bankrupt are concerned with security. They are buying protection against what they feel is an unkind and unpredictable world.
- Other people who build hefty bank accounts do so in order to feel free. They want options, to be able to say what

they want to say and do what they want to do. "If I have enough money, what's the worst that can happen?" they ask themselves. "The boss can fire me. So what?"

Rich Is More Important

In America we pride ourselves on being a classless society; and perhaps, compared to others, we are. Yet we still rank people according to the size of their income. Oh, we know better. We know that it's unworthy, perhaps even immoral, to honor the rich. After all, is a lawyer who makes $200,000 a year a more valuable human being than a janitor making but a small fraction of that? Of course not. The lawyer might bilk his clients while the janitor might donate dimes to the homeless. There's not one among us who would, without knowing a host of facts, say that the lawyer is "a better person." But most of us act as if he is.

ITEM In an experiment set up by social psychologists Anthony N. Doob and Alan E. Gross, an investigator alternated driving a sparkling new Chrysler and an old, worn Rambler. Regardless of which car he was driving, he planned to arrive at intersections in time for a red light. When the light changed to green, he delayed starting up for a full twelve seconds. An assistant in the back seat recorded how long it took the driver of the car behind them to begin honking. The result? Drivers were impatient and honked readily when the old car blocked their way, but they delayed honking at the drivers of the classier car. This, say the psychologists, shows that people pay deference to those they consider well-to-do.

ITEM During the mid-seventies San Franciscans became irate when they learned that street sweepers were earning an above-average salary. "Why should lowly street sweepers earn more than the rest of us?" protested the middle and upper class citizens. So great was the outcry that the sweepers eventually were downgraded to a lower salary.

The perceived relationship between wealth and worth has

been with us for a long time. In ancient Greece and Rome participants in religious ceremonies sacrificed bulls, giving part of the flesh to the gods and dividing the rest among themselves according to social rank. The bits of flesh were gradually replaced by metal coins: the most prestigious citizens were awarded gold, the next silver, and then bronze. So historically coins were used to confer status before they were used as a medium of exchange. And, since our society puts a price tag on human worth, we rate our own value in a similar manner. We begin to need money to bolster our self-esteem. Only the most secure among us seem able to resist.

> *ITEM* In order to belong to Mensa, a person must score in the top 2 percent of the population on intelligence tests. Yet a survey of these folks shows that they're only moderately successful in a financial sense. "They could probably make more," Mensa's executive director told *Money* magazine, "but they tend to work at what they like, not what pays best."

> *ITEM* Albert Einstein came to the United States just before World War II to work at Princeton University. When he requested an annual salary of $3,000, university officials were aghast. "But you deserve much more," they insisted. Einstein received $16,000 a year.

Most of us are more eager to accept the status that money confers. Diane Sawyer wants more money than Barbara Walters and Joe Montana wants more money than Dan Marino, not because they need dollars for dinner but because they need validation of their self-worth. "The money coming in is a communication of esteem in a language that cannot damn with faint praise, cannot hem and haw, cannot equivocate. . . . As such, it is sought most fervently by all those whose self-doubts make them crave official confirmation of their position," says Thomas Wiseman, author of *The Money Motive*.

Once that official confirmation is comfortably in the bank, we can begin to demonstrate our worth to others. We can purchase goods—clothes, cars, houses—that are visible proof of our worthiness. While we may be reluctant to tell people how much we make, showing our success through our possessions is acceptable behavior.

Or instead of buying material items, we can demonstrate our importance through the use of power. "Money is a metaphor for the ability to get things done," says the University of California's Nemeth. Stories of people who buy power regularly make the newspapers; they make us vaguely uneasy. We pass laws that limit campaign contributions in order to keep the rich from exerting undue influence, and we bemoan the fact that a person must be wealthy to run for political office. Yet these are only extreme examples of how we all use money to exert power. Rich people have more control over their daily lives. Whether they want a plumber to fix the bathtub, an immediate flight to Europe, or a special lunch with a legislator, they have the means to accomplish their goals.

Purchasing Love

Is money an aphrodisiac? Can love be bought? Probably not, at least not directly. In an interesting experiment to determine what resources people felt were equivalent to each other, social psychologist Uriel Foa gave participants cards that represented various resources such as love, status, and money. A person was asked to offer his cards, one at a time, to a partner who would decide which card he would present in exchange. Love and money were never considered equal trades. Yet love and status were frequently exchanged. Since money can buy status, it seems it can indeed be used to buy love.

ITEM Barters of money and status, masquerading under the name of love, is evident in the story of Anna Gould, daughter of railroad magnate Jay Gould. At nineteen Anna was lacking little except a husband and a title. Boniface, Count de Castellane, a charming and penniless European, was more than willing to change all that. The brief marriage cost Anna $12 million. It was, said the count, "the best investment the Goulds ever made."

The very rich are rarely at a loss for companions. Hundreds of women proposed marriage to J. Paul Getty, but he was under no illusion that they wished to spend their lives gazing into his blue eyes. "The magnetism I exert is of another color—green," he wrote wryly in his 1973 book, *How to Be Rich*.

And like Jay Gatsby, who believed that if only he were wealthy, Daisy would glide happily into his arms, many of us confuse the issue of love and money. We feel that if we can just send enough flowers, buy enough diamonds, give enough gifts, we'll have earned a person's everlasting love and devotion.

Saving for the What-Ifs

What if I get sick? What if the house falls down? What if the stock market drops, the company goes bankrupt, the boss gives me notice? Some of us live in a world of what-ifs. We worry all the time; and to alleviate these worries we want money, a lot of it, in the bank. Then if catastrophe strikes, we can get the best doctor, rebuild the house, live without a job. Money is protection. With a big enough bank account, we feel nothing can hurt us.

Like those who crave power, people who worry about security use money to feel in control. But rather than wanting to dominate others, they want to control the unknown dangers that lurk in the corners of their minds.

In a similar way some folks save money to buy freedom. This helps them feel in control over their environment because money gives them the means to change it. Money gives them an escape; they can do as they please. Every teen, struggling to break away from his parents, learns that he must have money in order to operate independently. It's a lesson few forget.

> *ITEM* San Francisco State psychology professor Henry Lindgren asked a group of young adults to name five important advantages they would gain if they became "instant millionaires." Every one included at least one statement that related to freedom.

Somerset Maugham summed it up best when, after earning substantial sums for his early writing, he was able to devote himself to his craft without worrying about the bills. "I found that money was like a sixth sense without which you could not make the most of the other five," he said.

What It All Means

Everyone needs to feel worthy, to have a certain degree of power, to be loved, to feel secure, and to be independent. There's nothing wrong with any of these goals, and many of us need money—or think we do—to achieve them. But sometimes we go berserk. Sometimes we defeat our own plans because we fail to see money for what it really is: a simple medium of exchange.

Most of us who want to restyle have to take finances into account. We simply don't have enough to walk off the job and live happily ever after. Even the best financial planner in the world can't structure a workable program if we're going to undermine it. And if we don't understand the money-emotion connection, we probably will.

If you're a person who spends excessively to fulfill your needs, you'll be unable to save enough money to responsibly restyle. If you're a person who has difficulty parting with your money, you may meet the prescribed financial goals but still be unwilling to give up your monthly paycheck.

Rich Henke makes restyling look very easy. He has a comfortable relationship with money. He plans but doesn't stay awake nights worrying about unforeseen developments; he is neither unduly cautious nor carelessly daring, and he trusts his own decisions.

Marian Gibson, on the other hand, was a risk-taker from the very beginning. Many of us would consider her actions foolhardy, but she knew her own money temperament. She never lost confidence in herself, and her risk brought handsome rewards.

. . . .

Profile: Marian Gibson—Child Care to Elder Care

*Don't let a need for material security keep you from taking
a chance on your dreams.*
                                        CHINESE FORTUNE COOKIE

*In 1981 Marian Gibson's dreams were considerably bigger than
her bank account. Still, at age forty-one she left the security of a
teaching position to start Temenos House, a personal care boarding home for old folks. She was divorced and had custody of her
two children, Andy and Krista, who were then in junior high
school. Her ex-husband provided $300 a month for child support.*

It's a few minutes before noon as my husband and I park the
car in front of an old, two-story, brick-and-clapboard house on
the outskirts of Denver. It is fronted by a large veranda and
surrounded by nineteen giant spruce trees; only a small plaque
on the door identifies it as Temenos House. "Come for lunch,"
Marian had told us cheerily. "You'll be able to meet all the old
people then; they love company."

Marian answers the door herself. She's dressed casually in
pants and a sweater; and at first glance she looks pleasant but
rather ordinary—medium height, light-brown curly hair, wire-
framed glasses. Then I notice her eyes. They shine with vitality,
glow with dedication. "There's an energy that comes from doing
what you want to do," she tells me later when I comment on
her intensity.

As we're taking off our coats, Mary, age ninety-one, walks
over to us, her cane tapping quietly on the floor. She extends a
frail welcome. Marian helps her get settled at the big dining
room table. "I'll be back in a few minutes," she says gently.

The staff is helping the other residents ride the stair glide
down the steps. It's a slow procedure, and Marian assures us
we have plenty of time for a quick tour of the house. "Eight old
people live here," she says as we enter the living room, a warm
blend of turn-of-the-century antiques, comfortable sofas, and
bright splashes of original art. "They stay with us until they
die, and we share the entire process with them and their fami-

lies. We help them through the transition between life and death. It can be very beautiful."

She stops and gives Orrin, ninety-two, a little hug. He responds by tipping his hat. "The greatest gift that any of these old people can give us is allowing us to care for them," she says softly. "It's wonderful; it's part of the human condition to be able to care for somebody. Somehow there's no separation between the person you're taking care of and you."

By the time we finish our tour, the staff has helped the old people get settled around the big dining room table. The conversation is animated; everyone is excited to learn that Temenos House will be mentioned in a book. "Tell them it's a fine place," says Orrin. I promise I will.

After lunch we go into an intimate parlor to the left of the living room, and I begin my questions. "On the phone you told me that for a while you and your children survived on not much more than spaghetti and beans while you were getting Temenos House set up. Weren't you scared?" I ask. Marian pauses for a few seconds before answering.

You know, as I was growing up, I used to wonder about my father. He was doing this humdrum job, but who was he? Where could his life have taken him that it never did? I sensed that the people I really admired were those who would take risks, get out of the humdrum. It's like from the outside it might look as though they're being really foolish, but to them, it's just a natural kind of path.

Following what I needed to do with my life became my priority, and money was underneath that. First things came first, and money could not be first. I was worried, and I didn't know where I was going to get money, and I can't say I didn't lose sleep over it. But not having it didn't change what I was going to do.

The bottom point came in 1984. I hadn't had any sort of job for over a year because I'd been devoting all my time to getting Temenos House ready. We were about to open, but we still didn't have any paying residents; and I'd used up every cent I had, about $40,000. I'd used a little of it for living, most of it for renovation, and then I completely ran out. I remember calling my parents, thinking I'd have to ask them because I had absolutely no money left and no one else to turn to. I got them on the phone and my mom started off by saying that they'd just bought a new car. She said, "We used the money that we had immediately accessible to us and now everything else is tied up in bonds or whatever. It makes me a little uneasy not to have some money we can get to immediately." So I never asked them for any money.

I decided I had only one choice and that was to go get food stamps. But I was rejected because I owned the house that was to become Temenos House. But the house wasn't feeding us. I went home and I didn't know what I was going to do. I was crying and this friend of mine, Dottie, said she had some pinto beans in her basement; and she came over and helped me cook up all these beans and put them in the freezer.

Then we had this wonderful hail storm and the roof got battered and so did my car. The insurance company gave me $1,500 for the car and $3,000 for a new roof. But the car still drove and the roof was only damaged, not actually leaking. So we had $4,500 and we made it through the summer!

My face must show my amazement, because Marian pauses and laughs. "Looking back, I don't know how I did it," she says, shaking her head. "But it seems as if my whole life was pointed toward doing something for old folks. It's like a seed was there; and as I grew older, it started germinating and finally started to flower." The seed for Marian was planted early, in the two-story house that she, her brother, sister, and parents, shared with her maternal grandparents.

Chicago is sort of a bunch of little towns—small ethnic communities—so since all my grandparents came from Czechoslovakia, it's like I grew up in a Czech settlement. There was something very special and respected about the old people there. They all spoke Czech, and it was disrespectful for us to speak English to them, even though they understood English. There was this sense that because they were older, you just did this.

I never knew why I really liked them, but I'm beginning to understand. It wasn't because of the wonderful stories they could tell or anything like that; it was because they were able to just be, to be in that settled spot where nothing had to be happening. It's the wisdom of old age; they can appreciate life in a way that other ages cannot.

My grandparents lived on the first floor of our house; we lived on the second. The downstairs was always a sanctuary for me. When my parents were cranky or unfair, my grandparents were always there for me, really understanding and giving. Even when I was in college, I'd come home from school and would go into my grandmother's room and just tell her what was going on. She was in her late seventies, early eighties at that time; and she always remained someone who was very interested in me.

You know, I was really fortunate to have her. I remember when she died I felt, There'll be nobody ever again who'll think I'm perfect. *[She laughs.]* It's always nice to have somebody think you're perfect, especially when you know you're not.

I had majored in Slavic Studies during college at Indiana University, and I really spent a great deal of time with the old Russian teachers, the White Russians who left Russia during the Revolution. They became real important to me. I realized I always seemed to be migrating to old people in spite of myself.

Despite her affinity for the aged, Marian, like so many women of her generation, ended up as a teacher of young children. She taught Russian and English in junior high school for a bit, got married, and then, while her husband was finishing his doctorate in psychology, she earned advanced degrees in special education and psychology.

Joe *[her husband]* got an internship at Fort Logan Mental Health Center in Denver, and we moved there. I got a job teaching in the children's division. Fort Logan was real progressive, an up-and-coming place at that point. Sixteen kids lived in a cottage and the social worker, psychologist, psychiatrist, teachers, and aids all worked together to help them. That's when I was introduced to residential care, and I really just felt that was the way to go.

I worked there for about two years, until my son was born. Andy was born in '68; Krista was born fourteen months later in '69. I was basically staying home with my kids, but some other women and I decided too many kids—mostly Chicanos— were dropping out of the school system, so we were going to reform the system. We ended up setting up an alternative education program in one of the Denver public schools. I really enjoyed that and, I don't know, maybe it helped me learn to deal with officials. There were a lot of them to deal with when I set up Temenos House.

When the kids got a bit older, I started teaching in the Denver public schools. I was working with disturbed elementary school–age kids. This was real important to me in terms of what became Temenos House because I got to set up this new program and I got to really work with what was going on.

By this time, 1974, Marian's marriage was in shambles. "It was," she says, "like everything I'd ever believed in had just gone up in air." She and Joe got divorced, and Marian knew she had to get in touch with what she really wanted to do with her life. She gradually became more and more interested in the teachings of Carl Jung.

This fit right in with what I was seeing happen in the classroom. In Jungian psychology, *temenos* is a sacred area around a cathedral. Jung says that within us we should all have a temenos, a secure spot out of which freedom can come. I realized I was creating a temenos for the children, that the tight structure in the classroom gave them security, and then learning ceased to be a problem for them.

So when I decided I really wanted to work with old people, I knew what I wanted to do was to create this secure environment where people are well taken care of in terms of structure. They'd have their food, their shelter, families who care about them, all the stuff they really need. I wanted to give old people a temenos, so we could see what really happens in old age, psychologically and spiritually.

In 1981 I took a sabbatical from teaching and during that year I volunteered in a huge nursing home. I ended up taking care of many of the people who were very close to death. I felt so good about what I was doing, and I remember telling this friend of mine, "There's something I have to do with old people. I'm not sure exactly what it is, but I have to work with them in some way." "You'll find the way," he told me. And I wrote a letter to the school district telling them I wasn't coming back. That was a real turning point. I was separating from the system and the security and saying, Okay, I really trust my life.

In the meantime, the kids and I were living in suburbia, and I felt so out of place. I felt we had to move into a neighborhood where there was much more of a cross-section, where there were old people, too. My daughter, Krista, and I were driving around one day and we saw this big old house—five huge bedrooms upstairs, two bedrooms and a bath on the main floor, a little apartment in the basement. The only way I could afford it was if we lived upstairs and rented out the basement apartment and the first floor bedrooms. So that was what we did. It was almost like the way I grew up, with extra people in the house.

But we didn't have much money at all. At one point I thought, Well, one thing I can do is go work at McDonald's. So I went to McDonald's and I got the job and I came home in my green and white uniform and told the kids. The McDonald's was right near their school and they said, "Mom, please don't do it, at least not at lunch time." I was really angry with them and I said, "I have to do this," but then the very next day I got a call from a home care agency that worked with the elderly. So I turned in my McDonald's uniform.

The home care agency was a good experience. I supervised the program where people went into the old people's homes and helped them out. One day I told the people at the home care agency that I was going to start a temenos for old people. They said, "What a wonderful idea. We can get a grant for this." I actually wrote a proposal, and one of the large foundations was really interested in it; but then I realized I'd just be working for another bureaucracy like the school system. I'd get funding for a year or two and then have to scramble to get money again. I'd be working for other people rather than doing my own thing. Saying no to any possible funding was almost a greater risk for me than leaving the schools.

Then I quit working at the home care agency so I could spend all my time starting Temenos House. That was probably the scariest time. I had no job; all I had was what I got from renting out the house and the $300 from Joe for the kids. It was about a year after that when the hailstorm saved us!

During that year Marian redid the house, dividing the five upstairs bedrooms into six bedrooms and a family room, adding a bath and an office. Then she put in adaptations for old people, such as a stair glide, call buttons, and hand rails.

A man helped me with some of the renovating, but I did all the painting myself, and a lot of the finishing, and all the draperies. This is what I loved; once again, I was creating an environment. I was really very happy that year in spite of all the money worries.

I also had to work with the state department to get the house up to code, set up the business with attorneys, make a brochure, hire staff. I'd never done any of these things before.

While I was doing all this, I pretty much isolated myself except for a very few friends. I didn't want to make it real public because I didn't want anyone questioning me. I felt people would be real judgmental; and there was part of me that was real judgmental of myself, that felt as though I wasn't being responsible. The fewer questions I had, the better off I was. I created a temenos for myself, because nobody understood how I could give up a secure teaching job to follow this idea.

The official opening was at the end of March 1984, but I gave myself till September not to panic. I was really scared though. We didn't get our first resident until July 7. It seemed the longest time; I really had to trust.

But I knew it was going to work when I got the first resident. That first resident—my God, how we loved her! We thought she was so wonderful even though she wasn't. She had Alzheimer's and she pulled people's hair. I wasn't evaluating well then; I accepted anybody at first!

It was funny though. I remember getting the check for her coming, and it didn't matter to me. I mean, you'd think this would be so huge—getting money—and it wasn't. I'll never forget that. It was like several days afterwards that I thought, My God, I really got some money. The fact that we had a resident was what was important; the fact that we got money for it just wasn't.

Right after that first resident came, the second resident came and then a third and a fourth. Because of those residents, people from the agencies stopped by and saw how well it was working. There was this wonderful enthusiasm, so I knew it was going to work. We were full in six months.

It's been six years, and I still owe money. But with six residents we can make expenses and pay me a living salary. If we have six we can survive; when we have eight, I can do more things and pay off my debts.

I don't know exactly what I'll do in the future. For a while I was thinking about taking in some unwed mothers. Old people can be so nurturing and understanding; they could give so much to these youngsters.

Now, though, I'm thinking more about opening a tea room for the frail elderly, like an old Victorian house where families could take their old folks for an afternoon outing. I'd serve the proper foods—pureed when necessary—maybe even have some entertainment. The employees would know how to treat and help old people. And I could do some teaching there too, give classes about old age, about this wisdom that old people have.

Marian pauses and looks around at the secure haven she's created. The inner glow that I'd noticed when we first met has turned into a fiery blaze, and I decide I won't ask how she plans to finance such a project. She'll find a way. She begins talking again in a quiet but passionate voice.

The decision for everybody is really whether or not you're going to follow the thread that is your life. Are you going to ignore it or respect it? I think if you make the decision to respect that part of yourself, then it's almost a choiceless path. It will take you rather than you taking it.

One of Marian's friends once commented, "Marian, I've learned so much about money from you." The comment puzzled Marian. "I don't know what she learned from me," she laughs, "except the one thing I say to a lot of people: 'Well, if you don't have anything else to worry about, you can always worry about money!'" She turns serious. "Let's face it," she says, "if your child is really sick, or you find out you have cancer, you're going to worry. You really are kind of lucky when you end up having to worry about money, because that means a lot of other things are okay."

· ·

Marian's approach to money is very different than Rich's. She's able to sleep at night while Rich would be scribbling numbers down on a well-organized form. And she's willing to take risks that would leave many of us paralyzed with fear.

Factors like these influence a person's money personality. In addition to spending and saving patterns, we each have different comfort levels when it comes to taking risks. The more aware you are of your own ability to live with uncertainty, the more likely you are to develop a plan that you can live with.

Crunching the Numbers

But even after you've figured out your fiscal style, you'll probably suspect there's a gap between how much you have and how much you'll need before you can comfortably leave your current job. You'll most likely need a plan.

The first task is to determine what your expenses will be once you cut the tether that connects you to your present job. Paul Terhorst, a former CPA and author of *Cashing In on the American Dream: How to Retire at 35*, maintains (and is living proof of the fact) that a couple can *fully* retire on a net worth of $500,000. "I figure $400,000 is enough, but that $500,000 is more comfortable for most of us. . . . That's total net worth, including home equity," he says.

Of course, most of us won't need that half-million-dollar nest egg. Like Ken and Shelley Cassie, we'll supplement our savings with monies earned through part-time ventures.

While some experts bandy around generalized figures (such as "a couple will need 70 to 80 percent of their pre-retirement income in order to maintain their standard of living"), it's safer to make a plan specific to your own situation.

Some costs will go down when you leave your longtime place of employment. You may no longer have to commute to work or dress to impress. You may be able to sell your house and move to an area where the cost of living is lower.

On the other hand, some costs may go up—or at least you may have to do some savvy planning to keep them under control. For example, if you're like most people, when you contemplate early retirement you worry about the cost of health insurance. For years you've relaxed knowing that your company-sponsored group insurance offered reasonable coverage at a reasonable price. Now you have visions of soaring premiums and fewer benefits. After all, under most conditions Medicare won't kick in until age sixty-five, and even then you may want to supplement the coverage.

But wait. It may not be as bad as you think. For starters, if you work for a large company, you can count on at least a year and a half of post-retirement coverage. According to the 1985 Federal Consolidated Omnibus Budget Reconciliation Act (COBRA), most employers with health insurance plans must continue to make the protection available to former employees for a minimum of eighteen months. (They can charge for this, but the charge cannot exceed the normal group rate by more than 2 percent.) In addition, you may be able to negotiate a retirement package that provides for insurance far beyond that point.

And there are other ways of getting group insurance. Restylers who begin work in another field may be covered by their new employer. Those who start their own business may find that their local Chamber of Commerce has a plan for members, or they may choose to go with a private insurer who offers group plans to businesses that consist of two or more people.

But the easiest way for most people to find group health insurance is simply to join an organization that provides coverage for its members. Your library will almost certainly have the three-volume *Encyclopedia of Associations* that provides addresses and phone numbers of organizations that appeal to every interest, from accordion playing to zoology. Check those organizations that appeal to you and find out if they offer health insurance to members. You'll find that the National Organization for Women (NOW) offers its members a comprehensive medical plan, as do many college alumni associations, professional societies, and trade unions. Joining the organization may be a small price to pay to be eligible for the group health insurance. Once again, it's just a matter of planning.

How much money do you need in order to cut the job tether? To answer this question, you need four types of data:

Expense Data—Present and Future

How much do you spend now? How do you spend it?

Which of these expenses will decrease after you leave your present job? Will you still need dress-for-success clothes, restaurant lunches, and commuter train tickets? If you move, will your housing costs decline?

What nonbusiness expenses will decrease as you get older? Will your children be financially independent? If you don't change locations, will your mortgage be paid off? Will you decrease, or possibly drop, your life insurance?

What expenses will increase after you complete your restyling? Will you need start-up money for a new venture? Will you travel more or spend more money on leisure-time activities? Will you be at home more and therefore see an increase in utility costs? Will you eat out more or less often? Will you have to replace your company-sponsored medical insurance with another, possibly more expensive, type of coverage?

Income Data—Present and Future

What company pension benefits are you entitled to?

How much will your personal savings and investments yield in the form of income?

What, if anything, do you expect to earn from part- or full-time work?

How many years do you have before you become eligible for Social Security, and how much money will you be entitled to from this source?

Asset Data

What will your assets be at the time of retirement?

Do you have any liabilities?

Are you willing to draw down these assets in order to finance your lifestyle, or do you want to keep them intact for your heirs?

Time Data

When do you want to leave your present job? Do you want to continue for a specified number of years until you become eligible for certain benefits? Until you have completed a designated project or reached a particular goal? Until a lease expires? Until your youngest child is old enough to allow you the freedom to travel?

How many years—given your present age and your life expectancy—will you be living on your retirement income? (Most financial planners recommend a person plan financially to live until at least age ninety.)

Until you have answered these (and related) questions, you can't possibly make a financial plan. But once you have, your plan becomes a relatively simple equation. You know where you are, where you're going, and how long you have to get there. If the numbers don't balance, you'll know what adjustments are necessary. Perhaps you'll have to scale back your lifestyle or choose to work a little longer. As Rich Henke says, "For most of us, there have to be trade-offs."

If you aren't sophisticated with financial calculations, you might ask a financial planner to help you. He or she will calculate into the above data your life expectancy, remembering that as a person gets older, life expectancy increases. Then detailed tax information, inflation rates, and possible and probable investment returns will be figured. The following table shows some of the possibilities:

How to Get from Here to There

One hundred dollars a month (one modest restaurant dinner a week for two people) can multiply into a tidy sum. Assuming an 8 percent annual return, saving $100 a month for five years will yield $7,397. The following table gives variations:

YEARS	5½%	7%	8%	9%	10%
5	$ 6,920	$ 7,201	$ 7,397	$ 7,599	$ 7,808
10	$16,024	$17,409	$18,417	$19,467	$20,655
15	$28,002	$31,881	$34,835	$38,124	$41,792
20	$43,762	$52,397	$59,295	$67,290	$76,570

Your Decision

At this point all you've learned about your own money personality comes into play. You are the one who must determine which assumptions about future inflation to use. You are the one who must consider whether you want to invest your money in a way that offers a possible 15 percent return or in one that offers a less risky 5½ percent return. And you are the one who must decide if the savings program you have set up is too stringent for your money behavior. Your insights into the interplay between your money self and your financial self are all-important. If your plan doesn't take them into account, it is certain to fail.

Gary Bowyer, a retirement counselor in Chicago, has a final word of encouragement. "If you leave your career when you are between forty-five and fifty-five years old, you have both the energy and time to recover if you find out you've made a financial miscalculation," he says. "But if you make a mistake at sixty-two and quit without having a large enough financial reserve, there's not a heck of a lot you can do about it."

E X E R C I S E S

Taking Your Risk Temperature

Are you the kind of person who is willing to take chances with money in pursuit of greater rewards? Or are you a more cautious investor who prefers to take minimal risks? This quiz will help you find out.

Be honest with yourself; there are no wrong answers. Then total your score and compare it to the key that follows the quiz.

1. You're the winner on a TV game show! Which prize would you choose?
   • $2,000 in cash (1 point)
   • A 50 percent chance to win $4,000 (3 points)
   • A 20 percent chance to win $10,000 (5 points)
   • A 2 percent chance to win $100,000 (9 points)

2. You're down $500 at a poker game. How much more would you stake to win the $500 back?

- More than $500 (8 points)
- $500 (6 points)
- $250 (4 points)
- $100 (2 points)
- Nothing—you'll cut your losses now (1 point)

3. A month after you invest in a stock, it suddenly goes up 15 percent. With no further information, what would you do?
- Hold it, hoping for more gains (3 points)
- Sell it and take your gains (1 point)
- Buy more—it will probably go higher (4 points)

4. You're a key employee in a start-up company. You can choose one of two ways to take your year-end bonus. Which would you take?
- $1,500 in cash (1 point)
- Company stock options which could bring you $15,000 next year if the company succeeds, but will be worthless if it fails (5 points)

5. Your investment suddenly goes down 15 percent one month after you invest. Its fundamentals still look good. What would you do?
- Buy more. If it looked good at the original price, it looks even better now (4 points)
- Hold on and wait for it to come back (3 points)
- Sell it to avoid losing even more (1 point)

Your score_____

Scoring key:

(5–18 points) More conservative investor. You prefer to minimize financial risks. The lower your score, the more cautious you are.

(19–30 points) Less conservative investor. You are willing to take more chances in pursuit of greater rewards. The higher your score, the bolder you are.

This Risk Tolerance Profile was devised by T. Rowe Price Associates, Inc. and is part of their Asset Mix Worksheet. Used with permission.

Financial Worksheets

These worksheets will help you get a rough idea of your financial readiness for retirement. Even more important, they will provide you with important numbers when you are ready to make more sophisticated calculations. Use a pencil when filling them out (or make several photocopies of each worksheet) so that you can update them as necessary.

1. Begin with the Annual Expense Worksheet. Complete both the "At Present" and "During Retirement" columns as accurately as possible.
2. Next, move to the Annual Income Worksheet. Fill out only the "At Present" column.
3. Compare your present disposable income to your present expenses as totaled on the Expense Worksheet. If your present disposable income exceeds your present expenses, you will be able to save more money for retirement.
4. Go back to the Income Worksheet. Assuming you invest these savings in a way that produces income, you will have additional investment income for retirement. Factor this into your calculations when you complete the "During Retirement" column.
5. Fill out the Asset Worksheet. If Step 3 showed that you will be able to save money between now and your anticipated retirement date, remember to include this when you calculate what assets will be available to you during your retirement.
6. Compare your anticipated retirement income to your anticipated retirement expenses as detailed on the Expense Worksheet. If your expenses exceed your income, you may want to explore dipping into your assets at some point in your retirement. If, for example, you have invested $50,000 at 7 percent interest compounded annually, you can withdraw $4,200 a year for twenty-five years before you deplete the principal.

These worksheets are only intended to be a guide. You may need the help of a financial consultant for a more detailed analysis that includes factors such as inflation, rate of return on investment, tax regulations, etc.

Annual Expense Worksheet
(Federal and state income taxes are included elsewhere.)

EXPENSES	AT PRESENT	DURING RETIREMENT

Housing
  Rent or mortgage
  Property taxes
  Gas/electricity
  Water
  Garbage
  Telephone
  Home furnishings
  Maintenance/repairs
  Improvements
  Household help		

Food
  Groceries
  Liquor/tobacco
  Restaurants		

Medical/Dental/Pharmaceutical Costs not covered by insurance		

Personal Care
  New clothes
  Cleaning/laundry
  Sundries
  Health club
  Hair cuts		

Transportation
  Auto payments
  Gas
  Maintenance/repair
  Parking		

(continued)

EXPENSES	AT PRESENT	DURING RETIREMENT
Insurance Premiums Life Medical Auto Homeowners Disability Long term nursing Other		
Child Care		
Parent Care		
Gifts/Contributions		
Education		
Entertainment Movies/theater Cable TV/video rental Sports events Books/magazines Newspaper Other		
Vacations/Travel		
Memberships		
Work-related expenses		
Debt interest on loans and credit card purchases*		
Other		
Total Expenses		

---

*List the purchase itself under the proper expense category.

Annual Income Worksheet

Sources of Income	At Present	During Retirement			
		At First	At 59½	At 62	At 65

Work-related Earnings
  Salary
  Bonuses
  Fees					

Investment Income
  Interest
  Dividends
  Rentals					

Pension					
Social Security					
Other					
Sub-Total					
Subtract estimated federal and state income taxes					
Total Disposable Income					

Asset Worksheet

ASSETS	AT PRESENT	AT RETIREMENT

Real Estate
    Home
    Other property		

Other Investments
    Stocks
    Bonds
    Annuities
    Certificates of deposit
    Mutual funds		

Cash Savings
    Savings accounts
    Money market accounts		

Pension Funds
    Company pension
    IRAs
    401Ks
    SEPs
    Keoghs		

Business Interests		

Personal Property
    Autos, boats
    Home furnishings
    Jewelry
    Art, precious metals, etc.		

Money owed to you		
Other		
Sub-Total		

Subtract any liabilities		
Mortgage		
Outstanding loans		
Installment debts		
Total Assets		

Resources

On the Emotional Aspects of Money

Your Money Personality: What It Is and How You Can Profit From It by Kathleen Gurney (1988, Doubleday; available from Financial Pyschology Corporation, 6 East Fourth Street, Suite 1204, Cincinnati, OH 45202, phone: 800/735-7935). Gurney, a former professor of psychological research at the University of California, divides people into nine money personalities: Entrepreneurs, Hunters, High Rollers, Safety Players, Achievers, Perfectionists, Money Masters, Producers, and Optimists. "You are a winner with money," she says, "when you understand how it works for you: when you control money instead of money controlling you; when your investments give you peace of mind as well as a piece of the action; when you learn to work smart as well as work hard; when you enjoy money whether you are making it, investing it, or spending it; when money becomes a vehicle to assist in realizing goals and dreams."

Money Madness: The Psychology of Saving, Spending, Loving, and Hating Money by Herb Goldberg and Robert T. Lewis (1978, Morrow; out of print but available in many libraries). Although Goldberg and Lewis wrote this book more than a decade ago and their numbers, when giving price examples, seem straight from Oz, it is still a clear look at the assorted "games, gambits, ploys and pastimes" that many of us use when dealing with money. Like Gurney, they divide people into groups—Security Collectors, Power Grabbers, Love Dealers, and Autonomy Worshipers—and show how the size of our bank account may depend more on our personality than on our job.

On the Financial Aspects of Early Retiring

Cashing In on the American Dream: How to Retire at 35 by
Paul Terhorst (1988, hardcover; 1990, softcover; both Bantam,
666 Fifth Avenue, New York, NY 10103, phone: 800/223-6834).
Terhorst, a C.P.A. who retired in the mid-eighties at age thirty-
five, encourages others to follow his example. He recommends
retiring on a net worth of $500,000 (including house and car).
The basic strategy? Laddered CDs and controlled spending: $50
a day for those without kids, and an additional $11 a day per
child.

Most books that line the financial section of bookstores focus
on specific investment strategies, such as stocks or real
estate. Which ones prove most useful to you depends, of course,
on your money personality and your risk temperament. But
there are a few books that discuss a variety of monetary
considerations.

Money Matters: Your IDS Guide to Financial Planning by
IDS Financial Services, an American Express Company (1990,
Avon Books, 1350 Avenue of the Americas, New York, NY
10019, phone: 212/261-6500). Most aspects of financial managing are discussed in this small pocket book: investments,
homes, insurance, debts, taxes, retirement, and estate plans.
A particularly good section for early retirees is the one entitled
"Taking Your Money Out," which discusses ways of taking
assets out of retirement plans.

The Price Waterhouse Book of Personal Financial Planning
by Stanley H. Greitbard and Donna Sammons Carpenter (1990,
Henry Holt & Company, 115 West 18th Street, New York, NY
10011, phone: 800/247-3912). In easy-to-understand language
the authors concentrate on helping the reader answer two basic
questions: What do I want and How do I get what I want.
They discuss all areas of financial planning from investment
strategies to insurance and taxes.

Sylvia Porter's Your Finances in the 1990s (1990, Simon &
Schuster, 1230 Avenue of the Americas, New York, NY 10020,
phone: 800/223-2348). In a thorough, organized fashion Porter

discusses a variety of financial concerns, beginning with setting goals in young adulthood and ending with preparing for retirement. What sets her book apart is the acknowledgment of and concern with different "life experiences that trigger financial moves." What special factors, for example, must the blended family take into account? What impact does caring for an aging parent have on financial planning? Porter doesn't always provide the answers, but at least she encourages the reader to ask the questions.

A Guide to Understanding Your Pension Plan by the National Pension Assistance Project of the Pension Rights Center with support from the American Association of Retired Persons (AARP, 1909 K Street NW, Washington, DC 20049, phone: 202/ 872-4700). In fifty pages you'll learn everything from why pensions are important to how your pension will be paid, how you can lose your benefits, and how to find out about your own plan's rules.

Look Before You Leap: A Guide to Early Retirement Incentive Programs (AARP, 1909 K Street NW, Washington, DC 20049, phone: 202/872-4700). As the title suggests, this booklet points out factors a person should consider before accepting an early retirement offer.

Retirement Builder: Guidebook to Planning and Financial Security (Available from most branches of Merrill Lynch, Pierce, Fenner & Smith, Inc.). Here's an easy way to get a free computer analysis of your financial situation. After reading this booklet, which gives a brief overview of retirement planning, just fill out the simple one-page form at the back and return it to a Merrill Lynch consultant. He or she will plug the numbers into a computer and—presto! a multi-page personalized report.

The T. Rowe Price Retirement Planning Kit (Free from T. Rowe Price Associates, Inc., 100 East Pratt Street, Baltimore, MD 21202, phone: 800/638-5660). Even if you're financially obtuse, you'll be able to get a reasonably clear picture of your financial situation by following the directions in this workbook. It starts by asking you to determine your assumptions (about inflation, taxes, and the rate of return your investments will bring), continues by helping you delineate your retirement goals, and then takes you step-by-step through financial factors you should consider before leaving a secure job. Additional information discusses formulating strategies and developing a plan.

On Health Insurance

Most of the overall guides to financial planning also have sections on health insurance.

The Complete Guide to Health Insurance: How to Beat the High Cost of Being Sick by Kathleen Hogue, Cheryl Jensen, and Kathleen McClurg Urban (1988, hardcover, Walker and Company, 720 Fifth Avenue, New York, NY 10019, phone: 800-AT WALKER; 1990, softcover, Avon Books, 1350 Avenue of the Americas, New York, NY 10019, phone: 212/261-6500). The authors open their book with a telling anecdote: "Overheard at a restaurant in a midwestern city: 'I went to the best clinic in town. With their skill they rebuilt my heart. Now the hassle with their paperwork is giving me another coronary.'" By reading the rest of this book, you'll make sure that "insurance gobbledygook" doesn't cause your first coronary and that the resulting paperwork doesn't cause your second. In a reasonably jargon-free way, the authors examine private health insurance, HMOs and PPOs, nursing home insurance, and Medicare.

Health Insurance Association of America (P.O. Box 41455, Washington, DC 20018; no phone orders.) Although HIAA is a trade association of insurance companies, the organization puts out several booklets for consumers: "The Consumer's Guide to Health Insurance," "The Consumer's Guide to Long-Term Care Insurance," and "Medicare Supplement Insurance."

National Insurance Consumer Organization (121 N. Payne Street, Alexandria, VA 22314; no phone orders.) NICO is a nonprofit public interest group that publishes a booklet entitled "Buyer's Guide to Insurance: What the Companies Won't Tell You."

Oh, what a tangled web we weave
When we first practice to conceive.

DON HERALD

4 | *FAMILY RESPONSI- BILITIES*

Hmmmnn. So maybe, just maybe, money isn't the stumbling block we thought it was. Maybe we *can* restyle. But still, we're concerned. Isn't restyling fundamentally a *selfish* idea? Do we have the right to make a major change that will, inevitably, force change upon those we love? What about our spouse?* What about our kids? We want our kids to work hard in school, so maybe we should work hard too. Don't we have to set a good example? Don't we have to be responsible pillars of the community? Horatio Alger may have lied, but his ghost hasn't died!

ITEM In 1946 our parents watched the two-hanky film *It's A Wonderful Life,* Frank Capra's classic starring Jimmy Stewart

---

*Throughout this book the word *spouse* means *husband, wife, partner, room-mate, significant other,* etc. Also, *he* is used when the person under discussion could be a *he* or a *she*.

and Donna Reed. The story centers around George Bailey, a man who repeatedly sacrifices his own dreams in order to help others. "So sad," thought our parents, as they reflected upon parallels between their own lives and that of Bailey. But, after all, isn't that what any good person would do?

Ah, how times have changed!

ITEM In *Field of Dreams*, an Oscar nominee for the best picture of 1989, lead character Ray Kinsella (played by Kevin Costner) outlines his problem: "I have a wife, a child and a mortgage, and I'm scared to death I'm turning into my father. . . . He must've had dreams, you know, but he never did anything about them."

Kinsella follows his dream, ultimately building a ball park in the middle of an Iowa cornfield. Sure, he's a bit crazy, even in the fantasy world of the theater; and yes, he's lucky he has an understanding wife. But he meets, if only barely, his obligations. Indeed, a heart-warming scene at the end shows husband, wife, and daughter, arms around each other, walking off to embrace what has now become a dream for them all. Why, they've even figured out a way to make that ball park into an income producer!

In the forties and fifties most mature adults practiced self-denial à la George Bailey. In the sixties and seventies, influenced by the new humanistic psychology popularized by Abraham Maslow and Frederick (Fritz) Perls, many "did their own thing," saying good-bye to responsibility in order to "fulfill their own human potential."

But now many of us are realizing that we can have our dreams and still not be ashamed to look at ourselves in the mirror. Midlife change, if managed properly, doesn't have to mean abandoning obligations. Instead it can be a protection against boredom and a healthy, even responsible, way to experience more of life's offerings.

Joint Expectations

No doubt about it—restyling affects both partners. At first it's likely to bring out all kinds of insecurities, all kinds of fears. For most people, restyling wasn't part of the initial contract. "If *you* restyle, *I'll* have to change," one spouse says with indignation.

Restyling forces change. If we change our spending habits, we may have to change our social habits. We probably won't join our friends for expensive nights on the town and, over time, we may see those friends less and less. After one partner has quit his job, we'll both miss out on work-related perks and events. And when one of us relinquishes a title—as doctor or engineer or executive—we both may lose status. To complicate matters further, restyling may involve a change in location.

Sometimes, as with the Cassies, Bades, and Pasins, spouses are eager to restyle together. But often, at about the time a man wants to plan for a new endeavor, his wife has just started to feel comfortable in her career. "Start something new?" she asks. "No way. I like what I'm doing."

In the past, men and women seemed to have different workaday patterns. They traveled parallel tracks when they were young: he being aggressive (to earn a living), she being gentle (to care for the young). Then, somewhere around age forty, the tracks converged and even crossed. The moneymaking master became a tender teddy bear; the nurturing nanny changed to a worldly warrior.

But is this roadmap still accurate when men and women more evenly divide both household and workworld responsibilities? Life cycle theorists aren't sure. While there is some evidence that hormonal changes activate midlife role changes, it's reasonable to assume that culture, too, plays a part. In other words, is this personality swap caused by biology or boredom?

The fact remains that a large number of midlife women have their own careers. According to the Bureau of Labor Statistics, in 1990, 75 percent of American women aged forty-five to forty-nine were working at, or looking for, paid jobs. The percentages dropped only slightly for older women: 67 percent of those aged fifty to fifty-four and 55 percent of those between fifty-five and fifty-nine were at work.

According to Kay Wright, a training specialist for AARP, dual-career couples frequently practice "staggered retirement." "We're hearing of more cases in which one person retires first, then the other retires when he or she is ready," she explains.

"There's no reason couples have to restyle in tandem," agrees Los Angeles psychologist Robert Shomer. "As long as they take each other's needs and wishes into account, they can pursue different timetables. The most important factor is talk—lots of it, and over a long period of time. Then you can develop a plan that takes the needs of both spouses into account."

Tom Christensen did exactly that. He spent years dreaming aloud to his wife, Sandra, and she understood his desire to start a business of his own. But, she said, she didn't want to be directly involved. She didn't want her own life, or that of their children, to be drastically changed. Tom listened, and he found a way to follow his own star without destroying his marriage.

· ·

Profile: Tom Christensen—Air Force Major to Travel Planning Entrepreneur

Nothing is really work unless you would rather be doing something else.

JAMES BARRIE

Tom Christensen, Air Force major, served as a pilot, social actions instructor, and acquisitions manager before leaving the service in July 1989, at age forty-four. He's using his savings to pursue his dream—a business of his own—and his pension money to provide security for his family. His wife, Sandra, does administrative work for a technical college. The Christensens live in New Hampshire; Tom's business is headquartered in Nutting Lake, Massachusetts. Their two oldest children, both boys, are already adults; his youngest, a daughter, is nine years old.

"I'm coming to San Francisco next week for a travel conven-tion," said Tom Christensen. *"Let's get together then. I'll show you my new product."* It was mid-afternoon on the appointed day when he finally rang our doorbell, a man of medium height with blond hair and a military bearing. *"Sorry I'm late,"* he said, full of the exuberance I'd come to recognize from our phone conversations. *"I've spent the day talking with wonderful people, and I have hundreds of new ideas."*

Other people might be exaggerating when they say *"hundreds of new ideas."* For Tom it's probably an understatement. This man generates ideas like McDonalds turns out hamburgers. Ever since he was a kid he's had more ideas than he's known what to do with, and now that he's retired he finally has the chance to see if they'll work. His current passion is Traveler's Concierge, his new travel information service. For a fee this company will give you a personalized itinerary for almost any city in the United States. You say you'll be in Atlanta on the third Sunday in July and you'd like to visit two antebellum homes, shop for miniature dollhouse furniture, see a sunset from a special vantage point, and eat at a Greek restaurant? Tom will tell you the hows, whens, and wheres. It's a gargan-tuan task, and he approaches it with gusto. He's been working on it like a demon for more than four years.

"I've always had the desire to have my own business," he says. *"Now I have put aside a certain amount of money, and when that money is gone, it's gone. I'll have fulfilled my lifelong goal of being an entrepreneur; and if I can't make it work, then I can't and I'll accept that. But until you have that chance to try, you always want to do it."*

"What about your wife?" I ask. *"Is she as excited about this as you are?"* He turns pensive.

My wife is not involved in my new endeavor. At this moment, today, she might be more willing to become involved, but before she did not want to. Simply because people are married to each other does not mean they can work well together in a business. In my situation, this is my idea, what I want to do, and there is no reason it has to be hers.

But when I got married, I took on the responsibility of a wife and then our kids. I may not necessarily have been the best husband or father; but when I take on a responsibility, I don't shirk it. So when I decided to start this business, I made sure my obligation to them was met. That's just who I am.

My wife gets all of the pension, so my new business is no risk to her at all. I agreed to that, and I'm an honorable type of person. Her needs and the household needs are being met. The money I'm risking has no bearing on her.

For years I felt I was a very creative person stifled inside a very structured organization. I always wanted to get out, but I was constrained by high pay inside, limited job opportunities outside, and my obligations to my family. I stayed wrapped in the military's security blanket. Now it doesn't make any difference. I can fly this idea around and if I lose my money, the wife and kids are provided for. It's my turn.

I've always liked organizing things, making things happen. I grew up in Worchester, Massachusetts. In high school I was the kid who organized the class trips. I organized the church bus trip to New York, the birthday party for the Scouts, and when the high school didn't have a ski club, I organized one so I could go on the trips for free.

Then in college I followed the same pattern. When there wasn't a college newspaper to express the needs of students, I organized one and became the editor. I even started a small business. It's sort of humorous and humiliating to think of it now. *[He chuckles.]* I'd go to the Salvation Army and buy ties for ten cents apiece. My wife would iron them, and I'd go to the college and sell them for a dollar each.

I spent one year at the University of Massachusetts, but then I transferred to a state college to become an industrial arts teacher. After college I taught for a time in a small Massachusetts town. I was unpopular there, not personally but professionally. The other industrial arts teachers had been teaching for thirty years; they taught their students how to cut, sand, and glue a single box. Then I came along, a young whippersnapper who wanted to use a production line. I wanted my students to understand how industry works, how mass production works, how efficiencies of scale work. Now that concept is popular; it's like the Junior Achievement program. But then it made me a rebel.

Tom didn't have very long to worry about his popularity with his colleagues. His teaching career was cut short by the Vietnam War. He was deferred at first because he was married and a father, but finally the draft caught up with him. He thought it over for a few minutes and decided, for reasons he can no longer remember, that he'd prefer the Air Force to the other services.

The local Air Force recruiter told me I could be either a pilot or a navigator. So I asked, "Who's in charge?" and he answered, "Pilots are in charge." I took a five dollar ride in a Cessna that afternoon and said, "Well, flying is okay," and that in fact is why I became a pilot in the Air Force. *[He hesitates; and when he starts talking again, his voice is softer than usual.]*

Sometimes people ask me what motivates me. I guess I think about those fifty-five thousand names on the wall, on the Vietnam Memorial. When I'm in Washington, I go look at those guys, those names. I could've been one of them.

In my case I had a couple of very harrowing experiences when I was in Vietnam. In fact, one of them that I remember quite clearly was when a missile exploded right underneath my airplane. The radar camera took a picture of it, and I have that picture up on my bathroom wall. I think about these things.

And there was another time I remember, a different type of war story but it also reflects my philosophy. I was on Guam after a grueling cycle of flying. I was really disillusioned at that time because I wasn't really a believer, just one of those guys who got caught up in the war, who did what he was supposed to do. A reluctant recruit, I guess you'd call me.

Anyway, there aren't many places you can go on Guam on a day off, but just for a change of scenery I wandered over to the Navy base and checked into the BCQ *[bachelor civilian quarters]*. It was a stark room with cinder block walls, and in the room there were only two pieces of furniture: a metal-type simple cot and a narrow, tall bureau. I walked into this room and closed the door and laid down—I was mentally exhausted—and there on the back of the door was a Snoopy™ calendar, one of those expensive ones you buy at Hallmark stores. I looked at that calendar and somebody who had lived in that room before me (probably some civilian who worked for the Navy) had X-ed off each day.

I lay there and all the frustration and despondency that I had disappeared. I decided at that moment I would never say TGIF—Thank God It's Friday; I would never cross off the days of my life. I didn't know then if I was going to be coming back from the next cycle of flying. All I knew was that I had that day. That wall calendar is a visual thing and it sticks in my mind. I'll always be grateful for the time I have.

Anyway, after that first tour of duty, I was planning to get out of the Air Force, but at that point my wife was very involved in Air Force social life. I was aircraft commander, so she was the commander of the wives of my crew. When I had fifty men under me, she was in charge of the fifty wives. And, about the same time, I got promoted to captain; and the salary jump from first lieutenant to captain is significant. My wife was secure and happy; so when I was ready to get out and do my own thing, she felt it was essential for us to stay in. So I did, to keep peace in the family.

And it wasn't too hard, really. I'd worn a Boy Scout uniform as a kid, and I'd been an ROTC cadet for a while in college, so it was easy for me to function in the rank structure of the military. For the most part, the Air Force was good to me.

Still, Tom dreamed of being an entrepreneur. In his off-duty hours, he dreamed and schemed, concocting one idea after another.

Let's see. First it was Dilleyville Toys. That company was going to build little cardboard houses for kids, four vertical pieces of cardboard that could be fashioned into a telephone booth or put against a wall to make an enclosure where a four-year-old could play. My idea was to form a cottage industry: one person in one house cutting the cardboard, another putting on the contact paper, a third putting the pieces together. The idea fit in well with my industrial arts background; but I lacked the marketing skills then, and I still do. But I always had the confidence I could make a business go.

Then when I was stationed in Ohio, I wanted to open a bike rental business. I figured that sometimes people want to bike around in a pretty place—say near a waterfall—but that it

within an hour, had two hours at the museum, and an hour's trip back to the airport to catch the next plane. People used to tag along with me just to see if I could make it!

Another time the government gave six of us $112 each and two days to get from San Francisco to Dallas. Three of the fellows flew direct and spent Sunday hanging around the motel. Two others came with me. We took a bus to Fresno, flew a cheap flight to Las Vegas, spent the weekend gambling, and got another cheap flight into Dallas. It's just a matter of planning it all out in advance.

Now, I'm not a bullshitter, so I was unable to simply declare myself as a company. I had to prepare. Every week I read all the travel industry papers—there's about eight—and I'd cut articles out of them all. I went to every major travel organization's trade show. Three times I actually had a booth just to test-market my idea. I didn't go to make money but to gain experience and knowledge. Then, too, I've asked questions of everybody in every phase of the travel industry—hotel clerks, travelers, visitor and convention bureaus, resort owners. I was—am—convinced I've uncovered a vital niche in the travel industry.

Then I had to learn about business. I read everything that had to do with automation, small business, marketing techniques, trade shows. And I developed mailing lists of all the people who exhibited at all the trade shows so I could see who's still exhibiting and what products seem to do well. I have over seven hundred file folders full of information.

I also developed an organizational structure for my company. People consistently laugh at me when I tell them I have an organizational chart that is twenty-six feet long, but that is what I need to help me articulate what skills my company must have. *[He smiles.]* Now I can only afford to hire three people, but just wait. In not too long I'll be able to have employees that will fill all twenty-six-feet worth of skills.

Tom has officially been in business for about six months. He finds that he misses certain things, especially the companionship and networking opportunities that a large organization provides. "When I go to the coffee pot, there's no one there to talk with," he says with a shrug. But overall he's delighted with the way things have been going. "Things are beginning to come together," he says with a grin.

My big task now is marketing. I have to make people realize that my program will save them a tremendous amount of time and energy—that it will cause their trip to be a smashing success, that they won't have to make thirty-two phone calls once they get there and waste a whole day arranging things. My dream is to be the Ray Kroc of the travel industry. Instead of McDonald's, I'll have "Coming and Going Centers" in every city so people can find out exactly what is available.

Is all this work worth it? *[His eyes sparkle, and he laughs out loud.]* Of course it is. I'm finally getting a chance to do what I've always wanted to do. That's really what it's all about.

· ·

Tom is living his dream; Sandra, his wife, is continuing to work in another field, holding down a job that she enjoys. As Tom's business grows, she may or may not decide to participate more fully. In the meantime, both are happy. They've found their own path to restyling. It's very different, for example, from the one chosen by the Pasins, who not only founded their Money Mailer business as partners, but also incorporated the talents of their two children.

This only underscores the point that there are no hard-and-fast rules to restyling, just a set of parameters. Each person faces a different situation; each person sees his responsibilities differently. The trick is to meet these responsibilities without forfeiting your own dreams in the process.

The Nest Stays Full

It used to be simpler. Twenty years ago Mom was only forty-seven and Dad was only fifty when the youngest child flew the coop. Plenty of time to try a new lifestyle, and kids were only a peripheral consideration. For some of us, this is still the case.

But if we neglect to plan, we may find that the empty nest we've dreamed about is . . . well, it's lonely. For years we've lived in a child-centered environment; as parents we fed our offspring, clothed them, and discussed them—endlessly. Now they're gone, and we sit in silence. If we can't talk about college plans and curfew hours, what will we talk about with our partner? We continue to share the same house; but without the kids, we may find we inhabit separate worlds.

But we all know when our children are leaving. We can count ahead to the year that, barring a traumatic accident, they'll leave for college or be old enough to move out on their own. And if we've restyled with their departure in mind, we can find new routes to togetherness.

Of course, for some of us, the children will be around until we officially become senior citizens. Many of us marry later; we postpone having children until our mid- or late thirties. We divorce and remarry, having "second families" at an age when our friends are waving good-bye to their first. Even those of us who are still young when our kids take off may be in for a surprise. Our children may not stay gone very long; they may move back in when the first rent payment comes due. In 1989 there were 18 million of these "boomerang kids," formerly independent adult children who returned home to live with Mom and Dad. For some of us it seems as if the nest will never empty.

David and Laura Rausch didn't want to wait. They'd planned for years and they were ready to go. Their youngest child, Michael, was thirteen. They packed up his bags and brought him along.

• •

Profile: David and Laura Rausch—Entrepreneur and Nurse to 'Round-the-World Sailors

Men for the sake of getting a living forget to live.
                                        MARGARET FULLER

David Rausch was forty-two and his wife, Laura, forty-one when they sold his business, traded their large home near San Francisco for a 42-foot sailboat, and set off for adventure on the high seas. They'd been planning this for twelve years. The original scheme called for an earlier departure date, but they decided it would be better to wait until their daughter, Paige, was securely settled in college. They enrolled their younger child, Michael, in correspondence classes, and on Halloween night of 1986 the three of them sailed off under the Golden Gate Bridge.

"I always knew we'd take off in our sailboat," says David Rausch, smiling and settling deeper into his easy chair. "It was a dream, that's all. You know, everybody has a dream that they've got to do." We're talking in the Rausches' new house in a Seattle suburb. After two and a half years of sailing, David and Laura reluctantly returned to the States so Michael could finish high school in a traditional setting. Now Laura has resumed her nursing career and David is back in electronic sales, doing essentially the same thing he used to do but on a smaller scale.

I admit that I'm disappointed. I'd met Laura seven years earlier, when she and I shared carpooling duties to our children's school. Laura had confided their sailing plans one day over lunch, and her tale inflamed my own dreams of a lifestyle change. My husband had also been intrigued, and he'd managed to speak with David at the next PTA meeting. "You're right," he'd told me afterwards. "They're just regular people who work hard and love their kids. If they can do it, we can do it."

But now Laura seems to be telling me that they couldn't do it after all, at least not until both of their children are off on their own. "No, that's not true," she says. "It was a glorious few years for all of us. And there's more to come. This house is just a rest stop. As soon as Michael graduates high school, we'll be off again." She gives me a happy smile, and her shoulder length black hair bobs as she nods her head emphatically. "It'll be even easier next time."

David motions us to sit down. He reminds me of a teddy bear with a salt-and-pepper beard, thinning hair, and a totally relaxed demeanor. "Should you have waited?" I ask him. "No," he says without hesitation. "If I had it to do over again, I'd leave even earlier."

LAURA: Having Michael along was great for us as a family. We enjoyed the same kinds of things, the diving and the traveling and taking off on a bus and going up into the rainforest in Central America. He loved it at first, even though there weren't a lot of kids his age. He met lots of local people, but as soon as he'd begin to make friends we were off again. And the people out sailing generally had younger kids or they were older and didn't have any children. The three of us became real close because he didn't have any kids to be with. What we didn't count on was the fact that he wouldn't like it forever. We were in Mexico when he told us he wanted to go back to the States for his junior and senior year of high school.

DAVID: He felt he'd hung out for two years with us adults, and he really wanted to be with people his own age. We'd always thought that if he really didn't like it, he could either go to a boarding school or live with his grandmother and spend his vacation time with us. Then as time went on when we were on the boat, it became obvious that we wanted to stay together as a family. So we decided to take a few years off from sailing. We got guilty is what it was!

LAURA: But in one sense he gained so much. He did so much diving and sailing, and he saw all these new places. We were gone for three school years, and yet he kept up with his correspondence courses. *[She laughs.]* We had great plans for a regular study schedule, but it just did not work out that way. When we were making passages, it was too rough to study; and when we were in port, there were always a thousand things to do that were more interesting or more fun. So he sort of did it in bunches, very hit-and-miss. But it worked. When we got back here, he was right where he should be. He's a junior in high school now and doing just fine.

It didn't bother him that we decided to stop in Seattle instead of returning to the San Francisco area. He just fit right in, going off and making friends with kids his own age. He doesn't have time to do things with us anymore, and at first I almost resented it. Yet of course that's the way it should be. *[She smiles.]* All I can say is positive things about what we did.

DAVID: It was just the right thing for us to do. Sailing was always in the back of my mind. It's what I was going to go for.

I guess it's hard for me to realize that people do just plod along with no goal. To me that's not natural. In 1974, when I started my business, the idea was to make good money for ten years and then call it quits. As it was we stayed twelve years so we'd be around while Paige adjusted to college.

Paige wanders into the room. She took a semester off from school to spend some time on the boat and now, a recent college graduate, she's about to leave for Washington, D.C., to look for a job. Laura excuses herself to talk with her daughter for a moment, and David takes up the narrative.

DAVID: I'm originally from Michigan. When I was fifteen, my parents moved to Santa Cruz *[California]*; but I stayed back there. I'd been going with this same girl from about seventh grade, and we were going to get married; so there was no way I was going to leave Michigan. I worked part-time, went to high school part-time and had my own little apartment—all at fifteen. Then I bought this new car and thought I'd go to California and see my folks. I took one look at how beautiful Santa Cruz was, drove back to Michigan to end my relationship with the girl, and moved out there.

Meanwhile, my Dad had taken early retirement. He bought a boat and he was going to sail around the world. During the time he was getting things ready, he . . . *[David pauses and swallows.]* He was going to leave in June of that year and he died on Mother's Day of a heart attack. He was fifty years old.

He always wanted us kids to go out sailing with him; and I always said, "There's no way you're ever going to get me on that boat out in the ocean. There's no way I'm going." So I never went, he never went, and eventually Laura and I just started getting this idea that there's gotta be a way. . . . *[He turns to my husband who has just asked the obvious question.]* No, at the time I never thought of sailing as living my Dad's dream, but you're not the first guy who's made that connection.

After Dad died, I could have had the boat. My mother would have given it to any of us kids if we'd wanted it, but at that time I didn't have any desire for a boat. I don't know what made me change my mind. I guess I've always wanted to travel. Even today I'll pick up and take off. Sometimes I'll just say, "I'm going to drive to Michigan to see my brother. I'll be back in a few days," and I'll drive across country. We've driven across country five times in the last year.

Anyway, I never graduated from college. I went to work for a company called Sylvania Electronics. I worked quite hard, did a good job, and had seventy to eighty people working for me. After a while they made a field engineer out of me and sent me overseas. I worked in the Philippines for a year. Then I came back and they sent me to a Minuteman installation in North Dakota. *[He smiles.]* Imagine from the Philippines to North Dakota in January! Finally I quit up there and moved back to California. That's when I met Laura.

Eventually I started my own company dealing in electronic sales. Let's say a company is building a military radar system. We know how the different parts work, and we represent a bunch of other firms that make the various smaller parts. So we can look at the whole picture and get five different guys to design the system. We get paid a percentage.

But, like I said, I only gave it ten years. That kind of business is a young man's business—a lot of work, a lot of entertainment, a lot of long hours, a lot of travel. Two or three nights a week you're out to dinner until midnight, then up at six in the morning. There's a lot of drinking, a lot of liquor. Just look at people, especially some of those Silicon Valley guys who started companies and were successful. You read about them in the paper all the time. They're dying, and they're just in their late fifties, early sixties.

Laura slips back into the room and rejoins the conversation.

LAURA: He said ten years, and I kept thinking, Oh yeah, right, sure. We'd talk about it, and we've got a library in there of all these sailing books, and I'd read these books and I'd think, Yeah, that's wonderful. But you know, I'd say we were going but I didn't really believe it. Up until the year that we actually left, I kept thinking, Well, we're going to wait one more year. Finally David said, "I'm going. You can come or you can stay." *[David, sitting across the room, chuckles.]*

You know, even when we were moving out of the house, I didn't really believe it. I kept thinking, Well, we're not going to go; we're not really going to do it. Then after we were gone for about six months, I thought, I don't know why we waited so long! I just loved it. I didn't miss the house. I actually didn't even miss our friends. I mean, that's an awful thing to say, but you meet so many new people and you go so many places, and it's just, it's just wonderful.

We were really prepared though. I went back to school and took a lot of classes—marine biology and oceanography, and navigation and celestial navigation. It was really interesting. I took all my books along when we left so I was always the professional tour guide. Michael and I both got our scuba certifications; and whenever we'd go someplace, we'd stop by the local yacht club or marina and talk to people who'd retired to sail full-time. So we had lots of role models; we knew it was possible. Then in 1984 David raced our boat to Hawaii.

DAVID: One of the sailing magazines interviewed me and asked me why I was in that race. I said, "Well, my wife told me if I could find Hawaii, she'd go cruising with me!"

The real point of no return came in 1982 when David agreed to sell his business. He found a young man who was interested in his company and arranged a four-year buyout agreement, gradually introducing the newcomer to the complexities of the operation. By the final year, David was "just a figurehead." He'd go to the office for a few hours in the morning and then spend the rest of the day fixing up the boat. "I never had second thoughts," he says.

DAVID: I'm trying to think if we were ever afraid of leaving. I don't think so.

LAURA: You weren't; I was. We had trouble selling the house—we ended up having to rent it for a year—and when it didn't sell, I was relieved because I thought, Well, good. If this doesn't work, we can always come back. I was concerned, too, about David's hip. He had a hip replacement in 1983, and it had to be redone in '84. There was deterioration from a lack of blood supply in the head of the femur; doctors don't know what caused the problem. But I was worried that he'd have problems with it on the boat.

DAVID: I looked at it differently. When I was lying around the hospital wondering if I was going to walk again, it made up

my mind for sure that I wanted to leave. I knew Laura sometimes worried about money, but I kept saying, "Sure, we could
stay and work longer and make much more money, but who
wants that?"

LAURA: We lived pretty well in the Bay Area. Our home had
a swimming pool, a tennis court, all that stuff. I think I felt
like I was supposed to have those things. I was living in a very
nice area, and it was a keeping-up-with-the-Joneses type of
thing. It's nice not to feel that anymore, and I think that's one
of the biggest advantages of getting away. It's like you don't
have to take yourselves quite so seriously or feel you need all
this stuff. You realize you just don't. You see how other people
live; and they're perfectly happy, and you're perfectly happy.

DAVID: Financially, the biggest thing we did to get ready to
leave was get the boat bought and paid for. That was about
$225,000. Once you have the boat paid for, sailing is a very
inexpensive thing to do. We were spending about $1,000 a
month, and we lived very well. That's eating out quite a bit
and renting cars and hotels sometimes. We traveled back to
the States a lot, too, because we had to sell the house and file
our income taxes, and once Paige got sick. I think, though, that
if we'd stayed out of the United States, we'd have had enough
money that we'd never have had to work again.

*"Do you want to see a videotape of our boat?" he asks. Without
waiting for an answer he flips on the television and adjusts the
VCR. The screen fills with pictures of a vast expanse of watery
blue, close-ups of smiling faces lathered with sunscreen, and
tilting horizons as the photographer swayed with the movement
of the boat. David is mesmerized as he gazes at the screen.*

LAURA: We sailed down the California coast, over to Mexico,
around Central America, through the Panama Canal. For me
it was the perfect life. I think the biggest benefit was the feeling of freedom and independence.

Then, when Michael wanted to come back, we had to decide
where to live. We didn't want to go back to the Bay Area; it
was too expensive. So we spent our last year on the East Coast
of the United States, just sort of traveling up and down, trying

to figure out if we liked it there. Then we went out to Washington to visit some friends, and we really liked the Northwest.

And the real estate is going crazy up here. Hopefully, hopefully, it will continue to do so and we can make a decent bit of money on this house. In our minds this house is just for resale. We're looking at it as an investment; we're looking at it as the next boat.

DAVID: We'll stay here at least until Michael graduates high school, and we can sell the house at a profit. In the meantime, we're working. I've started another business like the one I had before, and Laura is back into nursing at a big trauma center in Seattle.

LAURA: We're working because we have to do something, and we might as well make money out of it. That's not why we came back, but since we're here . . . I feel like I'm really working for a purpose now. I don't want to buy anything. I don't need anything and I don't want anything. I just want the money to be able to leave again. Next time when we go I figure it's catch us if you can! We'll just keep going and going and going. *[Her eyes sparkle in anticipation.]*

The Rausches' boat is up for sale now. David explains that it doesn't mean the end of a dream but the beginning of a new one. "We're selling this boat because by the time we leave again the equipment will be outdated," he says. "We'll take a tramp freighter to Australia and have a new boat built there. During the year that it takes to get the boat built, we'll tour the country by land. Then we'll sail around the South Pacific, visit all those islands . . ." He snaps off the video. "And the kids can visit us whenever they want to," he says with a smile.

• •

Children may not be a consideration for some of us. It's been estimated that by the year 2000, one out of three American households will be childless. But this doesn't necessarily mean we won't have people who need our care. Just as we're living longer, so are our parents. At least 5 million Americans, most often in midlife, are involved in time-consuming parent care at any given time; an additional 4 million assume a more limited but still necessary type of family responsibility for their elders. For many of us, restyling plans must take aging parents and relatives into account.

Oh dear. Once again we feel the doubts arise. Can I? Should I? Must I? I have so many responsibilities. But that's exactly why, for those of us who hear the muse, restyling is essential. It helps us recharge our batteries. Now that life is longer and our responsibilities are greater, we need to supply ample current for the years to come.

E X E R C I S E S

What's Important to Me

No real discussion of restyling can take place between spouses unless some time is spent laying the groundwork. Begin by making a photocopy of this exercise for your partner. Then each of you can individually explore some basic feelings and beliefs that will affect the course of your restyling.

Following are six pairs of statements separated by a row of numbers. There are also two blanks at the end for you to fill in other factors you'd like to discuss. The numbers represent points on a continuum. Circle the point that best indicates where you stand on each issue. For example, if you strongly agree with the statement that "the most exciting part of my life is ahead of me," circle 9 or 10. If "I worry that as I get older my life will be less interesting" more closely represents your feelings, circle 1 or 2. When you have finished, the numbers will serve as reference points and make it easy to compare your answers with those of your spouse.

I think the most exciting part of my life is ahead of me.	10 9 8 7 6 5 4 3 2 1	I worry that as I get older my life will be less interesting.
I want to change lifestyles.	10 9 8 7 6 5 4 3 2 1	Actually, I'm quite happy with my life just the way it is.

I am willing to cut back financially if necessary in order to change lifestyles.	10 9 8 7 6 5 4 3 2 1	It would be uncomfortable if we lowered our standard of living.
The children are able to fend for themselves.	10 9 8 7 6 5 4 3 2 1	I still have a big responsibility to our children.
My parents are able to care for themselves or can be cared for by others.	10 9 8 7 6 5 4 3 2 1	My parents need me to help take care of them.
I'd like to move to a new location.	10 9 8 7 6 5 4 3 2 1	I enjoy living in this area.
	10 9 8 7 6 5 4 3 2 1	
	10 9 8 7 6 5 4 3 2 1	

Slip List

Slip list is a tool that you can use over and over to help you organize your thoughts. It works well when used by a single person in order to prioritize ideas or tasks, and it is equally handy when two people use it together as a way of identifying their differences. Now it can help you and your spouse discover those restyling issues that are most important to each of you.

You and your partner should work separately as you begin this exercise, in different rooms if possible. You should also use different color inks. Each of you take a sheet of 8½ x 11-inch paper and cut it into four vertical strips. Now cut each strip into four smaller pieces. You should now have sixteen slips of paper. On each piece of paper, write down one of your feelings or "wants" that is relevant to restyling. The slips of paper are small for a reason: no piece of paper should contain more than five words. That way you will be forced to break up your thoughts into small, manageable bites.

Many of your thoughts may be conflicting. For example, one of your wants may be to "leave job in three years" and another might be to "stay in present house." But what if the only way you can afford to quit your current job in three years is to sell your house and move to a region with a lower cost of living? That's okay; write them both down, each on a separate piece of paper. At this point you're just jotting down your wishes. You'll have to tackle these inconsistencies eventually, but now you're merely trying to open discussion with your partner.

Once you have a pile of slips, stack them in the order of their importance to you. Put the most important "want" on top, the second most important directly below it, and so on. Move the slips of paper around as many times as you wish, but once you are reasonably satisfied with their order, turn them over and write down a rank number on the back of each one. The slip of paper at the top of the stack will be "1," the next "2" and so on.

It's a good idea to set a time limit for this portion of the exercise, perhaps half an hour. At the end of this time, shuffle your slips of paper and exchange them for those of your partner. As you look over his or her slips, you may be amazed to find that the statements are very different than yours. Nevertheless, without looking to see how your spouse ranked the slips, arrange them into your own ladder of importance. When you are finished with this, turn the pieces of paper over and write your rank numbers on the back next to those of your partner.

By now each of you should be well on the road to clarifying your own feelings, and you've almost certainly become aware of areas of both agreement and disagreement. Now it's time to discuss them.

Listen to Me

Whether you and your partner have totally opposing views
or merely slight differences in emphasis, restyling will be dis-
ruptive unless you each understand the feelings of the other.
This, of course, means talk—a lot of talk—and much of it about
issues that threaten the status quo. Counselors often suggest
that couples make communication easier by structuring a discussion according to certain rules.

1. To begin, one partner agrees to be the speaker while the
   other agrees to be the listener. Set a timer or alarm clock
   to ring in one half-hour. During that time the speaker is
   to talk about him- or herself; he can talk about hopes
   and dreams, anxieties and fears, anything at all. Many
   of the things he says may have an emotional impact on
   the listener, but the listener is not to interrupt. This is
   a monologue, not a discussion.
2. After the half-hour is up, both partners observe ten
   minutes of silence in order to think over what has been
   said.
3. Then reverse roles, and let the listener become the
   speaker.

This becomes, in turn, a listening exercise for one person and
a self-disclosure exercise for the other. The listener may find
he feels defensive, or scared, or pleased; but regardless of his
feelings, he cannot interrupt. Because of this, he can concentrate on what the speaker is saying rather than on what he
wants to say. This is more difficult than it sounds; most people
want to respond immediately.

Resources

Correspondence Schools for Children

If you will be traveling with school-age children, you may be
interested in correspondence schools.

American School, 850 East 58th Street, Chicago, IL 60637,
phone: 312/947-3300. (High School)

Calvert School, 105 Tuscany Road, Baltimore, MD 21210, phone: 301/243-6030. (Grades K–8)

University of Nebraska, Lincoln, Division of Continuing Studies, 33rd and Holdrege, Room 271, Lincoln, NE 68583-0900, phone: 402/472-2175. (High School and College)

Care for Aging Parents

If restyling involves extensive travel or a move to a new location, you may need a person to care for your elderly parent. Several organizations exist to help adult children find geriatric care managers who will arrange for and/or provide elder care in the child's absence.

Aging Network Services (ANS), 4400 East-West Highway, Suite 907, Bethesda, MD 20814, phone: 301/657-4329. Help for long-distance caregivers who need care managers in their parents' hometown.

Kelly Assisted Living Services (Subsidiary of Kelly Services), P.O. Box 331179, Detroit, MI 48266, phone: 313/362-4444. Provides home health care for elderly and ill; call for number of your local branch.

*Although men are accused of not knowing their own
weakness, yet perhaps few know their own strength. It is
in men as in soils, where sometimes there is a vein of gold
which the owner knows not of.*

JONATHAN SWIFT

5 | *A SENSE OF SELF*

For years now we've each been a something. Not a some*one,*
a some*thing.* Just think for a minute. The last time you were
at a party, did you introduce yourself by saying, "I'm Jane/
John Doe, and I have these thoughts" or "I like these things"?
No, of course you didn't. Instead you said, "I'm J. Doe and I'm
a doctor" . . . or a lawyer, or an Indian chief. We are what we
do.

"The definition of 'career' has increasingly broadened in our
culture to now include virtually all of life," says psychiatrist
Douglas LaBier, author of *Modern Madness: The Emotional
Fallout of Success.* "The implication is that our career should
be equivalent with our identity. . . . One's funeral, presumably,
would be the ultimate retirement party."

That's one of the reasons it's so difficult to leave a longtime
job. Even if we're getting a bit bored doing the same thing over
and over, even if we're yearning for the luxury of My-Time freedom, retiring is like having an amputation. And for people without a strong sense of self, it can be a crippling loss of identity.

"Having lived our life in a world where status and emulation,

126

work and success, activity and effort have been conditions necessary for self-justification and social approval, how can we preserve our acceptance of self without them?" asks psychologist Allan Fromme.

ITEM On July 20, 1969, eighteen minutes after fellow astronaut Neil Armstrong left the Apollo 11 lunar module, Edwin "Buzz" Aldrin became, the second man to set foot on the moon. Shortly after his return to earth, this man who made history suffered an emotional breakdown. In his 1973 book, *Return to Earth,* Aldrin explains his collapse: "I had gone to the moon. What to do next? What possible goal could I add now? There simply wasn't one, and without a goal I was like an inert Ping-Pong ball being batted about by the whims and motivations of others. I was suffering from what poets have described as the melancholy of all things done."

Aldrin eventually learned that there is indeed life after the moon; he learned to separate the astronaut from the man. And that task—uncoupling the workworld identity from the personal identity—is one of the most difficult tasks of restyling. As we shed our primary careers, we have to discover new standards by which to judge ourselves and other ways to express ourselves. In short, as we approach middle age, we have to find out who we really are.

. . . .

Profile: Dick and Fran Easton—Physician and Psychologist to Scuba Diving Writers

A man's work is his dilemma: his job is his bondage, but it also gives him a fair share of his identity and keeps him from being a bystander in somebody else's world.

MELVIN MADDOCKS

Dick Easton was fifty and his wife Fran was forty when in 1987 they scuttled their careers as physician and psychologist and began experimental careers as writers. Now Dick is writing medically oriented nonfiction, and Fran is working on her first novel and assorted articles. But their only dependable source of income is a small business, Health Information Services, that Dick started in 1974 to supply physician off-hour services to a local hospital. They've taken a 75 percent income cut, but they're reveling in the amount of time they can spend together. Married to each other since 1982, their children (from Dick's first marriage) are grown. They frequently visit Dick's ailing eighty-seven-year-old father, who lives in Kansas.

I walk outside on the small cement porch of our motel room and feel assaulted by the blast of hot air. Southern Virginia is sultry on this day in mid-October and, while I'm sure the area has much to recommend it, all I've seen so far is a motel room with a malfunctioning air conditioner. Why, I wonder, didn't we accept the Eastons' invitation to visit them next month when they'll be scuba diving near their vacation home in the Florida Keys?

Of course I know the answer; I didn't want to wait that long. From our short conversation on the telephone, I've concluded that Dick and Fran are quintessential restylers: two busy and successful professionals who forsook a six-figure income to enjoy a more relaxed mix of work and play. Dick, a physician with a master's degree in public health from Harvard, had been working for the city of Virginia Beach as the Director of Occupational Health Services. In addition, he'd been one of five moonlighting physicians employed by his own company, working two nights each week and one weekend each month to provide emergency care for the patients of off-duty staff physicians. Fran, with a doctorate in psychology from the University of Ohio, had a busy private practice as a psychotherapist.

Now Dick's hospital work, which he frankly describes as "scut work, the kind of thing that interns usually do," provides $36,000 a year and little prestige. It's the latter that particularly interests me; I'm eager to hear the Eastons' thoughts on the whole topic of professional identity.

At Fran's suggestion, we meet in the dining room of our motel. The Eastons arrive just as my husband and I sit down. Dick, who towers over his 5-foot 3-inch wife, is casually dressed in a brown-and-white-striped shirt and corduroy pants. Fran is neat *and comfortable in a red-and-white Oxford cloth shirt and blue jeans.*

After a few pleasantries, we order coffee and I plunge right in. "Did you retire," I begin, "or change careers?" Dick pauses for a very long moment before answering. "Well, that depends," he says.

DICK: On the day I left my position with the city, I would have answered, "I've changed from being a physician who takes care of patients on a daily basis to a physician who is going to write about taking care of patients in different kinds of settings, articles like 'How To Manage an Occupational Health Service' and 'How Employee Assistance Programs Deal with Absenteeism.'" Looking back on it, I felt then like a physician who did two things: who was a writer during the day and who employed his clinical skills at nights and on weekends to earn money to support his writing habit. Today, I don't know exactly how I envision myself . . .

His voice trails off, and I probe further. "If you went to the proverbial cocktail party," I say, "and someone came up to you and said, 'Hi, I'm a lawyer. What do you do?' how would you answer?"

DICK: I'd say, "I'm Dick Easton, and I live in Virginia Beach and try to get to our place in the Florida Keys to go scuba diving just as often as I possibly can." *[Fran laughs approvingly.]*

FRAN: And I have a Ph.D. in psychology—bully for me—but I'm trying to write a book, and I don't have a Ph.D. in bookwriting. There goes my professional identification. Psychology is something I can always fall back on. I don't believe that's been taken away from me. I'm not a therapist right now, but I am a psychologist.

Of course, I'm no longer in touch on a daily basis with colleagues. They think I've dropped out of sight. When I see them they ask me, "Do you think you'll ever go back into practice, ever go back and get a real job?" *[She laughs.]*

DICK: What they mean is, Will you ever return to useful work?

FRAN: Are you ever going to be of use to society again, or are you just going to hide your light under a bushel? This attitude is definitely something to consider when you leave a career. I had a standing in the community. Not that I was famous or anything; but I had professional contacts, referral sources, contacts that made me aware of a certain portion of who I was. And I liked that. Now I don't have patients who say, "Oh, thank you. This was so useful to me today." Instead I have a word processor with a cursor that goes blink, blink, blink.

DICK: We think, What do you mean stop being a psychologist or stop being a doctor? That is who I am; how can I quit? We need to give ourselves permission to change careers. But it's hard. There are so many "ought to's" and "shoulds" and "you better haves" that everybody's hammered into us all these years.

FRAN: It's the superego talking: If I'm not doing what I am trained to do, then I'm doing the wrong thing. Our society is committed to the idea that since particular professionals are trained and degreed and licensed, they should practice that profession. If they make a major shift in careers, people think they're wasting all that education, throwing it out the window. If you're trained to be a doctor, my God, you're supposed to be a doctor! *[She slaps the table for emphasis.]* Right now Dick's not a doctor so he's "playing around," wasting his life writing and traveling. That's the general feeling.

DICK: If I were sick and couldn't practice—if a cardiologist loses his hearing and can't hear heartbeats anymore—that'd be okay. But if I damn well just decide that I want to do something else, people don't think that's a good enough reason to quit being a doctor. So in subtle ways they withdraw their support. Whereas in the cardiologist example people would be very supportive, when I left people said, "What? You're leaving just to write a book?"

FRAN: His boss said, "You can't do that."

DICK: And I said, "Yes, I can. Read this." Then I handed him the letter that said I was leaving. When he said "You can't do that" he meant it on several different levels: you can't do that to us, you can't do that to me, this isn't what a doctor is supposed to do. But sure it is. Physicians are people, and they can do anything they want to do, be anything they want to be—if they're willing to pay the price.

[He takes a deep breath.] The point is that almost nobody's willing to pay the price. I quit my prestigious job. As director I had a title; I was one of twenty-six department heads so I used to go to staff meetings on Friday mornings and people would ask me for all sorts of answers to everything. I would get interviewed by newspapers and television, and I could walk into the police chief's office or the fire chief's office any time I wanted to. Well, all that's a big deal.

Now I don't have an office anymore; I don't even have a mahogany desk that's so big I can't reach across it. When I take night calls at the hospital, all those patients in that three-hundred-sixty-bed hospital belong to somebody else. I'm just there to cover emergencies that can't wait. I run full blast from six at night to six in the morning and on weekends when everyone else is off, and on federal holidays when everyone else is at the beach. But it's a way to pay the bills and it allows me more time and energy to do other things.

That's a good example of being able to do anything you want to if you're willing to pay the price. In this case, it's a monetary price, yes, but it's also a big reduction in prestige and ego.

Fran closed her office a bit prematurely in July 1985 because of a hysterectomy. Meanwhile, as Dick continued working for the city, they began examining their motivations—and their courage—for making a radical lifestyle change.

DICK: Ever since my junior or senior year in college, I've thought I was going to retire at age fifty. I don't know where that idea came from. *[He pauses, and a small frown creases his forehead.]* Wait a minute, maybe I do. I had a roommate in college named Jim Green who got sick when we were seniors and died when I was a freshman in medical school. He had kidney failure. It has to be about that time that I first decided I was going to retire early.

Then a lot of that was reinforced over the years by a memory I have about an actual patient I treated while I was in med school. This guy was an old-time Italian—came from Italy when he was a child—and he had a pizzeria. He used to save twenty-five cents a week, every week, when he first started out. Then over the years he was able to save more and more. The objective of all this was that when he got to be sixty-five, he wanted to take the whole extended family back to the old country. He saved for years and years and years for this. Then at age sixty-three, two years before he was going to retire and pass the pizzeria on to his kids, he got sick. In the next two years he blew every damn cent that he'd saved over thirty, forty years. He blew it all on medical care. He died at sixty-seven, never made it back to Italy.

This man made a big impression on me. I've thought about him over and over again. Every once in a while, about every two or three years, you get a patient like that; and it makes you think over again, Well, what the hell. I'd better do it— whatever "it" is—*now.*

FRAN: Dick sees people die all the time. Some nights at the hospital he'll see a half-dozen people die, and they won't all be ninety-five years old; some will be twenty-five. When you have experiences like that, you begin to realize that you're not immortal, that you're not even going to be fifty-three forever.

Then I think you just come to value an ordinary day, the kind of day when nothing outstanding happens. *[Her voice turns dreamy.]* Just think, no super highs that never last, no bottom-out lows that you think will last forever even though they don't, thank goodness. It's that stretch in the middle there that nobody talks about, when you've slept well the night before, when your shoes don't pinch. You must live through the traumas to know how to appreciate ordinary days, and this comes most often just with getting older.

DICK: What it amounts to is this: Fran and I measure our success differently than a lot of people do. "They" measure our success by asking, "Have you written your book?" "Was it accepted by the publisher?" "Did you make a lot of money from it?" "How many articles has Fran published?" and "How much money did she make?" and "How famous is she?" and "How many trips have you taken?"

I suppose by those standards we've failed miserably. But we don't look at it that way. Over the last couple of years we've come to measure success by personal anonymity, an adequate level of income, and the absence of hassle. What we've achieved is relief. We got rid of all the hassles of our practices.

FRAN: There were plenty of hassles. In 1985 I'd been in private practice for awhile, and I stopped to take a look at the finances. I looked at the actual income and outgo and to my surprise, I found I was working in order to work. I was grossing about $35,000 a year, but it was all going to pay the office rental and the bookkeeper and the receptionist and the malpractice insurance and the lights and the water and to buy the professional clothes.

In order to actually make a living at psychology, you have to work forty-five-minute sessions back to back every day, and I found out that's not good for me. I just don't have the energy level necessary to see that many patients and really be there for them and function on a one-to-one basis. But I can sit in a chair and write all day, or manage the books of Health Information Services all day. Those are things I love to do.

DICK: And I was irritated with some of the things that were happening with my job. There was a new city manager in Virginia Beach, and things had changed. But I could have taken any one of a number of similar jobs. I had literally fifty offers for similar jobs in administrative medicine when word got around that I was dissatisfied. One offered me a salary increase of fifty percent. But I didn't want to do that anymore; there were other things I wanted to do.

I'm just consumed with the fact that I am going to write my book on *Problem-Oriented Medical Record Concepts*. I wrote a book with that title in 1976, and now I want to do a total rewrite. Only five percent of it will be like the original book. I think about it all the time, when I'm at the hospital, when I'm at home, all the time.

FRAN: When someone in therapy used to tell me they were unhappy and they wanted out, my first question to them would be, What is working at this job—or being married to this person or whatever it is you want out of—keeping you from doing? In Dick's case, the job at the city was keeping him from rewriting his book. There was just never time to devote to doing that.

He was too tired when he got home; he needed to exercise instead of going downstairs and sitting at another desk.

DICK: A lot of people talk about going from the daily grind of hard work—hammer, hammer, hammer—to something more relaxing. They envision stopping the energy-draining activities and going to flake out on the sand while someone brings them a piña colada. But I bet that they won't do a thing unless they have a burning desire to do something that their present job is keeping them from doing. I think that's why people actually make the move. It has to be a very positive kind of thing, not running *from* something but moving *to* something.

Perhaps it was only natural that as soon as the Eastons began to feel vague dissatisfactions with their careers, they began to explore their options. After all, as Dick says, "The whole business of being a psychologist or physician is data acquisition and analysis and then formulating some kind of action-oriented plan."

DICK: I'd read about different seminars for career changers for two or three years before we finally went to one. It was a five-day intensive seminar, and it was useful for two reasons. First of all it gave the histories of how other people had changed, and that made change seem okay. And then it provided a framework within which to change.

Once we decided to quit, there were a whole series of decisions. We had to set a deadline and a time frame, and then we had to get real specific. We had to say, "We own twelve credit cards, and we owe on these two." Then we had to take the total amount we owed, look at the deadline, divide, and say, "We have to make this much more so we can pay it off by our deadline." Fran and I made a joint decision. Financially we agreed to get rid of all debts, all monthly payments, things like that. We stopped charging to credit cards; we went on a cash basis.

Then there was another problem. We used to have a yearly income of $112,000. In a global sense we had this huge income. But we also had a big outgo. For example, we had built some duplexes; we were going to rent them out and make all this money, but we also had big interest payments on them. One night Fran said, "Isn't it true that if we got rid of the duplexes and the $4,058.28 interest payments, we wouldn't need a $100,000-plus income to cover the outgo?" Of course she was right.

You get locked into a BMW and real estate and all these things, and then you have to have a big income to pay the interest. We said, "Aah, let's figure it the other way. What's the telephone bill? How much is the mortgage? How much food do we eat? What do we really live on?" We figured from that end and found we only needed $24,000 to $26,000 a year to live on.

FRAN: We also made sure we'd contributed enough to Social Security to get maximum benefits, and we have some retirement income put away for when we get older. It took us eighteen months to set aside enough money.

DICK: We were in a fortunate circumstance because I already had a way to make money by taking emergency calls at the hospital. Sure, it's a lot of hours, but it's a flexible schedule. I can work every night for the first week of one month and for the last week of the next month. That gives me a six-week vacation in between. Since I make up the schedule, I can arrange my hours however I want. I didn't start the company in anticipation of the change, but the fact that it was there certainly made the change easier. Otherwise though, I probably would have just worked for an emergency room somewhere.

We also did a trial run. From September 1986 through April 1987 I continued my position at the city, but I had the salary deferred. We lived completely on what we made from the company, just like we are now.

Yes, we have the place in Florida paid for and, yes, we have the station wagon and two cars and a whole bunch of stuff in our house, including computers and an organ, that is all paid for. But actually if the last hurricane that was threatened for Virginia Beach had gone through here and all that stuff got wiped out, who cares? All we really need is each other and enough money to eat and pay the bank so they don't kick us out of our house.

It's late afternoon now, and Dick keeps looking at his watch. "I really do have to go soon," he says apologetically. "I have to work at the hospital tonight. But there's one more thing I want to say. I don't think there are any mistakes in the world; I think there are just learning experiences."

DICK: If you do something and it doesn't turn out right, the real mistake is not that you did something and it didn't work. *[Dick leans forward to emphasize what he is saying, and his voice becomes slow and deliberate.]* I'm not so much a risk taker as I am a person who believes that if you want to do something, you first formulate a plan clearly so you know what every element of the plan is. Then you implement the plan with the idea that if any element of the plan doesn't work, you stop the plan and do something else. We went to the seminar and we made our plan. We paid off our debts and sold our real estate, and that part of the plan worked. Then I quit the city, and we began living on the money I make by providing off-hour services to the hospital. That part of the plan is working. If we ever hit a part that doesn't work, we'll change.

· ·

Personality Factors

Like Dick and Fran before they left their primary careers, many of us spend so much time at our jobs that we have little time for other activities. Ever since we entered the real world of adults, we've spent a bare minimum of forty hours a week, fifty weeks a year at work. At times our work consumes us, occupying our thoughts even when our bodies are at home or on the beach. So it's no wonder that we rely on these jobs to do much more than provide us with an income. We also look to them to fulfill many of our basic needs.

Back in the 1940s, for example, psychologist David McClelland identified three needs—aside from money—that motivate people to work: achievement (the need to compete against a standard of excellence), power (the desire to influence and control other people), and affiliation (the need for close interpersonal relationships). More recently Edward Scissons, the author of *Happily Ever After: Making the Most of Your Retirement,* expanded that list. In addition to competition and recognition (achievement), influence (power), and affiliation, he found that altruism, intellect, aesthetics, security, adventure, freedom, materialism, and religion are often motivational factors.

Quite obviously, it's "different strokes for different folks." Tom Christensen, for example, has a strong need for affiliation, a need that was amply fulfilled in the Air Force. Now, as he works to get his travel business on its feet, he finds himself in a different environment. "When I go into my office with not many people in it, I feel fairly—not lonely, exactly—but it's different," he says. "I was used to having a lot of people around me. Before I left the Air Force, I was bitching at staff meetings that we were wasting too much time at the coffee pot. Now when I go to the coffee pot, there's nobody there to talk with." He grins. "My phone bill is excessively high. I guess I use it to get that sense of camaraderie."

Like Tom, we'll all find that while our environment will change after we leave our primary career, our basic needs will remain the same. Those of us who enjoyed being around people in our first jobs will still crave the companionship of friends. Those of us who found pleasure by assuming responsibility and achieving goals will continue to seek activities that provide opportunities for measurable success, and those of us who enjoyed positions of leadership and importance will still want to exercise authority in one way or another.

Unfortunately, many people forget to take the personality factor into account. They believe that if they have the technical skills to do a job, they'll enjoy doing it. But that just isn't true. Although you may be *able* to sail a boat—you may have the intellectual ability to understand navigational techniques and the physical strength to pull the anchor and raise the mainsail—you may be downright miserable spending days on end out on the open sea. Ability and enjoyment do not always go hand-in-hand.

No Second Acts

While it's easier to learn new skills than to transform a personality, successful restylers still build on their past. They are able to dissect the tasks they performed in their first job, break them into component parts, and reassemble them to fit new situations.

A dentist who is in the process of restyling explains it this way: "At first I thought all I was capable of doing was drilling and filling teeth, talking with patients, and working with the three members of my staff. Now I see that 'drilling and filling' is evidence of manual dexterity, 'talking with patients' is a communication skill, and 'working with staff' is a management skill. It's almost like a game, figuring out how a skill that seems specific to dentistry can be transferred into a more generalized ability that is applicable to other things."

By analyzing his skills with an eye to their transferability, this dentist realized that he had more options than he ever imagined. Like most people, he realized that, as F. Scott Fitzgerald said, "There are no second acts in American life." There's not often a need for one. The radical change that may, at first, look like a whole new story is really just a variation of Act I: the same props but with a brand new stage setting.

. . . .

Profile: Gene Estess—Investment Banker to Director of Project for the Homeless

I think I can—I think I can—I think I can.
          WATTY PIPER, *The Little Engine That Could*

In the summer of 1987 Gene Estess, then fifty-two and an investment banker for nearly twenty years, took "at least a 50 percent pay cut" to do what he'd always wanted to do: something "charitable." He's now the executive director of the Jericho Project, a New York City program to aid the homeless. His wife, Pat, the editor of a consumer finance magazine, gave him her full moral support. They have been married to each other for twelve years; for most of that time four of their eight children (Gene's five and Pat's three) lived with them. When Gene left Wall Street, the children ranged in age from nineteen to thirty.

"Now you have to understand," says Gene when I phone him to arrange a meeting, *"I'm not sitting around relaxing. That*

disappoints some people. Like the producers of 'The Today Show' and '60 Minutes'—they hear about this quirky man who supposedly has given up everything on Wall Street to do something else. They think it's this side of kinky. But after they find out that I'm working hard, that I'm not sitting on a beach, they lose interest."

I assure Gene that my husband and I would like to hear his story, even if he's working forty-hour weeks. "Oh, it's more than forty hours some weeks," he responds quickly. "But this is so rewarding that I don't think of it as stress. Stress is not wanting to do something anymore and not knowing how to get out of it. That's stress."

We arrange to meet on a Sunday afternoon at his apartment in midtown Manhattan. "Come about 11:30," he says. "We'll have brunch."

My husband and I find their apartment building with no trouble at all. An elevator takes us right into the Estesses' living room, which is filled with paintings, plants, and books. Gene greets us warmly. He's a large gray-haired man, dressed in khaki slacks and a turquoise and white sport shirt. He leads us into the dining area where Pat is setting out a typical New York deli feast: bagels, lox, cream cheese, coleslaw, potato salad, coffee cake.

The four of us sit down at the table, and Gene starts off with a rush.

GENE: Jericho is a private, nonprofit organization. It was founded in 1983 to provide permanent housing and rehabilitation for homeless single adults with substance abuse problems. As the executive director, I'm responsible for raising all the money, for the program, for community relations. Everything falls into my lap. *[A big smile lights up his face.]* I can tell you I love it.

What's interesting to me is how this position fits me so perfectly. You know, way back in college on page one of some business textbook we read about interchangeability of skills, but then we forget it. We go and raise our families and do our thing, and forget that our skills are interchangeable.

This idea of using your skills in a different situation is very exciting. I mean, when you come right down to it, if I had been sort of an executive all these years on Wall Street, well, I'm still an executive; I still hire and fire people. If I had been somewhat creative over the years—and you have to be somewhat overordinarily creative to develop a financial package that's good for a family—then I most certainly am being creative as I work to find programs for the homeless. If I had been in sales all these years, which I had, well my God, I'm selling every day now. It's just that it is so much easier to believe in this product.

I either raise money dressed casually like you see me now; or once in a while when I go into corporate America, I put on a three-piece suit. My understanding of both worlds has been real good because I know, for example, that businesspeople like to hear about return on investment. So, okay, I can clearly show them in terms that they'll understand what an investment in Jericho will mean. It doesn't disturb me that they consider it an investment; it doesn't disturb me that a person expects a return. I mean, even if you give one dollar on the street to someone who looks real hungry, you should be concerned about where that dollar is going. Is it going up their nose or into their stomach? I can talk to businesspeople in language they understand.

There is no skill that I possess that I'm not using now. I do a lot of public speaking. Well, I did a lot of that on Wall Street. I trained people all those years and I talked before investment groups, so I don't completely collapse when I get in front of a group and talk about Jericho. I can do all this stuff; it's real simple because it's really what I've been doing all along.

[His voice drops to a husky whisper.] The other day I said to Pat, "This is just such a great job because when I was a little kid, like all little kids, I wanted to be a policeman. Well, now I'm a policeman; I really am." I don't walk around with a gun, but I have definite police things to do because some of our clients are always getting into trouble. Then I got a little older and I said, "I want to be an entrepreneur," and I am that. I'm running a large project; it's getting larger all the time. Then I wanted to be a shrink at one point, and I'm doing that. It goes on and on. I'm doing all the stuff that I always wanted to do.

It's true; I've been able to roll all these little fantasies into one. But skillwise, there is no skill that I have found that I was lacking—not because I'm so skillful but because I've done all this stuff before. It's just that I never realized I could transfer them to something as far afield as this.

[Gene has been talking rapidly, the words tumbling out in his excitement. Now he begins to speak more slowly.] You know, changing careers is just a question of focusing on what our skills are and how we can use them in different ways. You just have to wake up and find out how you can do what you've always dreamt of doing without sacrificing the world to do it.

Stepping off the fast track wasn't as hard for Gene as it might have been for others. He'd always seen it for what it was, a way to make a living, not a life. From an early age, he'd known that one day he would, in his own way, follow in the footsteps of his grandfather and uncle.

GENE: I was born and raised in Rock Island, Illinois. My grandfather was sort of like "The Last Angry Man." He was a real ethnic character, very successful in business and very charitable. He would give you literally the shirt off his back if you needed it. He was responsible for many local business successes because when people were up against it, they'd come to him and he would help them out one way or another.

Then there was his son, who was my uncle. He was a bigtime financier in Chicago. When he died many years ago, my aunt found things in his pile of papers that showed he did the same kind of helpful things. The behind-the-scenes things that he did were just unbelievable. Many people owed their college education to him. *[His voice catches and tears come to his eyes.]* At his funeral people stood in line to tell my aunt exactly what he had done for them.

I became an investment banker for all the reasons anybody else does anything. When I grew up my father was a businessman; he expected me to go into the family business, which was a department store. When I decided to go to college, I sent in two applications: one to the University of Arizona because I really wanted to play in the sun, and the other to the Wharton School of Finance and Commerce at the University of Pennsylvania. I was accepted to both, and I said to my father, "Which one do you think I should accept?" He gave me one of those guilt trips. "It's up to you," he said, "but let your conscience be your guide." So I went to Wharton; and at that time when people went to Wharton for four years, they went into business afterwards.

I worked in my father's business for eight years and decided, "I gotta get out." I was married to my first wife then, and she was from New York so we took the children and moved to New York. There were financial pressures, and I fell into investment banking because that was the way to make a buck. I became real successful at it, and I liked it at first. It was very, very exciting because I was dealing with a lot of exciting people, and they were taking over companies and there were all these buyouts and all this stuff. But after a while it became more of a standard kind of investment milieu, and I didn't feel it was rewarding in any way except financially.

But at that time I could not just up and leave. I could not have done it financially, and I could not have done it emotionally. Our kids were still young; it was a demanding time and I needed to be home more. I just couldn't have done it then.

PAT: You have to do these things when the time is right. Eight years ago Gene started to work toward a master's degree in social work. He went to one course and loved it. We couldn't shut him up about it; that's all he wanted to talk about. But it was just not possible for him to continue. There were too many familial responsibilities.

GENE: We still had four kids living with us—teenagers—and that's a huge responsibility.

PAT: The school wanted him to give up a year to do field work in social work, and there was no way in the whole world we could have afforded for him to go for a year without earning any money. You've got a responsibility with children, and you can't negate that responsibility.

GENE: I dropped out after one course. I just couldn't see my way clear.

PAT: But two and a half years ago it was the right time in his life to make a career change. We still had one child in college but after having so many, one seemed like nothing. You're never financially clear, really, when you have kids, but at least it's not day-to-day responsibility.

Pat, a soft-spoken, immaculately dressed woman with short blond hair, excuses herself to work on an article she's writing for a major magazine. "This is really Gene's story anyway," she says with a smile. Gene glances up at her, and his eyes shine with affection.

GENE: I think the reason I was able to make a switch, when so many people just talk about it, is this woman right here. I really can't tell you how much I feel I owe her. In the final analysis it was Pat who asked me, implored me, to do something else. I'm not trying to be overly dramatic, but I can't imagine anybody making a big change in their life unless they have the support of the people who care about them. Pat and the kids gave me support when I needed it, and now I'm running with the ball.

About 1983 Pat heard about a seminar in lifestyle planning. She thought I should take the course. I said, "I don't do things like that. I hate group encounters." Pat talked me into at least trying. I went to classes a couple of evenings a week for eight weeks and, I must admit, it exercised my mind.

I credit that class with showing me you can take charge of a situation. Listening to the stories they told of other people was an eye opener. I don't know if I really needed that seminar or not. I do think you need a third party though. When your spouse or close friends say something, you might not hear it; but if someone else says it, you listen. But I still didn't make a move for several years. These things play on your mind, and I think that's okay.

First you have to decide what you want. I've been interviewed for local newspapers, and the hook is always, "He gave up a six-figure income on Wall Street to devote his life to the homeless." There's more to it than that. It's not just financial. It's not just that the kids are out of the house. It's a mindset question. It's "Geez, I've done this thing for twenty-five years; now what?"

Pat and I had some soulful discussions, culminating in the first part of '87. She said to me, "I just read in the paper that the New School [*a New York school for social research*] is having a wine-and-cheese party for new possible applicants." I went and liked the people I met, and I said to Pat, "I'm gonna do this," and she said, "Go for it." I said, "That means I'm gonna leave making money and go to school full-time," and she said, "Fine."

So I made up my mind that in September '87 I was going to leave Wall Street and go to the New School for a master's in public policy and urban analysis. I thought maybe I could eventually get some kind of government position where I could influence the way dollars were spent or the way public policy was set. I wanted to use my financial background to help a social situation. That made sense to me then, and it still does.

Even before Gene and Pat began their lengthy discussions, Gene was becoming more and more involved in the plight of the homeless. He and Pat lived in the suburbs at the time and commuted to work through Grand Central Station. Gene found himself spending more and more time talking to the homeless who lived in the station.

GENE: I began sort of indiscriminately giving out money to the people who panhandled there. I was giving out a dollar here and a few dollars there. Then one day I saw a woman lying on the ground, and around her waist was chained a black poodle dog. I summoned up the courage to introduce myself, and I found out she was named Patricia and was in her mid-forties; her dog was named Ebony, and they were in fact homeless. I asked her how much it cost her to live in the station and support her dog, and she said "About six dollars a day." So I said, "Well, until I find out what it takes to house you permanently somewhere, I will provide the money for you to live," which in fact I did for many, many months.

Then one day I got a call from a woman who was helping Patricia. This woman invited me to a meeting of an agency called Jericho. I went to the meeting and soon began donating quite a bit of my time to the project on both a people basis and a fundraising basis. I was subsequently elected to the Board of Directors.

About the time I decided to leave investment banking to go back to school, the executive director of Jericho resigned. I told my fellow board members that I wanted the job. I submitted an application and out of seventy applicants, they finally said, "Okay, it's yours."

Sure, I was frightened. There was the question of, How the hell am I going to do this? I mean, my office now is really in a single-room-occupancy hotel. There are strange people walking around the halls; there are cockroaches that every once in a while walk around me; there's all this strangeness. And, my God, I had secretaries before; I had *stuff*. So I was scared. Was I going to be able to really do this?

I'd wake up in the morning and say, "Yeah, it looks good," but then I'd wonder if I was like a kid saying, "Oh, Daddy, Daddy, I love ice skating." So Daddy schleps this child every weekend and rents skates and watches him practice, and then the kid says, "Oh, Daddy, Daddy, I want to buy the skates." So Daddy buys the skates and that's the last time the kid touches them. I think my fear was, Gee, I think I want this; but once I take a taste of it, will I still want it?

Also I knew I could be accused of being self-centered, especially financially. Pat could say, Hey, we're giving up all this Wall Street money for a field that is slim pickins from a financial standpoint. I mean, we are certainly not Rockefeller, and we have certainly decided in some areas to tighten our belt. Obviously there are economic realities. We watch our money much more carefully, but the net-net is that we really can still enjoy the things that we enjoy. We are very lucky about that.

But let's assume that Pat wanted a mink coat or to eat out every night or that she put demands on me that our children go to Europe every year. If she'd been that kind of person, then there would be no way that I could have done this except by splitting up our marriage—and now you're talking about tripling the anxiety.

[Once again, a huge smile envelops his face.] But I can still hear the door close on the day I walked out of my Wall Street office. I had a feeling of such euphoria that I wanted to jump up and smash my heels together. I have never looked back. Frankly at this point in my life, knowing what I know now and being as happy as I am, if I were ever confronted with the fact that I would have to change my style of living dramatically or go back to Wall Street, I would hope that Pat and I would decide to just sell everything we own and repattern our lives.

I hope we would be able to do that because I would never go back.

"Just one more thing," I say to Gene as we get ready to say good-bye. "What happened to Patricia and her dog, Ebony?" He smiles. "They're still around," he says. "Unlike our typical client, she's mentally ill and will never be out of the program. She's not really well, but on the other hand she has her own room and is fat and sassy. Ebony is fat and sassy, too. In her own way, Patricia is very thankful. . . . And I'm very thankful, too."

. . . .

Gene's transition was exceptionally smooth. He left investment banking to do something that matched his interests, his personality, and his skills. Although he was moving from the gilt-edged world of the rich to the despair-filled streets of the homeless, he was confident he could do the work his new position demanded. After all, he'd done it all before.

E X E R C I S E S

Career counselors offer a number of tests that are designed to give information about a person's aptitudes, personality, and interests. Some people find that these tests help them clarify their thoughts; others feel that they can gain enough insight into their behavior and ability by reviewing their past experiences and noticing patterns. After all, one of the advantages of midlife is that we have a history of experiences that can, if mined, provide revealing information.

Career Review

Journey in memory through a typical day at your present job. Try to forget the daily hassles, and concentrate on the overall picture. You open the door . . . and what happens? What do you do first? As you mentally progress through the day, jot down the activities that give you pleasure. Do you enjoy the social interaction at staff meetings? The physical exercise as you take a brisk walk at lunch? The creativity of a new project? The accountability procedures that keep everyone on track? The existence of goals that you strive to meet? What will you really miss when you leave this job?

If you had other positions or jobs before this one, do a similar review of those. This will give you a good idea of the types of activities that you'll need to structure into your postretirement life.

Parenting Review

Another "primary career" that will end for the majority of us during our midlife years is that of being a parent. While we'll remain in the role of "parent emeritus," we'll retire from the daily management role we enjoyed when our children were younger. Spend a few minutes doing a review similar to the one above. What will you really miss about being a parent? Will you miss being needed? Giving advice? Being in daily contact with youngsters? Participating in competitive sports with your teen?

How can you structure these activities into your empty-nest lifestyle?

Fly on the Wall

Divide a piece of lined paper into six vertical columns, one quite wide and five very narrow. Choose a midweek day—Tuesday, for example—when your activities will be as normal as possible, and title your sheet of paper with the name of that day.

NEXT TUESDAY					

When that day arrives pretend you are a fly that can quietly buzz through your day observing your every action. Use the wide column to list *all* your activities, even the ones that seem the most inconsequential. Did you make breakfast, cuddle your toddler, drive in commuter traffic, and 'yes sir' your boss? Talk to a customer, place an order, wash the dishes? Write it all down.

Now it's time for the narrow columns. According to the *Dictionary of Occupational Titles,* a nearly 1,500-page tome from the U.S. Department of Labor, all jobs or activities require a person to relate in some way to people, things, or data (information). So label the first three columns as follows: "P" for "People"; "T" for "Things"; "D" for "Data." Now look at each activity you listed and decide whether it required you to use people skills (such as teaching, supervising, persuading, or helping), things skills (such as operating, manipulating, tending, or handling) or data skills (such as analyzing, compiling, computing, or comparing). Put a check in the appropriate column or columns.

Later, if you wish, you can refine this technique to give more specific information. You may find it useful to make another chart in which you subdivide the "People" category into "Children" and "Adults," for example, or "Customers," "Boss," "Co-workers," and "Assistants."

The last two columns provide space for you to indicate which activities you feel you do well and which you consider weak points. Mark one column "S" for "Strength," the other "W" for "Weakness." (You may prefer to use these columns to chart your "likes" and "dislikes.")

Repeat this exercise three more times—once on a Saturday or Sunday, once while on vacation, and once for a typical day in your past. What do you do in your "off hours"? What is your life like when you travel abroad or visit a resort? Was it different before you had children or when you had another job? Observing yourself in four different situations allows you to find talents that otherwise might be overlooked.

A quick tally of the results will give you insight about the skills you can bring to future undertakings.

NEXT TUESDAY	P	T	D	S	W
Make breakfast		✓			✓
Help Davy dress	✓			✓	
Drive him to day care	✓				
Commute		✓			✓
Look over papers			✓	✓	
Dictate letter			✓	✓	
Phone call to FMC	✓		✓	✓	
Phone call to travel agent	✓		✓	✓	
Staff meeting	✓				✓

Different Strokes for Different Folks

All of us enjoy accomplishing our goals, and all of us enjoy developing relationships with people. But which pleases you more: a feeling of achievement or a feeling of affiliation?

Are you motivated more by your interest in a task (the challenge of mastering it and the knowledge that you can do it well) or by people (the assurance that people like and respect you and the satisfaction of working harmoniously with others)?

Look at each pair of words below and check the word that you believe best describes your usual mood. Work rapidly and put down first impressions. The words are *not* meant to be opposites. Don't worry about responses that seem contradictory. When you are finished, you should have made exactly thirty check marks.

Column A				*Column B*
forthright	___	1	___	accepting
able	___	2	___	neighborly
companionable	___	3	___	industrious
quick	___	4	___	agreeable
at ease with others	___	5	___	competent
effective	___	6	___	grateful
laughs easily	___	7	___	energetic

(continued)

Column A			Column B
firm	__	8 __	friendly
like being helped	__	9 __	disciplined
team worker	__	10 __	inventive
bright	__	11 __	sharing
acute observer	__	12 __	chatty
congenial	__	13 __	logical
peace-loving	__	14 __	precise
creative	__	15 __	caring
enterprising	__	16 __	pleasant
approachable	__	17 __	busy
calm	__	18 __	enthusiastic
trusting	__	19 __	aggressive
clever	__	20 __	giving
ambitious	__	21 __	self-sacrificing
kind	__	22 __	dominant
generous	__	23 __	resourceful
loyal	__	24 __	conscientious
considerate	__	25 __	firm
ambitious	__	26 __	friendly
capable	__	27 __	sympathetic
persevering	__	28 __	understanding
intelligent	__	29 __	cooperative
amiable	__	30 __	thorough

Now use the following key to score your answers. When your answer agrees with the key, circle the number of the question. When your answer does not agree with the key, do not circle the number.

1. A	7. B	13. B	19. B	25. A
2. A	8. A	14. B	20. A	26. B
3. B	9. B	15. A	21. A	27. A
4. A	10. B	16. A	22. B	28. A
5. B	11. A	17. B	23. B	29. A
6. A	12. A	18. B	24. B	30. B

Test developed by Henry Clay Lindgren, professor emeritus of psychology, San Francisco State University. Used with permission.

Your score is simply the number of items you circled. For example, if you circled twelve numbers, your score is twelve. Write your score here:_____

People who score between twenty and thirty have a high need to achieve. They tend to enjoy activities that involve initiating and completing tasks that they find personally worthwhile and interesting. Often they like to work alone with a minimum of guidance, support or encouragement. When they do work with others, they find competition stimulating.

People who score between zero and ten have a high need for affiliation. They enjoy working with others to achieve mutually satisfactory goals and would rather collaborate than compete when working on projects. They value close friendships and are able to maintain warm relationships with co-workers.

Behavior that is too exclusively one-sided in either direction may be counter-productive. The person who single-mindedly pursues his or her own goals may irritate others. On the other hand, the person who is overly eager to be liked may be unable to think or act independently.

By looking at your score, you should understand more about the choices you have made in the past and the ones that are likely to bring you the most satisfaction in the future.

Transferable Skills

The key to understanding your nontechnical strengths is to identify your transferable or functional skills. Once you have done this, you will be better prepared to identify what it is you want to do and are able to do.

Many people view their skills in strictly work-content terms. Consider, for example, a professor who knows a particular subject such as Greek history or Renaissance music. If he decides to leave education, he may find that there is little demand for his expertise. On the other hand, he very likely has many skills that are directly transferable to other endeavors: the ability to communicate, plan, innovate, write, manage time, and so on.

The skills and traits on the following list are valuable in a variety of situations. Which ones best describe you? Place a "1" before those that strongly characterize you; a "2" before those that describe you to a large extent; and a "3" before those that describe you to some extent. After completing this exercise, review the lists and rank order the ten characteristics that best describe you on each list. By capitalizing on these strengths, you will greatly expand the choices before you.

Organizational and Interpersonal Skills

___ communicating

___ problem solving

___ analyzing/assessing

___ planning

___ decision-making

___ innovating

___ thinking logically

___ evaluating

___ identifying problems

___ synthesizing

___ forecasting

___ tolerating ambiguity

___ motivating

___ leading

___ selling

___ performing

___ reviewing

___ attaining

___ team building

___ updating

___ coaching

___ supervising

___ estimating

___ negotiating

___ administering

___ trouble-shooting

___ implementing

___ self-understanding

___ understanding

___ setting goals

___ conceptualizing

___ generalizing

___ managing time

___ creating

___ judging

___ controlling

___ organizing

___ persuading

___ encouraging

___ improving

___ designing

___ consulting

___ teaching

___ cultivating

___ advising

___ training

___ interpreting

___ achieving

___ reporting

___ managing

Personality and Work-Style Traits

___ diligent	___ honest
___ patient	___ reliable
___ innovative	___ perceptive
___ persistent	___ assertive
___ tactful	___ sensitive
___ loyal	___ astute
___ successful	___ risk taker
___ versatile	___ easy going
___ enthusiastic	___ calm
___ outgoing	___ flexible
___ expressive	___ competent
___ adaptable	___ punctual
___ democratic	___ receptive
___ resourceful	___ diplomatic
___ determining	___ self-confident
___ creative	___ tenacious
___ open	___ discrete
___ objective	___ talented
___ warm	___ empathic
___ orderly	___ tidy
___ tolerant	___ candid
___ frank	___ adventuresome
___ cooperative	___ firm
___ dynamic	___ sincere
___ self-starter	___ initiator
___ precise	___ competent
___ sophisticated	___ diplomatic
___ effective	___ efficient

Lists from *Careering and Re-careering for the 1990s* by Ronald L. Krannich. Used with permission.

Resources

Aptitude and Personality Tests

If you'd like professional help in assessing your talents, the National Board for Certified Counselors can send you a list of certified career counselors in your area and/or a list of agencies accredited by the International Association of Counseling Services. Send a self-addressed stamped envelope to NBCC at 5999 Stevenson Ave., Alexandria, VA 22304, or call 703/461-6222.

APTITUDE TESTS

Career counselors generally use one of three types of aptitude tests. The first two are likely to be most useful for restylers.

- tests that rate your ability on mechanical, spatial, verbal, and mechanical skills (such as the California Aptitude Survey, the General Aptitude Test Battery, the Differential Aptitude Test Battery, and the Johnson O'Connor Research Foundation Tests).
- tests that measure your adeptness in areas such as problem solving, scholastic aptitude, and professional judgment (Wide Range Achievement Test, Otis-Lennon Mental Abilities Test, Nelson-Denny Reading Test, Watson-Glaser Thinking Appraisal).
- tests that measure your ability to perform certain jobs.

Discover What You're Best At by Barry and Linda Gale (Fireside/Simon & Schuster, Inc., 1230 Avenue of the Americas, New York, NY 10020, phone: 800/223-2348). The authors provide a series of tests to help you define "your own true career abilities, not merely your interests." The Business Test, for example, probes for aptitudes in coordinating, delegating, managing, negotiating, persuading, selling, and supervising. The Logic Test looks at your ability to find similarities and differences, systematize, solve problems, draw conclusions, and infer information. Other tests look at clerical, mechanical, numerical, and social skills. These are followed by a directory of careers keyed to different aptitudes.

PERSONALITY TESTS

Professionals often give the Myers-Briggs Type Indicator test, which categorizes people according to four pairs of preferences: extraversion vs. introversion, intuition vs. sensation, thinking vs. feeling, and judging vs. perceiving. Various mixtures of these character traits lead to sixteen groupings, each of which can be related to occupational profiles.

Please Understand Me: Character & Temperament Types by David Keirsey and Marilyn Bates (1978, 1984, softcover, Prometheus Nemesis Book Company, Box 2748, Del Mar, CA 92014, phone: 619/632-1575). Keisey and Bates offer nonprofessionals a simplified version of the Myers-Briggs Type Indicator test. (See above).

Thank God It's Monday by Leonard H. Chusmir (1990, softcover, New American Library, 120 Woodbine Street, Bergenfield, NJ 07621, phone: 800/331-4624). Chusmir begins with a "Manifest Needs Questionnaire" consisting of fifteen quick-to-answer questions, and ends with a lengthy list of jobs that fulfill each need. Based on Chusmir's own research which, in turn, is based on the motivation theory of David McClelland (achievement, affiliation, power), this slim volume is mostly directed to unhappy employees and their managers; but it can also help restylers gain insight into their own needs.

To stretch the octave twixt the dream and deed. Ah, that's the thrill.

RICHARD LE GULLIENNE, *The Decadent to His Soul*

6 DISCOVERING YOUR DREAMS

Admitting to ourselves that we can indeed do what we want to do is a scary proposition. We're so used to being confined by "shoulds" and "have to's." We *should* live in a big house with a large front yard that needs mowing every Saturday. We *have to* wait until the kids are off on their own before we can even think of ourselves. And we must, absolutely must, keep plugging away at the same old job.

But as the previous chapters have shown, many of these "shoulds" are illusory; many of the "have to's" disappear when they are examined more closely. And our "can do" skills are much greater than we dared imagine.

So now what? The range of possibilities is unlimited. If we don't have to go to a specific job every morning, then we don't have to live within commuting distance of that office or business. If we don't have to sing to the boss's rhythm, we can orchestrate our own tunes. But over the years most of us have become deaf to our personal wants and desires. Once we accept the feasibility of change, the next step on the road to restyling is to discover what it is we want to do.

A World of Choices

Restyling isn't about stopping; it's about starting. It isn't about yesterday's job; it's about tomorrow's pleasure. "Most of us have secret dreams about things we'd like to do," says Freda Rebelsky, professor of psychology at Boston University. "We're like suns—great, round things—with many rays coming out. By middle age we've only had time to follow a few of our rays."

Those of us who are lucky know just which rays we want to follow once we get the chance. Rich Henke, for example, had more hobbies than he could count when he left his position at the aerospace company; Marian Gibson was determined to work with old folks; and Tom Christensen had been devouring information about the travel industry long before he retired from the Air Force. Ken Cassie voiced his appreciation of the fact that his resignation from teaching didn't leave Shelley and him at loose ends: "It helped that this wasn't a complete break for us. When we left teaching, the craft fairs were there waiting for us the next weekend. The pottery had been going on before; it was a continuation of something we knew."

But some of us have been so wrapped up in our careers and families that we've let other interests slide. Oh, maybe we play golf now and again, or maybe we spend the occasional hours reading a book or visiting a museum. But we don't see these activities as providing the foundation for a full, enriching life. We have to imagine ourselves as we'll be five or ten years from now and figure out what we really want to do when we finally have time for My-Time.

ITEM Some people are doers. Others are dreamers. What differentiates the two? According to a study done at Ohio State University, the main difference between those who actually started a small business and those who only talked about it was conceptual. The doers could conceive of themselves making the move. They could envision.

Years ago when we envisioned the future, our teachers called it daydreaming and rapped our knuckles because we weren't paying attention. But visualization, the fancy name for daydreaming, is a technique that helps people turn dreams into reality. Adelaide Bry, author of a book on this subject, calls it "directing the movies of your mind." Because it enables us to see ourselves in different roles and different costumes, it's an important part of restyling.

In order to successfully plan our futures, we have to try on the clothes of midlife and look at them in the mirrors of our imaginations. Is the financial belt too tight, the security coat too loose? Does the new style match our personality, whether it be daringly wild or conservatively proper? In short, are we comfortable with the fit?

For years Kinney Thiele saw herself attired in the vibrant fabrics of Africa. Over and over again her mind replayed an imaginary movie, "African Adventure starring Kinney Thiele." Gradually her desire to live her dream became stronger than her fears of leaving a secure job; and when the Peace Corps accepted her application, the reels became real.

· ·

Profile: **Kinney Thiele—Research Analyst to Peace Corps Worker**

I believe that . . . dreams are more powerful than facts.

ROBERT FULGHUM

Kinney Thiele was forty-four when she left her $26,000-a-year job as a research analyst and conference coordinator for Stanford Research Institute [SRI]. She'd finally found a way to fulfill her dream of living in Africa. By joining the Peace Corps she was able to spend twenty-six months in the West African nation of Sierra Leone, working in a small village as a health and rural development volunteer. She'd been divorced for twelve years; and her son, Rett, was eighteen.

For Kinney Thiele, going to Africa started as a joke. "It must have been about sixteen years ago," she says with a chuckle. "I *was broke, dead broke, and Rett, my seven-year-old son, came up to me: 'Mommy, can we go to the movies?' Well, of course we couldn't. I didn't have any money, but I didn't want to tell him that. It was too depressing. So I said, 'No, Rett, we're saving to go on a safari.' Then I started laughing at myself because going to Africa was the most impossible thing I could think of."*

We're in the living room of Kinney's small apartment in Menlo Park, California, a few miles from Stanford University; and I note that the surroundings look like those of a professional student. Books line the wall, plants sit casually in nooks and crannies, and marvelous African masks stare down from the wall. Only the television, a large, overbearing console model, seems out of place.

Kinney notices that I'm looking at it. "I won the TV," she explains. "It doesn't go well with African artifacts, and I never would have bought such a large one, but I do watch it. I'm embarrassed to admit how much I watch it."

She doesn't look at all embarrassed. In fact, everything about Kinney suggests a woman totally at peace with herself. She's unabashedly gray-haired, wears little makeup, and is comfortably dressed in a cotton skirt, oversized sweater, and sandals. There's a wonderful lilt to her voice, a delightful sparkle to her eyes.

We all settle deeper into our comfortable chairs and, with a broad smile, she continues her story.

My son was born when I was twenty-six. About the time he started kindergarten, I said to myself, Obviously he's going to grow up and move out, just the thing that should happen. So what can I do when that happens? What I really wanted to do, I decided, was to go off and live in Africa. I knew that wasn't something that was possible for me, but still . . .

That's probably why "safari" popped into my mind when I had to tell Rett we couldn't go to the movies. Then, the next time I saw a book on Africa, I read it. *[She gestures toward the overflowing bookcase.]* Ninety-nine percent of those books are on Africa. Over the years I read something about Africa every day and attended every seminar I could find to learn more about it. I just started reading and preparing myself so I'd be comfortable if I ever got there.

It was a series of little steps, one at a time. First I was learning about Africa; and then I began realizing that it was going to be very hard to actually get there, but I started to think about it anyway. And finally, in 1978, I took Rett on that safari.

She hesitates and a dark cloud passes briefly over her face. Then, with a no-nonsense shake of her head, she continues. "You just don't know what an achievement that was for me," she says. "I had no self-esteem whatsoever. Going on that trip alone—not with another adult but just with my child—was a real turning point for me." She stops for a minute to collect her thoughts, and then in a soft, matter-of-fact voice she begins talking about her early life.

To summarize my beginnings, I had a really lousy, rotten, awful childhood. When I was four, my parents went off to World War II and left my sisters and me with some very old relatives. I can understand now why they did it; they didn't want to traipse a bunch of kids around while my mother followed my father, who was on a secret wartime program. But it felt miserable to be dumped.

By the time my parents came home from the war, my father was an alcoholic. They split when I was about eight, and my mother went to work and again left me with these same people. So I was mostly raised by this old lady and her brother, who had only one leg, in a brown house when everybody else had a white house. What I learned from all this was that I was different, that I wasn't worth shit.

I went to college for a couple of years, but I didn't get my degree until much later. Instead I got married. My husband was a college professor, a theoretical physical chemist.

I enjoyed being a young mother. I remember when Rett was about one and a half or two, we lived on the top floor of an apartment house in Baltimore, in the cheapest two-bedroom place we could find. It was full of families with little kids, and a lot of women sat there and bitched and said, "Life is so boring and my husband is always at work." I'd say, "I'm taking Rett to the apple cider farm this afternoon. Do you want to come along?" "Well," they'd say, "not really. I have to polish the silver." *[She shakes her head at the absurdity of the comment.]*

That became a phrase in my life: I have to polish the silver. It helps me remember what's important.

Anyway, when my husband and I split after eleven years of marriage, I was completely devastated. I really didn't think I could do anything without someone else as a partner. I knew I had to re-raise myself. I didn't want those old tapes, the not-worth-shit tapes, playing all the time. So I decided that when I wanted to try something different, even if it scared the heck out of me, I should try it. I should listen to the people who say, "You can do it," instead of to my old self.

That's probably what got me out of Baltimore. I went to the University of Massachusetts at Amherst and finished up the work I needed for a master's in education. Then I moved out to Northern California where some of my relatives were living. I had no money and was desperate for a job. After about three months of getting lots of nibbles but no work, SRI offered me a job as a typist. I was pretty desperate—I had no income at all—so I said, "Sure." Then one day they said, "We need this information, so go find it." Suddenly I was a research analyst.

A few years after that I took Rett on the safari. He was eleven years old; if I'd waited another year, till he was twelve, it would have doubled the airfare. So I decided just to borrow the extra thousand dollars I'd need and go. I went down to the travel agency; and as I gave the agent the money, it occurred to me that I'd never thought I could really do things without my husband. Yet here I'd just made this major, major decision. That moment is still etched in my mind. From that point on you couldn't keep me back!

The following year I was elected chairperson of this staff advisory group at SRI. It was big-time as far as my life was concerned; the president and all the vice-presidents would be listening while I ran the meetings. I started having panic attacks. Then I said to myself, "If they believe I can do it, if they elected me to this position, then I can do it." And I did. Chairing that group put me over the cusp. Shoot, if I could do that, then I can do anything. If I want to, I can. [She unconsciously straightens her back and sits taller in her chair.]

Joining the Peace Corps had also always been in the back of Kinney's mind. She'd been fascinated with the concept from the

*time President John F. Kennedy first proposed it in the early
sixties. Now it seemed the perfect—possibly the only—way for
her to get to Africa. With her new-found self confidence, she
turned to the five-year planning calendar that was in the back
of her Daytimer™ and wrote "Apply for the Peace Corps."*

Why didn't I wait until I was older and could draw full retirement? Why did I want to go in my mid-forties? A lot of people
ask me that, especially since I didn't think I'd be able to ever
again work at SRI. In fact, my self-esteem told me they'd never
want me back. I really expected to be unemployed when I
returned, and that scared me. You always hear that no one
will hire you if you've got gray hair, so I was very anxious
about that.

But if you look at it really coldly, there's a good chance statis-
tically that if you wait, some medical problem will come about
that could keep you out. *[She puts her finger to her head as if
a gun is finishing her off.]* I've already had a bout with skin
cancer. I've just had enough happen to me that I know I'm
mortal, and I didn't want to risk not getting to go.

Maybe I'll go later, too. There was an eighty-year-old and a
seventy-three-year-old in my group. Let's hope that'll be true
of me; but if it's not, I've been once.

Actually though, I'd planned to wait three more years. My
son's escapade with the National Merit Scholarship triggered
the actual departure date. Rett was invited to apply for a
National Merit Scholarship, but he "forgot" to submit the
papers on time. His school found a way to bend the rules for
him, and we all worked to help him get the papers finished;
but he still didn't hand them in. I looked at him and thought,
I have been raising you on a secretary's salary, and I think it's
time for you to wake up and take some responsibility. I told
him I was going to join the Peace Corps and stop running
interference for him.

Within six months of my saying, "This is it. I think you're
terrific, but I really am going away," he shaped up. He knew
I was not going to be there to make it all real easy for him.
He was eighteen, and he went to a local community college
and then to the University of California at Santa Cruz.

Still, it wasn't easy. Just before I left he sprained his foot.

Here he was sitting with this purple club at the end of his leg, and I thought, I am terrible. I am getting in an airplane and going a third of the way around the world, and my son is wounded. But I went. *[She grins mischievously.]* Sometimes the kids leave home; in this case the parent left home.

Kinney applied to the Peace Corps almost fourteen months before she actually boarded that plane, and she spent those months envisioning herself in a West African village.

Before I went I spent hours imagining myself there. I used to take myself and put myself mentally into a village situation. I thought about how I'd have to use a latrine and how I'd have to "brook my clothes." I realized I'd have to walk everywhere, so I practiced walking from my house to the ocean by doing it in small pieces. First I walked from my home to a friend's house, and she drove me back; the next time I walked from even farther and another friend drove me back home. I steadily built up my endurance. Finally, the last few weeks before I went overseas, I even broke my habit of having tea in the morning because I didn't want to feel lousy if there wasn't tea in Sierra Leone.

But mostly I tried to imagine just how insignificant I would be. My do-gooder side wanted to go and make big changes right away, but I knew that wouldn't be possible. I tried to imagine what I would be asking of the people if I were to say, "You are dying because you are drinking water from that river without cleaning it up." I realized that for African villagers to clean that water, they'd have to use their only pot, the one that they need to cook food in, and instead use it to boil water. And in order to boil the water they'd have to go out to the bush and get some wood to build a fire. I made myself realize all these things; and this was one of the best preparations I made for myself, because then I was able to feel very good about very small accomplishments. If I hadn't been able to do that, I would have been discouraged fast. But I was able to keep my perspective.

Since I had done all sorts of volunteer work over the years— in mental hospitals, disaster shelters, and earthquake preparedness projects—the Peace Corps decided I had a "demonstrated interest in health." They taught me the health needs of the country and how to teach about them and what resources were available. Then I took my SRI experience, the training in organizational development that I had from my master's program, and my vast interest in Africa, and I just kind of stirred the pot.

I was assigned to an inland chiefdom headquarters of about three thousand people. What they really needed was someone to help them find resources to bring in things like Planned Parenthood, UNICEF, UNESCO. There are a lot of organizations ready to help and a lot of places that need help, but how do you get a little chiefdom in Africa together with them? How do you develop a plan, write a proposal, do a needs-identification survey? All the research analyst work I'd done at SRI really fit. I think I facilitated quite a number of connections for them, and I am real proud of that.

But there's so much left to do. A lot of the time we didn't have enough to eat. *[Kinney lost forty pounds while she was in Sierra Leone.]* You want a little dinner tonight? First you go out and slash down two or three acres of bush with your one machete. You take the one hoe that the blacksmith made, and you plow the land. Then you scatter all the seeds and hope it rains. Every day of the year you have to chase away the birds, so you go out and throw huge clumps of dirt at them. Then you chase away the little animals, and then you chase away the thieves.

One day I woke up really hungry, and I also woke up to the fact that I hadn't the foggiest notion what it was to be hungry because I always had a ticket home. *[She shakes her head.]* I learned so much.

Although SRI was willing to give Kinney her old job back after she returned to the States, she had no desire to work full-time. She decided instead to devote about half of her time to publicizing the Peace Corps.

I'm a freelance whatever-they-need at SRI right now. Sometimes I do research work; sometimes I just answer a lot of phones. As long as I work fifty percent of the time on average over a twelve-week period, I get all the benefits—and that's what's really important to me. Last year my taxable income was $13,000, and I survived just fine.

When I'm not at SRI, I work on my book, one that will tell

about the unfolding of a middle-aged woman and will also give an accurate view of Sierra Leone. And I've given over a hundred and fifty talks about the Peace Corps to churches and schools, and I've had a photographic exhibit about my experience. I've also been on television several times. I want to get people interested in the developing world. *[She smiles contentedly.]* I have a composite career now, and I'm having fun!

As for the future, I'm in a quandary about what's next for me. If somebody would give me $3,000 a year clear for my retirement, I'd probably spend half of the rest of the years of my life in the Peace Corps. Only half, because it is nice to be home, too. I missed my sisters, my friends, this climate, hot water. It's great to be here, it really is, and there isn't a minute of the day I don't appreciate it. But there is no way to describe the satisfaction of sitting down there in a village and waiting it out till you know enough and have made enough friends that you can help them and share their lives. I was living out my fantasy.

[After a thoughtful pause, she continues.] When I was younger I didn't think I could do so many things; I was trying to conform to whatever it was I thought I was supposed to be. But I think the person that I am now was there all along; I just carefully kept the real person under wraps.

Finally I recognized that I was scared to death but that making the break was more important than being afraid. I wanted to prove to myself that I could endure something really tough. I remember watching people like Jane Goodall and just aching to know what it was like to be there, to be inside another culture, to do something that was difficult and to really achieve something. I wanted to know what that was like more than anything else in the world. And now I know; I really know.

[A few tears sparkle in the corners of Kinney's eyes, and she stops to consider her next words carefully. Then she smiles.] You know, if there's one gift I could give people it is the idea that you don't have to keep things the way they are. You can go out and have a good life. If you're basically a nice person, you're not going to hurt anybody by developing yourself.

As we say good-bye, Kinney hands me her business card. On it is a quote by G. K. Chesterton: "An inconvenience is an adven-

ture rightly viewed." She laughs. "I guess that about sums it up," she says. "I just decided to have a midlife adventure instead of a midlife crisis."

● ●

Greener Pastures

Kinney found the setting for her dream deep in the bush of the Third World, others find it right in their own backyards, and many look somewhere in between. Without a job to hold them down, early retirees are free to choose a location based on other considerations, and a great many pack up their household goods at about the same time that they pick up their last paycheck.

Deciding where you want to live can be a time-consuming, albeit pleasant, activity. *Places Rated Almanac* lists ten factors that should be weighed: cost of living, jobs, crime, health care, environment, transportation, education, the arts, recreation, climate. Only you know which things are most important to you. Do you want to live near the mountains or the ocean? Do you prefer fishing or boutiques? Do you want to live near your children or your parents? If you'll be starting a second career, where are the opportunities the greatest? The questions go on and on.

Of course, relocating is often not so much a matter of choice as it is a matter of necessity. Restylers who live in areas where real estate has boomed may find they can only finance their early retirement by selling the family home. "After all," says John Howells, author of *Retirement Choices,* "the capital you have sitting in your equity is just that, *capital,* and you have to account for the income your capital is losing by not being invested elsewhere."

Whether you choose to move because of climate, recreation, or dollars, cutting ties with the family home isn't an easy decision. The well-regarded Holmes and Rahe Social Readjustment Rating Scale, which assigns numerical values to stressful events, indicates that a combination of retirement and a change in residence is more stressful than the death of a close family member or a marital separation. Not only are you losing the friends and structure of the workplace, but you're giving up the friends and familiarity of your residence as well.

By planning for these changes well in advance of their actual occurrence—in other words, by restyling—you lessen the traumatic impact of a double change. You can spend many comfortable evenings in front of the fireplace discussing what you'd like to find in a new area; you can spend relaxed hours at the library researching what exists in various places; and you can, over the years, visit the most promising locales.

David and Melanie Thimgan had visited Vermont several times and they had, quite simply, fallen in love with it. It seemed to offer everything they wanted—simplicity, friendliness, beauty. Although financially things have not turned out as well as they had hoped, they're still delighted with their new home. "Sure," says David, "in retrospect there are a few things we might have done differently, but staying in California isn't one of them."

. . . .

Profile: Dave and Melanie Thimgan—Architect and Educator to Ice Cream Store Owners

Unless one says goodbye to what one loves, and unless one travels to completely new territories, one can expect merely a long wearing away of oneself and an eventual extinction.

JEAN DUBUFFET

David and Melanie Thimgan were forty-six and forty-three, respectively, when they traded the congestion of the San Francisco Bay Area (population 6 million) for the picturesque serenity of Bennington, Vermont (population 16,500). David was an architect; Melanie was the co-owner and director of a large day care center. Now the Thimgans are proprietors of Mother Hubbard's, an ice cream shop that features light lunches and fresh-baked cookies made from Melanie's own recipes. The Thimgans, both divorced since the late seventies, tied the knot in 1985, shortly before moving to Vermont. David's two daughters and Melanie's older son were grown; her younger son, Greg, was seventeen and about to enter his last year of high school.

It's late Friday afternoon when we arrive in Bennington, and a few flakes of snow promise to turn this quiet New England village into a scene from the front of a Christmas card. The white-steepled Congregational Church looms in front of us, and my husband unconsciously begins to hum "Over the river and through the woods," as we turn right and then left to reach the Thimgans' new home.

I must admit I'm a bit disappointed when that home turns out to be a modern condominium. My fantasy had David and Melanie comfortably ensconced in a traditional colonial setting. David, a large man with light brown, rapidly thinning hair, glasses, and a wide smile, opens the door; it's almost as if he reads my mind. "I'll bet you were looking for a two-story house with giant maples and a babbling brook, weren't you?" he grins. "Well, the upkeep on this is easier. Come on in." He leads us into an attractive contemporary living room done in tones of tan and white. Melanie, who has been on the telephone, comes in to greet us. She's dressed in casual black pants and a deep pink sweater and is, I note, unbelievably slender for someone who spends her days surrounded by ice cream and cookies.

After a few minutes of get-acquainted chatter, we pile into the car and head for a nearby restaurant. As we wait for a table, five different couples come up and greet David and Melanie with a big hello. Once again David reads my mind. "Yep," he says, "you can live in a place like the Bay Area forever and still, when you go someplace, you never see anyone you know. Here there's a sort of intimacy. Here people know us and we know them."

A waiter leads us to a table just the right distance from the blazing fireplace, and Dave and Melanie begin telling the story of their move.

MELANIE: For us place was the major change, the most important one. We wanted to live here; what we did here was secondary.

DAVID: I'd been thinking about moving to some idyllic region for six or seven years—not necessarily to Vermont. Some parts of California are also very attractive. I think I equated fulfillment with being more in control of my environment. The press of population and congestion and pressure and activities that were going on during the last ten years I was in the Bay Area made it not fulfilling. I wanted a more simple setting.

My trip to New England in the fall of '83 sort of solidified that in my own mind. I toured the whole Northeast—rented a car in Boston, went through New Hampshire to Bennington, north to Burlington, cut back across to Maine. The place I liked best was Bennington. In Bennington I went to a Rotary meeting and started talking with a man whose wife was a real estate agent. She had a day off and she volunteered to show me around. I liked what I saw.

David met Melanie soon after he returned from his exploratory trip to the Northeast. Their romance and their decision to begin a new life in Vermont progressed hand-in-hand. The next Valentine's Day David asked Melanie to visit Bennington with him. "It was my fantasy," she says, "like all the Vermont pictures of snow and everything. I just thought, Oh, wow, and I fell in love with it." By the following January they had decided to get married, move, and open an ice cream shop.

DAVID: I just didn't want to do architecture when I moved. I'd been doing it for twenty-five years. When you've been trained specifically to do something, at first it's all a whole new world; but after you've done it for years, you're an expert. Architecture was easy for me, but it was getting pretty tiresome. I wanted to do other things.

It's real easy to get into a deep rut if you've pursued a profession or business your whole life. You can't see over the edge; and boy, what a curse in later life that you have only one thing you can relate to. I didn't want to let myself be limited by my professional background.

We chose Bennington first; then the rest followed. First we thought about opening an inn, but we discarded that idea pretty quickly because of the capital required and our lack of real knowledge about how to run one. But ice cream and cookies were of direct interest to us. We *like* cookies and ice cream. *[They both laugh.]*

MELANIE: And it was something we felt we could do.

DAVID: It was something we could understand and grasp, yet it was still creating something altogether different than anything we'd ever done before. It was the excitement of giving birth to something different.

MELANIE: It just seemed like a natural transition for both of us. I had a day care center in California that fed two hundred children breakfast, lunch, snacks, and supper. I'd been involved in all the food services, and that experience—in buying, inventory, knowing different vendors—was helpful. I'd done food on such a large scale that a small ice cream and cookie shop seemed tiny. It was no big deal to develop recipes or make twenty-five-gallon batches of dough.

David had never been into food ordering and preparation, but he knew all about remodeling and floor plans and how to order kitchen equipment and supplies.

DAVID: That part was right down my alley. When we designed the store, I could analyze traffic flow and stuff. I'd done a lot of office planning and contract furniture [where the architect provides furnishings] in the Bay Area, so I knew where to get the kitchen equipment we needed because I'd outfitted other buildings. We purchased all the public furniture in California before we left and had it shipped here, because I was familiar with vendors on the West Coast.

MELANIE: So we spent almost a year researching the whole thing, reading volumes of books, all this analytical stuff on business structure. Then David and I went to every ice cream store for miles around and spent hours doing all kinds of analyses on them. What types of people came in? What did they buy? What times of day were the busiest? We parked outside one store so often that the owner finally came out and said, "What are you doing?" We told him and he said he didn't care, but he acted a little uncomfortable with us scrutinizing his store.

DAVID: We made pretty valid observations about traffic patterns and sales.

MELANIE: We looked at the product mix each store had, whether it was cookies and ice cream, or desserts and ice cream, or sandwiches and ice cream . . .

DAVID: . . . and whether they made their own product or purchased it.

MELANIE: Then we got to know this lady who had a shop with Famous Amos™ cookies and some line of ice cream. I just went in there one day and asked her a bunch of questions and told her what we were going to do. I asked her if I could come help, just volunteer for a few days. I did and I learned a lot, observing how they did everything and talking to her.

DAVID: We read all about the importance of location, location, location. So we concentrated on trying to locate our building as advantageously as we could. We thought we'd picked a very good place: downtown, near a crosswalk, with a junior high school down the street, and a high school close by.

MELANIE: Then we came up with the name and had a name search done; and we did all the graphics and designed the floor plans and hired a contractor. We had to modify the building extensively.

DAVID: It was a busy year.

But despite the Thimgans' research, planning, and experience, Mother Hubbard's didn't turn out quite the way they expected. David and Melanie confide that their projections failed to take into account three things: David's personality (as opposed to his skills and interests), certain details about the market, and local taxes.

DAVID: When we came here, we thought we were achieving some kind of retirement or slow-down. We thought we'd just be kind of gentlemen farmers. It never turned out that way.

MELANIE: We thought it would be the kind of thing where we would have a store and hire someone to run it. But Mother Hubbard's is not making enough money to support a manager. So now I'm involved with everything. I open the store at 9 A.M. and am usually there till 3 or 4 P.M. I only go in three hours on Saturday, and I try not to go in on Sundays at all.

DAVID: Originally I was going to work in the store, too, but I found I was real short with people. I didn't last long behind the counter, because I couldn't tolerate some of the unreasonable demands people would make. "I didn't order that; I ordered this." "Give me a taste of this, this, and this." I'd get impatient. I'd rather be behind the scenes doing something in the back, certainly not out in front behind the counter.

It goes back to my value system. I have a fixed idea about the role I play in the grand picture, and if something contravenes my concept of the way things should be, I can't compromise. And, man, you've got to compromise a lot in a retail business.

MELANIE: It's easier for me to flow with things; I enjoy working with people. But what we didn't research well was this town: how much volume it would generate, if this was really the place for an ice cream store.

DAVID: We were researching in California, for example, where it's warm year-round, and in Boston and New York and other urban areas where ice cream is consumed year-round even though winters are cold. Here in Bennington, ice cream goes way down in volume in the winter, and we completely missed that.

MELANIE: And we forgot about the impact of tourism. One of the problems is that this year New England tourism is down twenty percent and that has significantly affected us.

But not thoroughly investigating the property tax situation may have been the Thimgans' most serious mistake. Although Vermont's tax bite is slightly lighter than California's, it's much higher than that of neighboring New Hampshire, which has one of the lowest state taxes in the country.

The Thimgans, who own both their condominium and the commercial property that houses Mother Hubbard's, could have saved more than $7,000 a year if they'd chosen to settle in a small town across the state border.

DAVID: The taxes were a shock all right. *[He shakes his head, and begins tapping his fingers on the table.]* We're having to dip into our savings. Now our overall monetary goal is to reach the point where our assets will support us. That's our objective; we're not there yet. If we'd stayed in Silicon Valley, we probably would have been there by age fifty-five; now we probably won't be, not at the rate we're going.

I guess my advice to others is to be a little more objective about where you locate. We were not. We were not super-objective about all the things that control the quality of life here, like taxes for instance. We knew we wanted a New England town, but we didn't explore what differentiates this New England town from another one.

Now while Melanie works in the store, David practices architecture part-time and works on becoming a property developer. Although their move to Bennington has been a setback for their bank accounts, neither regrets their decision to experience a new location and to start a new business.

DAVID: The term "wrong decisions" is relative. I don't think there is such a thing as a wrong decision. This was a new adventure. When we first got here, every day—and I am not exaggerating—was a real experience because we were discovering new things. If we were to face the decision again, we'd probably do it again because we'd have never done it before. It was exciting then, and it is still exciting.

MELANIE: The people here have been wonderful to us. We'd heard New Englanders were very reserved, but it was real easy to fit in here, phenomenally easy. When we opened the store, we must've gotten thirty-five plants and flower arrangements, even though we never sent out announcements. People asked us to dinner, to sit on boards. . . . Almost overnight we got totally overcommitted. In the Bay Area we were only involved in professional things. Here we are more active on a community basis.

I felt accepted right away. There's a certain town quality that's here; everything's much more relaxed, more appealing. I love walking out the back of my store and crossing the street for my dentist appointment. In California any place you go is at least a half-hour car ride away. Here there's no traffic, no pollution. Of course we like it.

[She stops to catch her breath and then continues.] And we were at a place in our lives when we could make the move. I never would have done it five years earlier. First of all, I was involved in the whole education thing. I really wanted to do a child care center; I was doing just what I wanted to do. And

then there were the kids. I would have felt moving to Vermont and opening an ice cream store would have disrupted their lives too much and been too risky.

But when Dave and I discussed moving to Bennington, my oldest son, Jonathan, was twenty-three and my youngest, Greg, was seventeen. I told David I couldn't possibly consider moving here for another year till Greg was out of school, but then I realized there was another alternative: Greg could live with his dad and finish school in California. That's what he finally chose to do; he came out to Vermont later. David's kids were both grown; this was a good time for us.

DAVID: *[He nods his agreement.]* You know, your values change as you get older. Now being happy—doing what we like to do, having a good time, enjoying ourselves, feeling purposeful and fulfilled—is what's most important to me. Ten, fifteen years ago, it wasn't. Not in that sense. Then I was interested in developing a practice, in "getting there." Now getting there is not as important as the ride going there.

MELANIE: That hits it right on the head. We're more interested in the journey than in getting to the destination.

DAVID: We're already "there," relatively speaking.

He stands up and walks to the window. Outside the snow is beginning to fall in earnest, and for a few minutes David seems lost in thought, hypnotized by the wintry landscape. Then he turns and looks at us with a smile. "You know," he says, "to shudder in fear to try things is terrible. We are here on this earth to enjoy ourselves and to experience all we can absorb."

Melanie nods her agreement. "And then," she says, "there's the beauty of this place. I stop every day and say, 'God, this is beautiful.'"

. . . .

For the Thimgans, place is primary. Their script is more concerned with the setting than with the action. In this sense, their move is a complete success. They remain charmed by Bennington and consider the shaky state of their ice cream store but a blip on the screen. For them a dream has been realized.

Perhaps Henry David Thoreau summed it up best when he said, ". . . if one advances confidently in the direction of his dreams, and endeavors to live the life which he has imagined, he will meet with success unexpected in common hours."

Once we've acknowledged our dreams, it's time to find ways to fulfill them.

EXERCISES

Pie in the Sky

Whether we're employed, restyled, or retired, whether we're rich or poor, young or old, we all have 168 hours per week. When we make a major lifestyle change like restyling, we simply redistribute these hours.

Begin this exercise with the here and now. The following circle is divided into seven parts, with each large pie-shaped piece representing one twenty-four-hour period. Each square represents one hour. Use colored pencils to answer the following questions by coloring in the appropriate number of sections for each day. Use a different color to represent each activity.

- How many hours each day do you spend in work-related activities? Don't forget the work that you bring home with you to do in the evening or on the weekend or the time you spend commuting.
- How many hours each day do you spend on activities of daily living (eating, showering, exercising, etc.)?
- How many hours each day do you spend sleeping?
- How many hours each day do you spend tending to household chores? Include the time it takes you to do occasional jobs, such as paying the bills or repairing a leaky faucet, as well as the time you spend on more regular chores like cooking dinner and washing clothes.
- How many hours each day do you spend talking with your spouse? With your children? With friends?
- How many hours each day do you spend on leisure-time activities (reading, sports, hobbies, etc.)?

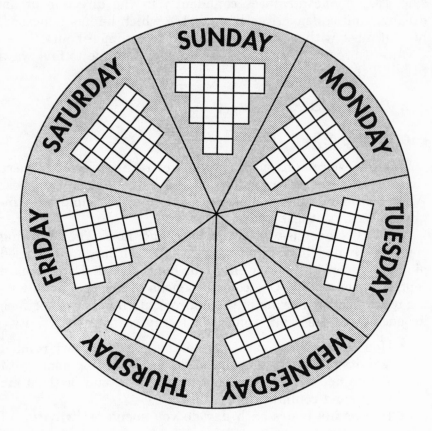

Are you surprised to see just how much time you spend doing things you think you *have to do* and how little you spend doing things you *want to do*?

Now, fill in this second pie chart as you would *like* it to look.

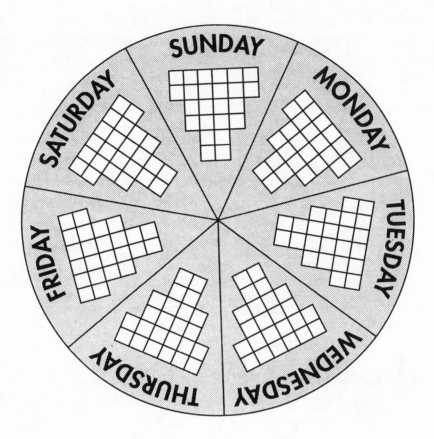

When, at the end of this book, you formulate a personal restyling plan, look back at this exercise. Does your projected lifestyle match your desired time allotments?

Resolutions

The following list includes a sampling of factors that most people consider important for personal happiness. There are lines at the end for your own additions. In the first column put a check (√) next to those that you have now. In the second column put a plus (+) next to those you'd like to increase or improve upon in the future.

	Have Enough	**Need More**
Time with family		
Time with friends		
Money		
Recreation		
Exercise		
Solitude		

The Sixteen-Year-Old You

Think back to your own sixteenth birthday. What were your ambitions? What did you want to do with your life? Teenagers often are not very realistic. That's okay. This isn't a time for realism. This is a time for dreams.

Flip through an old photo album. As you see your sixteen-year-old self grinning at the camera, try to remember the person you were at that time. What did you discuss with your friends? Who were these friends? What did you do in your free time? Where did you go? Did you go alone or with friends? What were your hobbies? Was there a movie star or sports hero whom you admired? Why? Which classes were your favorites? Which ones bored you silly?

Take your time reminiscing. Flip back a few years. Photos of a sixth grade science project may remind you of a latent interest in environmental activities; mementos of an eighth grade trip to Washington, D.C., may encourage you to think about political activism. As you leaf through the pages of your life, you'll be reminded of the myriad opportunities that once existed for your future. Many of them still are viable.

Brainstorming

The *Random House Dictionary of the English Language* tells us that the word *brainstorming* began to be used in the late 1950s to mean "a conference technique of solving specific problems, amassing information, stimulating creative thinking, developing new ideas, etc., by unrestrained participation in discussion." Actually, a similar procedure was practiced in India more than four hundred years ago.

When you brainstorm, you give yourself permission to go quite crazy with ideas. Begin by stating your problem in clear, concise terms. For example: "I want to quit my job in five years and spend two years traveling around the world. But I won't have enough money to travel around the world if I retire." Let your proposed solutions run berserk; put forth every answer you can think of, with no evaluation, no criticism. But your ideas are impractical? No problem. They would never work? Not to worry.

The purpose of brainstorming is to free your mind of preconceived notions. As the name implies, you want a windstorm of ideas, one that will blow away the musty leaves of "can't" and freshen the air like a cleansing rain. Later you can evaluate; later you can see if maybe there's a glimmer of possible in the heap of crazy.

Some people try to brainstorm alone; but as the dictionary states, it is really a technique that is best used in a group. Tests show that adults produce from 65 to 93 percent more ideas when they free associate with others than when they try it alone.

So gather a group of friends and enter a world where anything goes. As in the following exercises, the idea is to suspend reality and see what comes up in the land of fantasy.

The Magazine Cover Test

Several years ago mail order catalogs began featuring a new item: a mirror fashioned to look like a *Time* magazine "Person of the Year" cover. There, in the upper corner, is the headline banner; around the edge is the famous red border.

Imagine yourself looking in that mirror. What have you done to merit this attention? Would you, perhaps, prefer to grace the cover of another magazine—*Rolling Stone, Fortune,* or *Vogue,* for example? What do your answers say about your dreams and ambitions?

The College Catalog Game

Many universities have orientation programs for incoming freshmen. The young people are asked to write down any majors that might possibly interest them. "Don't worry," say the counselors. "This isn't for real. This is just so we can get to know you better."

This isn't for real either. You don't have to score 1,600 on the SAT or pay the tuition, so you can choose any college or university in the country. Find a copy of its course catalog at the library, or write a letter to the admissions director asking for one.

Now pretend you are an incoming freshman. You're not restricted by distribution requirements or prerequisites, so you can take any classes that interest you. You'll most likely see courses that weren't available when you were in college. Stanford, for example, has a relatively new interdisciplinary program concerning the relationship between technology and Third World countries.

Make a list of all the courses that sound exciting. Do you see any patterns? Are you more intrigued by people, things, or ideas? Do you prefer hands-on classes? Seminars that require active participation? Lecture classes where students sit back and listen? What do your choices reveal about your interests? About your skills? Your personality?

The Mythical Job

At regular intervals the United States government puts out a hefty tome entitled *Occupational Outlook Handbook*; it is available at most libraries. Prepared by the Department of Labor, it's a detailed inventory of jobs that are expected to be in demand in the coming years.

Thumb through this book in the same way you did the college catalog. What positions look the most fascinating? Which would interest that sixteen-year-old in your old photo album? Do you prefer a job that is mostly physical or mostly mental? Are you looking at jobs that require you to work alone or in a group? As a manager or as a laborer? Indoors or outdoors? In the United States or abroad? Full-time or part-time?

Remember, you've no intention, at this point anyway, of applying for an actual position; this exercise is only meant to stimulate your imagination. Change the job descriptions to make them fit your dreams.

You can also do this exercise by looking through the employment ads in the newspaper.

Sentimental Journey

Close your eyes and take a mental walk through the city or town in which you now live. What do you like best about it? The fact that there are four distinct seasons? The crime-free neighborhoods? The nearby mountains? The city college? The low cost of housing? Try to be as specific as possible.

Think back to the place you lived before this one. Again, focus on the things that made this place special. Was it the four golf courses? The proximity to an international airport? The multicultural atmosphere?

Repeat this for every location you have lived in since you have been an adult. Then move forward in time. What would enhance your present surroundings? Would you like to live nearer to your adult children? Are you planning a second career that would influence your choice of location? Are you concerned about health services or state tax laws?

Then, using the slip-list method explained in Chapter 4, rank your preferences. Now, with your priorities in mind, you are ready to look at specific cities or regions.

Resources

On Discovering Your Interests

TESTS

Career counselors can give you a test which is designed to discover your interests. Interest tests generally come in one of two styles. The type most likely to be of use to restylers rates the test-taker's interest in a variety of categories such as art, science, business, etc. The Strong-Campbell Interest Inventory is such a test. Other interest tests are tied more directly to certain occupations and rank the respondent's answers against those of people in different jobs and professions.

EXERCISES AND TECHNIQUES

Imagineering: How to Profit from Your Creative Powers by Michael LeBoeuf (1980, Berkley Publishing Group, 200 Madison Avenue, New York, NY 10016, phone: 800/631-8571). "Imagineering," explains LeBoeuf, "is a coined word adopted by the Aluminum Company of America that means 'You let your imagination soar and then engineer it down to earth.'" The sections on brainstorming and goal-setting are exceptionally good.

Wishcraft: How to Get What You Really Want by Barbara Sher with Annie Gottlieb (1979, Ballantine, 201 East 50th Street, New York, NY 10022, phone: 800/726-0600). For more than a decade this book has been a favorite with those who want to "pinpoint [their] goals and make [their] dreams come true." The chapter on brainstorming is a gem.

On Second Careers

Earning Money Without a Job: Revised for the '90s by Jay Conrad Levinson (1991, Owl/Henry Holt and Company, Inc., 115 West 18th Street, New York, NY 10011, phone: 800/247-

3912). "This book is dedicated to all people who understand and affirm freedom," says Levinson, who advocates picking up spending money by a variety of methods such as cleaning aquariums for pet store owners, tending bars, writing books, or starting a mail order business.

The Fifty Minute Career Discovery Program by Elwood N. Chapman (1988, Crisp Publications, Inc., 95 First Street, Los Altos, CA 94022, phone: 415/949-4888). This series of exercises helps you pinpoint career possibilities for any stage of life. Chapman discusses life goals as well as career goals, and talks about interests, aptitudes, and talents. (Aptitude, he says, "implies a natural inclination for a particular kind of work . . . an ability to quickly master a particular skill," while talent is "a superior, often natural, ability.")

The Occupational Outlook Handbook by the United States Department of Labor (updated regularly, distributed by VGM Career Horizons, Division of NTC Publishing Group, 4255 West Touhy Avenue, Lincolnwood, IL 60646-1975, phone: 800/323-4900). Your tax money has helped prepare a 492-page compendium of more than 200 different occupations, from able seaman to zoologist, with information on such things as working conditions, employment opportunities, and sources of additional information.

What Color Is Your Parachute?: A Practical Manual for Job-Hunters & Career Changers and *The Three Boxes of Life: An Introduction to Life/Work Planning* by Richard Nelson Bolles (*Parachute* is updated annually, *Boxes* is copyright 1981; both from Ten Speed Press, P.O. Box 7123, Berkeley, CA 94707, phone: 800/841-2665). These books, both classics in their fields, are packed with exercises and advice. It's hard to imagine a restyler who wouldn't benefit from selected sections. Both books contain a wonderful prioritizing device that shows how to decide what is very important to you, what is sort of important, and what really doesn't matter much at all.

Where to Start Career Planning: Essential Resource Guide for Career Planning and Job Hunting by the Career Center of Cornell University (updated every two years, distributed by Peterson's Guides, Inc., Dept. 7101, P.O. Box 2123, Princeton,

NJ 08543-2123, phone: 800/338-3282). The folks at Cornell's Career Center have prepared a "one-stop source of current career planning and job hunting materials." The sections most likely to be of interest to restylers are the ones on second careers and overseas employment.

Jobs and Careers for the 1990s is a catalog of more than 1,000 books and videos that will help you plan your future. Free from Impact Publications, 10655 Big Oak Circle, Manassas, VA 22111-3040.

On Relocating

NEWSPAPERS

The true flavor of a town is often best reflected in its local newspaper. *The Gale Directory,* published annually and available at most libraries, gives the addresses of newspapers throughout the country.

BOOKS

Several authors have logged thousands of miles in order to tell you about prime retirement-living spots. The danger in these books is that the details can change almost before an updated version is off the press. Still, they're a good place to start and can be especially helpful for people who want suggestions of places they might otherwise never consider.

Adventures Abroad: Exploring the Travel Retirement Option by Allene Symons and Jane Parker (1991, Gateway Books, 13 Bedford Cove, San Rafael, CA 94901, phone: 415/454-5215). From Thailand to Ireland, from Poland to Mexico, the authors give practical information on vacation and retirement living in countries where Americans can find a happy blend of adventure and affordability. Also included are worksheets to help you decide if foreign living is right for you.

The Rating Guide to Life in America's Small Cities by C. Scott Thomas (1990, Prometheus Books, 700 East Amherst Street, Buffalo, NY 14215, phone: 716/837-2475). Thomas concentrates on the 219 "micropolitan" areas, his name for cities with between 15,000 and 50,000 residents. He grades each on ten factors: climate/environment, diversions, economics, education, sophistication, health care, housing, public safety, transportation, and urban proximity.

Gypsying After 40: A Guide to Adventure & Self Discovery by Robert W. Harris (1987, John Muir Publications, P.O. Box 613, Santa Fe, NM 87501, phone: 505/982-4078). Author Robert Harris and his wife, Megan, are two of the restylers profiled in this book. You'll find out more about them—and "gypsying"—in Chapter 7.

Retirement Places Rated by Richard Boyer and David Savageau (updated frequently, Prentice Hall Travel, 15 Columbus Circle, New York, NY 10023, phone: 800/223-2348). More than 300 metropolitan areas are reviewed with emphasis on living costs, job outlook, crime, health, environment, transportation, education, the arts, recreation, and climate.

Sunbelt Retirement, Retirement Edens Outside the Sunbelt, and *Travel and Retirement Edens Abroad* by Peter A. Dickinson (1986, 1987, 1989, AARP/Scott, Foresman and Company, 1900 East Lake Avenue, Glenview, IL 60025, phone: 708/729-3000). Dickinson is an avid researcher, and he fills his books with details on climate and environment, medical facilities, housing availability and costs, cost of living, recreation and culture, and special services for seniors.

Touring Europe by Motorhome: The Grandest Tour of All by Helen Vander Male (1990, Mills & Sanderson, 442 Marrett Road, Suite 6, Lexington, MA 02173, phone: 800/441-6224). Vander Male is a retired artisan who has spent three years exploring Europe in a motor home. Although she writes as a traveler rather than as an expatriate, she's full of tips for roaming restylers.

Where to Retire, RV Travel in Mexico, Choose Latin America, Choose Mexico (with Donald Merwin), and *Choose Spain* (with Bettie Magee) by John Howells (1991, 1989, 1986, 1988, 1990, Gateway Books, 13 Bedford Cove, San Rafael, CA 94901, phone: 415/454-5215). Howells covers most of the same information as do the other where-to-live authors, but he writes in a more conversational tone, interspersing facts and figures with lively opinions.

World's Top Retirement Havens edited by Marian Cooper (1991, Agora, Inc., 824 E. Baltimore Street, Baltimore, MD 21202, phone: 301/234-0515). Scores of people contributed to this overview of eighteen countries, mostly in Europe and South America. They discuss the nuts-and-bolts issues of foreign living, from property prices, medical care, and taxes to cost of living, immigration procedures, and how long it takes to get a telephone.

HOME EXCHANGE ORGANIZATIONS

Often the best way to decide if you like a new location is to try it out, but hotels can be expensive, as well as impersonal, for an extended visit. For information on people who are interested in exchanging homes (and often cars) for several weeks or longer, contact the following organizations:

Better Homes & Travel; 185 Park Row, Box 268, New York, NY 10038-0272, phone: 212/349-5340.

Intervac U.S.; P.O. Box 590504, San Francisco, CA 94159, phone: 415/435-3497.

Vacation Exchange Club, Inc.; 12006 111th Avenue, Unit 12, Youngtown, AZ 85363, phone: 602/972-2186.

NEWSLETTERS

Greener Pastures Gazette, a quarterly newsletter published by William Seavey, is dedicated to "the search for countryside Edens where the Good Life still exists." For subscription information: Relocation Research, Box 1122, Sierra Madre, CA 91025, phone: 818/355-1670.

International Living is a monthly newsletter full of practical tips on living abroad, whether for a brief interval or for an extended stay. For subscription information: Agora, Inc., 824 E. Baltimore St., Baltimore, MD 21202, phone: 301/234-0515.

RELOCATION CONSULTANTS

Lifestyle Explorations gives one- and two-week tours to popular easy-living spots in Argentina, Costa Rica, Uruguay, Ireland, and Portugal. In addition to a quick look at popular visitor sights, the tour includes talks with expatriate Americans, real estate agents, businesspeople, doctors, etc. For information: Lifestyle Explorations, World Trade Center, Suite 400, Boston, MA 02210. Twenty-four-hour information and reservation hotline: 508/371-4814.

Bill Seavey, publisher of *Greener Pastures Newsletter* (see above), does individual telephone counseling about small to mid-sized towns and country living in the United States. Contact Bill at Relocation Research, Box 1122, Sierra Madre, CA 91025, phone: 818/355-1670.

Jane Parker, founder of Lifestyle Explorations (see above), no longer leads tours but is an authority on spots around the world where Americans can live well and inexpensively. When Jane is not exploring, she can be reached at 3722 Blue Lake Drive, Spring, TX 77388, phone: 713/288-1529.

You have brains in your head.
You have feet in your shoes.
You can steer yourself
  any direction you choose.

DR. SEUSS

7 | TAKING ACTION

Restyling, for most of us, is a bumpy road. We go along smoothly for a while, and then we hit a psychological rut. The fears come back: "Am I doing the right thing?" We stop, backtrack, turn off the motor: "Maybe this job isn't so bad." Then another friend dies, another "youngster" gets promoted ahead of us, and we lurch forward again, with a detour here for a workaholic week and a pause there for a spending spree. If we don't have a road map, we risk getting lost forever.

Most of us get derailed in the wishing stage. We know that choices exist, and we spend quite a bit of time dreaming about what we'd like to do with My-Time. But that's all we do, dream. And, as Leslie Camerson-Bandler, author of *Know How: Guided Programs for Inventing Your Own Best Future,* says, "Between wishing and having there must be doing." Most of us persistently run from the doing.

Even the thought of devising a plan for doing is enough to make our hands get clammy and our stomachs churn. We procrastinate because of our fears, because—as wag Roy Blitzer has said—"the only person who likes change is a wet baby."

188

Though we know change will come, that as an inevitable part of life it *has* to come, we prefer not to think about it. We choose not to plan for it.

But the restylers profiled in this book are different. They're no richer, no more talented, no more dynamic than many of us; yet they did what most of us only talk about doing. In addition to wishing, they explored their options, they planned, and they acted. Instead of waiting for change to happen to them, they took steps to control that change.

Now it's our turn to commit to a plan of action. That doesn't mean we have to go into the office tomorrow morning and give notice to the boss. Not at all. Remember, restyling is a process, not an act. Depending on our individual road map, we may have five, six, or even more years to reach our destination. We just have to accomplish certain things so that when we reach midlife, we'll be able to enjoy the renewal of a planned change.

Setting Goals

There is an old saying that "life by the yard is very hard, but life by the inch is a cinch." By setting goals we can inch our way through restyling, advancing a little bit each month, moving a little closer each year, so that all the myriad decisions will be made and the hundreds of tasks accomplished by the time we want to leave our primary careers. In this way we can give substance to our dreams. Then the future won't look nearly as scary, and the present won't look nearly as drab.

Most of us already know our primary restyling goal: to leave our present jobs at a certain (if only approximate) date in the future, at which time we will embark on specific other activities. Now we have to identify the secondary goals that will help us attain this goal.

- Are there certain skills we need to acquire? (Ken Cassie spent years improving his pottery while his wife, Shelley, honed her marketing skills.)
- Is there information we need to gather? (Tom Christensen read ferociously in order to learn all he could about the travel industry before he left the Air Force.)

- Are there classes we need to take or things we have to learn? (Gary Wood mastered the Morse Code long before he left on his sailing odyssey.)
- Are there places we want to explore? (Dave and Melanie Thimgan made several trips to Vermont before they left their positions in California.)
- Are there business arrangements we need to complete? (David Rausch found a person to buy his company four years before he actually turned over the reins.)
- Are there financial goals we have to reach? (Dick and Fran Easton sold their duplexes and reorganized their financial portfolio before Dick resigned his position as a medical administrator.)

These restylers were thinking years ahead when they took the actions that enabled them to move smoothly into a new lifestyle. Most of us have to work backwards to formulate the restyling goals that will help us do the same. "In order to reach my primary goal," we say, "I have to accomplish certain secondary goals; and in order to accomplish these secondary goals, I have to perform specific activities." And so we continue until we reach the level of small, manageable tasks that can be done right now.

If, for example, you are going to move to another location, you will have to sell your present home. This may involve painting the outside of your house to make it more attractive to buyers or perhaps planting a new backyard. Both of these chores are ones that can be done several years in advance of your actual leave-taking, and therefore they become small steps on the road to restyling.

When we worked to develop our dreams, we wrote the scripts for our own movies-of-the-mind. Now in order to bring these movies to life, we must become first-class directors and producers.

• •

Profile: Gary Wood and Dorothy Cloud-Wood—High-Tech Entrepreneur and Marketing Manager to Captains of a Ship

If you have built castles in the air, your work need not be lost; that is where they should be. Now put the foundations under them.

THOREAU

Gary Wood and Dorothy Cloud-Wood left their high-tech positions in Northern California's Silicon Valley in October 1989. They had been married to each other for eight years and were living in a lovely four-bedroom house with Gary's two daughters, Lisa and Stacy, both of whom were young adults. Now the girls live alone in the family home; and Gary, forty-three, and Dorothy, thirty-five, have moved to a 34-foot sailboat, currently moored in Cabo San Lucas, a small town on the tip of Baja California.

It's three days before Christmas when Gary Wood calls me on the phone. "Dorothy and I flew back to spend the holidays with my daughters, and John told me you'd like to talk with us about a book you're writing," he says in a deep, measured voice. "We can visit with you today or tomorrow if you wish."

"What are you doing right now?" I ask eagerly. "Would you like to come over for a cup of coffee?"

I'd first heard about the Woods three months earlier. "They're masterly planners," our friend John had told us. "You'll enjoy speaking with them. Of course, it might be a bit difficult since they're somewhere in Mexico. But if I ever hear that they're back in the area, I'll have them get in touch." John obviously had been as good as his word.

Dorothy and Gary arrive looking tan, fit, and relaxed. Dorothy's light-brown hair is long; she wears it pulled back so that it doesn't overwhelm her finely sculpted features. Gary has what he later tells us is a "Mexican haircut," close-cropped and definitely in sync with his neatly-trimmed mustache. Both are dressed casually.

"It's good to be back for a week," says Gary as we all take

*seats around our dining-room table. "It's given me reassurance
that the girls are doing well and that the house is being properly
maintained." He clasps his hands and leans forward. "Where
would you like us to start?"*

*"Wherever you like," I say as I reach to turn on the tape
recorder. With a nod Dorothy begins and, with little interrup-
tion from me, the Woods proceed in a clear, well-organized
fashion.*

DOROTHY: Intel, a company that makes microprocessors, had
been my first and only serious job. I started working there in
1975; at first I was in finance and then, about the time I got
my MBA, I switched to the marketing department. When I quit
I was in what you'd call a mid-management marketing position; I'd done product marketing as well as customer marketing
and handled major accounts.

But getting to the top in marketing is tough for women. Moving up the ladder would have demanded more energy and dedication than I was willing to commit, so I felt I was at my peak.
I was content but also ready for a change.

GARY: I have a BS and MS in "double E," electrical engineering. I was at Intel for seven years, but then I left to be
the co-founder of a start-up company. It was very exciting, but
there are two sides to success. There's failure. *[He laughs.]*
When the company was doing this *[his hand zooms up]* and
you're the vice president, you go into banks and instead of
waiting in line, you get ushered up to a special room. That's
the power of wealth, or potential wealth. But when the company starts to do that *[his hand zooms down]* and this great
team you've built starts to disintegrate, it's not fun.

Still, I was never driven by power. That doesn't mean I don't
enjoy some of the perks of high positions, but I see them for
what they are.

DOROTHY: The pace of this whole industry is stressful. My
work was fascinating, but the trade-offs were heavy. Every
week was a fifty-hour work week, plus commuting time. Even
though the kids were not small, it was time away from them,
from our hobbies, from the things that keep you healthy, like
working out and eating well.

GARY: Sailing is very appealing if you live in a real complex environment and work in complex areas. It lets you take your problems and reduce them all to thirty-four feet. In cruising, all you really have to worry about is the safety of the boat and the crew, finding a good place to anchor before dark, figuring out the proper navigation to get to that point, having enough food on board. It's a very simplified life.

But *[a quick smile flashes across his face]* not too simplified. In sailing and boats there's enough technology involved to keep it interesting for me. I have not yet been bored for one moment on that boat. There's always something I can go fuss with. I can trim a sail or I can sit and read; I can go down and plot our next course or I can put the ham radio on. There's all kinds of toys that keep me involved, but it does reduce the complexities of the world.

The hectic pace wasn't the only thing that motivated us, though. There were myriad reasons. I was also driven by a sense of adventure, by the idea of captaining my own boat on the high seas. That has a lyrical quality to it, a romantic one.

[He pauses.] You know, you can have a job and you can earn a great deal of money and then you can retire at age sixty-five, but at age sixty-five you may not have the physical abilities to do the things that interest you.

DOROTHY: It was Gary who finally set a departure date. When he realized the start-up company was going to fold, he took a look and said, "It's time for a change. We'll work here for a bit more, to get to where we need to be financially, but then I want out."

GARY: Everything kind of pointed to: "Hey, the fall of 1989 is a good date to set, a real date for sailing out of here and cruising to Mexico or beyond." Dorothy would be entitled to a sabbatical then and that would mean extra pay; certain stock options were coming due at the same time; and I figured that my daughters would be somewhat self-sustaining by then, not only financially but also emotionally.

Gary was perfectly clear about his intentions when, after disengaging himself from the start-up venture, he applied for a position at 3Com Corporation. He was, he said, only going to

be around for two years. And while he'd certainly work hard,
he was also going to spend a lot of time planning his getaway.

GARY: I very much enjoy having a deadline, a known deadline.
It made me take the job at 3Com a little differently. I told
them right up front, "What would you like me to do? I don't
care what it is. It doesn't matter because I'm not going to be
here that long."

It turned out that I did climb the ladder. I became director
of a whole division and that made me feel good, feel confident
that I could compete and do a good job. But I didn't have the
pressure of worrying about "Gee, if I mess up, I won't get that
next position." It gave me a great deal of freedom in the way
I behaved. I probably did a better job because of it.

DOROTHY: I think we excelled in the planning part, and the
process was fun. It was great therapy for both of us. No matter
how bad a day we had at work, we knew that within two years
we'd be gone.

Yes, we knew maybe the deadline would change; maybe we
would get close to it and realize we needed two more months.
But if you don't give yourself a deadline, you will almost never,
ever achieve your goal.

GARY: First I'd daydream. I'd sit there and mentally envision
the forepeak of the boat *[he touches his fingertips together to
indicate the front of a boat]* and I'd say, "Oh, I could add some
additional storage there," or "Wouldn't it be fun if we'd do that
there." Sometimes I'd get so excited about a new idea for the
boat that I couldn't fall asleep. I was constantly working things
out in my mind.

DOROTHY: We also read an awful lot and gathered a lot of
information that way. Then we could dream in a logical way.

GARY: And then I'm a list generator; my favorite thing to do
is to make lists. They put down in front of you what you need
to do, and the action of generating them makes you think of
things you never would have thought of otherwise. I planned
the cruise the same way I planned projects at work, by saying,
"These are the steps we have to take." I spent at least an hour
a night, every night, fiddling with lists. I'd work on the boat

lists, on the lists to help the girls remember certain things, on the financial lists.

DOROTHY: I'm not as analytical as Gary is, but I also keep lists because that's the only way to get things done. I learned that in the time management classes I had to take while I was in industry. If you really want to make a move, you have to set a time frame and break everything down into small elements, action items that need to be completed.

Little milestones were set up along the way; these were checkpoints in the planning process. In order to take off and travel, you have to get the house ready so you can leave, the boat ready so you can go, the family ready, yourself ready, and your finances ready. All the steps involved in doing these things are the milestones toward achieving the ultimate goal. We got pretty detailed and then just ticked things off one by one.

For the Woods the financial part was the easiest. They knew just what they wanted—safety, simplicity, and income—and with the help of a financial advisor, they were able to go about getting it.

GARY: How people handle money is very personal. I'm just not emotionally equipped to lose more money on speculation. We'd been in the stock market and after five years we ended up with less money than we'd had before. And we got into limited partnerships, and every single one lost us money. So we realized that what we had to do was stop the hemorrhage, quit investing to gain more money and invest so as not to lose any more money. We were tired of taking chances. And I wanted to stop paying interest so we paid off the cars and all of those things. I don't like to be paying someone else; I want someone else to be paying me.

For us financial planning was mostly a matter of getting out of obligations and getting into a cash position that would give us income and safety. We put most of our savings into bonds and CDs and those things that generate money.

DOROTHY: We also did a budget, a projected budget on a spreadsheet on our PC. We took a look at inflow vs. outflow . . .

GARY: . . . and the result is that we have enough, enough money to do what we want to do as long as what we want to do is sail on a boat. A boat is your housing, your transportation, and a great deal of your entertainment. As long as it's paid off, sailing is a low-expense way to live. Our plan says that as long as someone will live in the house and pay the expendable bills, we have the finances to sail and never do anything else.

[Once again the quick grin crosses his face, and he looks at Dorothy.] My daughters are taking care of the house now. Stacy is nineteen and Lisa is twenty-three, so it's proving to be quite a learning experience for them. Before we left, we often became very frustrated with them and their attitudes. They seemed to think we were "tight" because we wouldn't let them keep the furnace running at eighty-five degrees. Finally one morning I said, "You know, when we're gone, you're going to have the opportunity to pay your own gas and electric bill; and you can have the house as warm as you want."

DOROTHY: Guess what? *[She chuckles.]* When we walked in the other day, it was freezing!

GARY: To help them understand the kind of expenses they would be responsible for, I went through my checkbooks for the last five years. I made lists of what had to be paid when and what repairs were likely to be needed. Then I prepared a folder for each month. "Here's when the motor vehicle registration comes due, so expect it. Here's when you might need to call out the ant man . . ." Finally, I asked them what they thought they could afford to pay toward rent. So far they haven't paid any rent at all, but hopefully they'll feel obligated to do so soon. I want them to find out how tough it is to live in this area on a secretary's salary. Maybe then they'll become more motivated.

I also spent a lot of time teaching them about the house. I generated a major list about the house systems: how the pool runs, how the pool filter works, how the water heater works, the fireplace, everything. Then on several days the girls and I walked through the house, and they took their own notes. I showed them how to maintain things: "Move the black thing till it stops; turn the red thing to the left."

They've been doing great. Now they can snake a toilet,

plunge a toilet, do all sorts of things. Of course, I know they can call on my friends to help out if something gets too bad.

DOROTHY: We have a ham radio on board to give us contact back to the States. Once a week we connect with the girls and find out how things are going. As long as they tell us they're okay and there are no problems with the house, we can sail off happy for another week.

GARY: Still, I worry all the time. I can't get rid of that; the girls are here and that's a responsibility I will always have. Even though their mother lives nearby and we have friends who are looking in on them, I have normal parental concerns.

From a planning standpoint, readying the boat was the biggest challenge. Although Gary had learned to sail as a youngster, and although they had owned their boat for several years, a day's outing on the San Francisco Bay is a far cry from an ocean cruise to Mexico.

GARY: I didn't build the big things, but I made a lot of modifications. I added electrical systems and a lot of safety things. For example, you don't need satellite navigation in the Bay, but you do to sail to Mexico. And I took a class in celestial navigation. In a pinch I could navigate by the sun or stars. Then I installed the convenience and entertainment things: the storage, the TV, things like that.

DOROTHY: I knew I would not be comfortable living with spartan cooking and sleeping facilities. I like to have certain conveniences; we have a microwave on board, for instance, and a TV and VCR and cassette player. But everything had to be measured before it was bought—even the spice rack, because it could only go in one spot! That was all part of the planning process.

GARY: And there was a need to get my ham radio license. That requires two things: you have to take a radio theory test and also a code test. Being an electrical engineer I knew the radio theory would not be a difficult thing for me to pass; but the other test required rote memorization of the Morse Code. So I spent at least fifteen minutes a day for over a year just listening to dots. I'd tape the lessons, and on my way to and from work I'd play this endless da-dot, dot, da-dot. Finally I got proficient at it. So that was one of the things on the checklist.

We even took a check-out cruise. We raced the boat from Oakland to Catalina Island and found out that, yes, it is seaworthy and capable and that we are also seaworthy and capable.

Finally we concerned ourselves with the "what ifs." What if this breaks? Do I have a spare? Or if I can repair it, do I have the tools?

DOROTHY: We had overboard drills, too, so we'd know what to do if one of us got thrown overboard. And we planned medically and dentally. Since my fillings were giving way, I had crowns put on before we left. I didn't want any trouble while we were gone.

Now that the Woods have embarked on their sailing odyssey, they're finding that new situations call for new analyses, new plans.

GARY: We really had no idea how we would react to long-term sailing. Neither one of us had been away from a job for more than normal vacations. We didn't know how we would react to the confinement of a thirty-four-foot piece of fiberglass or to Mexico. So we were unable to plan very far past taking off.

Now I don't think we're going to be capable of just doing nothing for the rest of our lives. We can't just snorkel and sail and sun ourselves all the time.

DOROTHY: Our goal is to find a job of some sort that is a lot closer to what we'd like to do all the time, a job that we might not even need financially but that we need to occupy time. We're thinking of possibly looking for one down in Baja.

GARY: We just bought a condo in Cabo San Lucas; it was a very spontaneous move for us. But the Mexicans just changed some regulations that allow Americans to own property and businesses. The area is just gorgeous, and it's exploding with Americans and Japanese.

DOROTHY: Tourism is a big part of business down there, and I think with my marketing skills I might be able to find something associated with the tourism business. For Gary, with electrical engineering, it might be more complex. They haven't reached the level of technical sophistication to need someone to set up computer systems . . .

GARY: . . . but that could be a challenge. I have skills in problem-solving and, yes, right now they're pretty well confined to the computer business; but that doesn't mean I can't solve problems in other fashions.

DOROTHY: We need more information before we can make decisions about the possibilities for living and starting a business, or participating in a business, in Baja. Right now, we just don't have enough information.

GARY: And buying the condo has reduced our monthly interest income. So that's another term in the equation that we're going to have to figure out. If we sell our home in California, we can live in Cabo San Lucas and not work at all. But we can't afford one home in California and one in Cabo unless we rent out one of them or unless we go back to work. So again there's a number of trade-offs we have to study.

Lately when I lie there before I go to sleep at night, I say to myself, "Okay, here's where we are today, and we have decisions to make." There's this huge decision tree *[he uses his hands to depict a tree with branches going off in all directions]* and I've got to begin to prune that tree and make some decisions. And I have to decide what the conditions are of those decisions; but that's not easy. The emotions that you're dealing with are not measurable in units; you're trying to weigh things that are not weighable. "How much do I hate driving in traffic?" "How much do I like living in Mexico?" It's all these intangibles.

One thing we've learned is how complex human beings are, how complex we personally are. No one can sit down and tell you, "Okay, this is the way to run your life; here are the steps you must take to go from point A to point B," because everyone's point B is different. The things I can do, you can't do; you may have no interest in them or you may not have the skills to do them.

But even after a relatively short time away, I think my definition of success has changed. In the past I probably would have looked at "How big a car do you have?" and "What is your home like?" and "What toys do you stock it with?" Now my feeling of success is based on having the time and health and the money to go do the things you want to do. *[The quick smile returns.]* This is another variable we have to factor in.

· ·

Ready, Set, Go

Perhaps because of his engineering background, Gary was extremely logical and organized in pursuing his dream. Most of us need a little push. It's so easy to procrastinate chores that aren't urgent and, no doubt about it, when we're still in the throes of our primary career, restyling just doesn't seem that essential. There's always, we think, tomorrow. But in order to have a smooth transition into midlife, it's important to invest a little of today's time and energy into preparing for tomorrow. How about, let's say, an hour a week? We can block this time out on our calendars—a bona fide appointment—and we can schedule our restyling activities into these periods.

At first, we'll probably spend our hour-a-week just thinking and talking, discussing all of the possibilities that lie before us. That's okay. We're acclimating ourselves to change, and that's a slow process. But gradually, out of this talk and intro-spection, goals will begin to emerge. When we can formulate these goals clearly enough that we can write them down, we will, say the experts, have reached a turning point. The act of declaring our intentions on paper signifies that we have made a commitment and that our restyling dreams have started to take shape.

Sure, our list of goals will need revising now and again. As we gradually refine our plans, we'll change these goals to reflect our new decisions. Bob and Megan Harris, for example, refined their plans time and time again. Each time they took yet another break from work until finally Bob realized that he was a gypsy who part-timed every few years as an architect rather than the other way around.

• •

Profile: Bob and Megan Harris—Architect and Home-maker to Gypsies Abroad

Saying is one thing and doing is another.

MONTAIGNE

Bob Harris was forty-four when he closed the doors of his architectural practice and with his wife, Megan, and two youngest sons went to live on a Greek island. Megan, who was working in a folk art gallery at the time, and the boys—David, sixteen, and Daniel, thirteen—all considered it a grand adventure. The family (minus their oldest son, Kirby, who was in the Navy) set off in the fall of 1969. They returned to the United States after a year when "the coffers were empty"; two and a half years later, having earned some money and taken care of details at home, they were off again. It's been like that ever since. Bob and Megan, now sixty-four and sixty-six and about to celebrate their thirty-eighth wedding anniversary, have spent eleven of the last twenty years in Europe.

It isn't easy catching up with the Harrises. I'd first "met" them through Bob's book, Gypsying After 40, *published in 1987. Largely a guide with advice on matters such as "Getting There Economically" and "The Roads, The Rules, The Conditions," the book also offers tantalizing glimpses of the Harrises' personal adventures.*

"The vision of Gypsying strikes hard when your career and hopes have reached an anticipated level of success and the once distant challenge has become reality," wrote Bob. "The lure of starting a new life strikes again when retirement beckons. At such times we need to step out towards vital new directions. Listen carefully to that voice whispering inside you. It begs you to take risks, start afresh, and seek new vistas."

I knew instantly that I wanted to talk with these people. I finally tracked them down not in Santa Fe, their nominal home, but instead on Orcas Island, off the coast of Washington. "We're thinking of moving up here to the San Juans," said Bob when I finally connected with him on the phone, "but first we're trying it out by house-sitting for some folks who are on vacation. We're used to three hundred and fifty days of sunshine a year in Santa Fe and here there's only about two hundred, but it's beautiful. Come take a look."

On the morning of our scheduled visit, my husband and I find ourselves dodging raindrops in Seattle. But as we reach the coastal town of Anacortes (about eighty miles north) where we're to catch the ferry to Orcas, the sky clears and we are bathed in crisp, brilliant sunlight. For an hour and twenty minutes the ferry glides over sapphire waters studded with emerald isles, and by the time we reach the island, we agree with Bob. This is God's country, all right.

We call Bob from the grocery store of the no-stoplight town, and he gives us directions to their borrowed home. He's waiting in the driveway when we arrive, a small man with white hair and a neatly trimmed beard. He's rustically outfitted in blue jeans and a turtleneck sweater that, we learn later, was purchased seventeen years ago in Gibraltar for one dollar. He welcomes us enthusiastically as does Alex, the boxer dog that accompanies him everywhere (including, on occasion, to Europe).

"You know," he says as we settle into the comfortable living room, "planning is destructive." I am momentarily taken aback. I've heard the bare outlines of Bob and Megan's story on the telephone, and it appears to me that most of their actions have been the result of careful forethought and, frequently, extended tryouts. Even their move to Orcas, I think, is being prudently considered, explored by means of a six-month house-sitting arrangement.

Then I realize that to Bob, an architect-planner by profession, a "plan" is a blueprint, something that must be religiously followed. Even a slight deviation can cause the whole structure to collapse. His next words show me that our differences over the word "planning" are largely semantic. "Planning as a direction is useful," he says, "but it must be a process that starts and continues, that adjusts continually. It must accept new input every moment." I readily agree, and he seems pleased.

Now, while Megan sits off to one side quietly knitting with a burgundy yarn that matches her pants and shirt, he begins to tell their life story.

BOB: Most of us are programmed. As Jung said, we're given a push by our culture, our family, our peers, and so on to do something, to enter a profession or whatever. Architecture was the profession I was extremely talented at and it was just the way it worked out.

But I started when I was sixteen. By 1967 I'd been doing architecture for more than twenty years. I was pretty successful, but you know, I'd almost used up the program; the challenge was gone. Architecture was beginning to be less meaningful. I wasn't terribly unhappy, but I was beginning to say, "What's next? What's the new program?" The lack of a program can cause a crisis.

Then came the epiphany. Bob went to the funeral of an architect whom he had known since he was a child.

BOB: This man had been one of the town's leading architects. He'd gone to MIT, was extremely well trained, had been head of the Historic American Building Survey for the whole state of Texas. But by the time he died, he'd gone out of fashion as an architect; and he'd grown rather morose.

His funeral was in a neo-Gothic church that he had designed in the late twenties. It was an excellent building, a superb building, but it was in a neighborhood that had become run-down. All around me were fellow architects, but they didn't care about him. They were just there as a perfunctory thing. Suddenly I had this shift, and *it was me in that coffin!*

Bob walks over to his desk, picks up a piece of paper, puts on his reading glasses and begins to read from the manuscript of his next book.

"Watching and listening to the organ's groans and then to the minister's carefully worded eulogy, I became aware first of the building and then of my assembled fellow architects while my cold body lay numb. Is this what it all came to, a few words of late praise, a huddle of almost strangers, a well-constructed building in a rotting section of the city? All my years of difficult training, of scratching a barely adequate living, of working sixty-hour weeks, of always hoping to create magnificent buildings while having to accept the less-than-perfect reality. This was the funeral of a man who had succeeded and faded, leaving competent and careful work harshly judged by fickle fashion. This was my coffin. Those were my mourners. I felt deader than any embalmed corpse.

"I knew something had to be done. I was depressed at a time when my career was blossoming. Yet this had been, without a doubt, my own funeral, the death of hope, really."

Bob puts down the paper and gives an ironic laugh. "Now you begin to see the whole thing," he says. "I thought, So this is what it all comes to."

BOB: I said, Whoa, something is wrong, and Megan and I started talking about it all.

MEGAN: *[She looks up from her knitting—a trim woman with a gray-blond pageboy—and nods her head in agreement.]* We just asked each other, "What's this all about? What's a nice kid like me doing in a situation like this?"

BOB: I guess I came up with the idea of just taking off; I tend to come up with the wilder ideas. But it's hard to say. Basically, Megan had really always wanted to travel, but it just wasn't included in our lifestyle. You know, we'd take off for a couple of weeks every year, but that was all. So we both wanted to make a move, but there are all these questions: How do you do it? How can you afford it? What happens to your identity and everything? If your work is involved with your identity, which unfortunately is the way it was with me—then you have to find an identity outside your work.

MEGAN: We came from a generation that was all geared into this Puritan ethic of work, work, work.

BOB: It was a couple of years of questioning. We'd talk, set it aside for a while, say "Oh, we can't do that," and then go back to it.

They spent nearly two years "just batting it all around." Then they made a four-part decision. Bob would complete work on the architectural project with which he was then involved; this would bring them a comfortable nest egg of $60,000. He would apply for a grant to study neighborhood planning in Greece (a

country which was then doing some of the most innovative hous-
ing projects in the world); this would help cover living expenses
as well as maintain Bob's self-identity as an architect. They
would rent out their Santa Fe home (an old house they'd bought
for a pittance but that Bob, with his architectural savvy, had
successfully renovated); this would provide additional spending
money. Finally they would enroll their two teen-age sons in
correspondence school classes, close Bob's office—"Bang. Click.
Good-bye"—and take off for Europe.

BOB: In the beginning, it wasn't smooth. I mean, when I said,
"We're going in May," Megan said, "Well, but is this done?"
and "Are we going to have enough of this, that, and the other?"
Finally I said, "All you can do is go, because there's never going
to be a perfect time." So we set a date, because if you don't
you never will go. It gets scarier and scarier. There was fright
on both our parts; I just hid mine better than she did. *[He
chuckles, but Megan interrupts.]*

MEGAN: I don't think I had fear.

BOB: About not having enough money . . .

MEGAN: Well, I thought we were going to have enough money.
If I had known. . . . *[She laughs.]* If I had known we weren't
going to get that grant—we were counting on that—I don't
know if we'd have gone.

BOB: And I thought money was coming in from that job,
$60,000 . . .

MEGAN: So we thought we had money when we went.

BOB: Yes, but not having money taught us. It taught us many
things.

MEGAN: One lesson we learned from this is that if you can't
handle your business before you go, don't expect anybody else
to take care of it for you. Don't even expect anybody to forward
your mail.

BOB: I'd finished my part of the architectural project. Another
fellow was supposed to complete the work, and I was due all
that money. Instead, all kinds of things went wrong, and when

we came back, I found myself $20,000 in debt. And other people did strange things, too. We had an accountant who just wrote checks out for anything anybody wanted. He never questioned a single bill. It cost us a lot of money. *[He grows thoughtful.]* I think you create a tremendous jealousy when you leave. Maybe that's why people act the way they do.

MEGAN: People think you're shirking your duty by going.

BOB: You're shirking, they think, and therefore you ought to be punished or something. It is crazy, absolutely crazy.

MEGAN: The whole year was a financial disaster but a personal triumph.

BOB: It was. When I first got to Greece, it was hard to make the change, to shed the old identity. I couldn't sleep. I'd wake up about 3 A.M., sure I'd heard a telephone ringing. There wasn't a telephone for five miles. Then I'd wake up in the morning and start rushing around as if I had an appointment at my office. But there wasn't anything I had to do but walk an eighth of a mile to the beach and watch the sun come up. One of the things that happens when you make the break is you discover your identity is not specifically what you thought it was. It's not tied up in the work you do. Once you find out what your identity is—that you're just you—then you can do anything. The world just opens up for you. But it took a while.

MEGAN: It wasn't as hard for me. I was a curator in a museum, but it wasn't my identity.

The Harrises spent a year in Greece, living for the most part in a small apartment on one of the islands. Once they took a three-week trip to Turkey on a fishing boat. Then, sated and broke, they returned to Santa Fe to "figure out what to do next." This had been their trial, and they liked what they had learned.

BOB: When we tried living abroad for that year, we found out it was an entirely new life for us. We had so many adventures and learned so much, and it was the beginning of a new relationship between ourselves. We realized that this was just the beginning of growing. So we decided, by golly, we'd better go again.

MEGAN: We just knew there were certain financial obligations we had to clear up first.

BOB: And you have a cycle. An architectural cycle is about three years from starting to completing a big project. So we figured in about three years we'd go back, and we did. We sold up what we could, and we worked very hard to get our finances back in shape. Then it came to a point where one of us had to set a time to leave. I mean, it was the same as the first time. You finally get to a point where you have to face yourself and say, "On this date we go," and get a reservation and on and on. We were gone six and a half years that time. That's pretty much what we've been doing ever since, back and forth for twenty years.

We've been to Europe six times for a total of about eleven years. Travel for us is a slow thing. We stay in a place a month, six months. In the summer we usually use a very small camper. In the winter we spread out; we rent a little place in an area where it's warm and inexpensive.

For a while, about four and a half years, we had a sailboat. I'd always wanted to do sailing, but as a young man you detour; you drop those ideas when you get so busy. I mean, I was a flier in the Navy, but I didn't even try to get a private license when I got out. I had to concentrate on being an architect.

We've been all around Europe—as far east as Greece, Turkey, and Israel. And we spent some time in North Africa. In between travels we came back to the States and worked. I've always been able to find jobs in architecture.

Living in Europe was a wonderful experience for our boys. The first time we went they were in junior high and high school, and we took over books from a correspondence school. After two weeks we realized what a huge mistake that was. They never looked at them; there were too many other things to learn. When we returned to the States, neither boy had to make up the year's worth of classes he had missed; both were able to advance with their former classmates.

After that first trip, they had two school years in Santa Fe; and then we all flew to Frankfurt for our second trip. The boys were sixteen and nineteen then and full of self confidence. They wanted to go to school in Europe, so we said, "Fine, here's a little bit of money; go find a school." They'd learned, while we were in Greece, to live on almost nothing.

The older one went to University College in Wales and was there two years and then came back to the States and graduated from Bennington. The younger one went to a school for a year in England and then came to Spain where we'd heard about a very good school. Then he spent some time bicycling and working in France and Switzerland. He came back to the United States and applied to six Ivy Leagues. He was accepted by five and three offered him a big scholarship. He went to Yale. Both boys went on to graduate school and are now teachers—good ones. They're interesting guys.

Bob realizes he is fortunate that he can always find architectural work when he comes back to the States, but he firmly believes that if you have trust, good things will happen. In addition, he and Megan simply refuse to worry about money.

BOB: We never earned any money while we were in Europe. The only income we had was the rent money from our home back in Santa Fe.

MEGAN: Bob did one article for a travel magazine, and it was such a hassle that we said, "That's ridiculous."

BOB: When you have discovered what is important in life, then you spend so little money. We have no debts, we don't charge anything, we don't spend more money than we have. We haven't owed anybody anything for over twenty years. We have no image to keep up.

There's this whole idea in our society that any material thing will make you happy. If you really want to see what hell is like, it's a shopping mall.

The point is, you can live and travel this way for so little. It's so cheap that if people ever would learn this, everybody would leave the United States and quit living in their homes. If you can get rid of your mortgage, then you can rent your house and that will give you income for a long time.

We spend the night with the Harrises, suitably settled on mattresses on the living room floor. The next morning we're reluctant to say good-bye. It's obvious that our hosts are comfortable with themselves and with each other; they're easy people to be around.

"What's in your future? Do you think you'll ever stay put?" I ask as we prepare to leave. "Re-read the last page of Gypsying," *answers Bob with a smile. On the ferry to the mainland I pull my well-worn copy of his book out of my overstuffed bag. "We don't ever want to 'retire' in the usual sense of withdrawing from the action, from work which connects us to the world," I read aloud. "We won't stop Gypsying. Curiosity and a passion for what lies over the horizon keeps us on the move. Imagine what each of us has yet to experience!" My husband and I grin at each other and walk out on deck to experience the vibrant beauty of the San Juan Islands.*

• •

Most of us aren't as lucky as Bob Harris. We can't try out a new lifestyle and then return to our old job for a few months or a few years. Our old bosses don't want us back. Oh, some of us may be able to return to a different position or a different company, but we're likely to be faced with a loss of both salary and status. For the majority of us, early retirement is a one-way street.

Yet retirement will come to all of us sooner or later. We can choose to take it early and, through restyling, plan for a rejuvenating interlude at midlife. Or we can wait until it is forced upon us when we may be too drained and too habituated to make the most of our remaining years. Either way, as we approach midlife we have to select which path we want to follow into the future. As W. James once said, "When you have to make a choice and don't make it, that in itself is a choice."

E X E R C I S E S

My-Time Goal

Every restyler should have one major compelling goal which can be stated in simple, concrete terms. "I'm going to sell my business in ten years and go sailing," said David Rausch. "I'm going to resign in five or six years and devote my time to my hobbies," said Rich Henke. "I'm going to retire from the Air

Force when I reach the twenty-year mark and start my own business," said Tom Christensen. Each of these restylers knew exactly what he intended to do and when he intended to do it.

You may not know the exact date that you will be able to leave your present career, but you should be able to give a ballpark figure. (For most of us, that ballpark figure is primarily based on the ages of our children and the size of our bank account.) State your goal in twenty words or less.

Are You Sure?

Before you go any further, you want to verify your goal. Is it compatible with your values and interests, aptitudes and skills? Look back over the exercises you completed earlier in this book.

- "The Two Main Routes," at the end of Chapter 1, asked you to list the pros and cons of restyling vs. staying in your present job for as long as possible. Do you have any additions or changes to this list?
- "The Years to Come," at the end of Chapter 2, was a preliminary exercise in goal setting. Is your current goal in harmony with the life goals you stated earlier?
- "Taking Your Risk Temperature," in Chapter 3, showed how willing you are to take financial gambles. Does your current goal require a risk so great that it will cause you sleepless nights?
- "What's Important to Me" and "Slip List," in Chapter 4, revealed some of the "wants" that are important to you

(and your partner) in your midlife years. Will your present goal fulfill these wants?

- The various self-discovery exercises in Chapter 5 were designed to give you insight into your personality, your aptitudes and your skills. Does your present goal make use of your strengths and downplay your weaknesses?
- The exercises in Chapter 6 pointed out your dreams and desires. Will your present goal fulfill these dreams?

To illustrate many of the following exercises, we're going to use the example of a fictitious restyler named Sam. Sam, now a physician in the suburb of a large city, is eager to move away from freeways and congestion and open a bookstore in small-town America. His wife, Marge, who teaches English to high school students on a half-day basis, is in full accord. Yet she worries about moving because she feels responsible for her elderly father, who lives nearby. Sam and Marge have three children; the youngest is fourteen. They figure that if they make their move in five years, all of their children will be more or less independent.

All in a Night's Sleep

Did you have trouble stating your goal? Are you lying awake nights mulling over a host of possibilities? Instead of tossing and turning, go to your desk and review each option by looking at the best possible outcome (sweet dreams) as well as the worst likely result (nightmares). Then heed the words of J. Paul Getty, who once remarked, "When I go into any business deal, my chief thoughts are on how I'm going to save myself if things go wrong." Leaving your present occupation and embarking upon a different lifestyle may be the biggest "business deal" you'll ever make, so you want to also consider alternatives in case your nightmares come true (sleeping pills).

The easiest way to complete this exercise is to divide a piece of paper into four vertical columns: "My Options," "Sweet Dreams," "Nightmares," and "Sleeping Pills." An example for Restyler Sam follows:

A Night's Sleep for Sam

My Options	Sweet Dreams	Nightmares	Sleeping Pills
continue as a doctor in private practice in this location	remain financially secure; have status and friends	I burn out and do something foolish or die without ever trying something new	if I burn out, open bookstore then
continue but work fewer hours	ditto	patients will go elsewhere if I'm not always available	open bookstore
move to small town and work for another doctor	moving would be a breath of fresh air; would still be earning money	I'd hate working for another doctor after being on my own for so long	open bookstore
move and open bookstore in small town	I'd be a wild success and work only part-time	business could fail	get job working for another doctor to recoup financial losses
retire and concentrate on hobbies	a chance to do what I like to do	I could get bored	open bookstore

Tomorrow's Résumé

Now that you've stated your primary goal, you need to know what skills you must learn and what information you must possess in order to be successful at your post-retirement activity. Project yourself into the future and pretend that you are applying for the position you dream of holding. Write an imaginary résumé showing your qualifications. Make them so strong that it is obvious to anyone that a person holding such qualifications would be an obvious success at the activity you dream of doing. Then go out and make your résumé come true.

An example of Sam and Marge's future résumé for becoming the owners of a bookstore follows. The italicized parts indicate things that Sam and Marge must accomplish before they will be ready to open a bookstore in a new location.

Name: Sam and Marge Smith

Address: A new home in small-town America

Position Desired: Owner of a bookstore

Experience: Marge has learned the bookselling business by working part-time at a large bookstore for three years. She understands all aspects of running such a store. As a high school English teacher she also has a good background in British and American literature.

Sam has been a doctor for twenty years and in this capacity has been running a small business. He knows how to work with employees, negotiate leases, and communicate with patients (customers).

Education: Marge is a graduate of Northwestern University with a B.A. in English literature and an M.A. in education. *She has been reading* Publishers Weekly, *a trade journal for booksellers, for nearly two years.*

Sam is a graduate of the University of Illinois and Washington University Medical School. *He has taken numerous business and management courses at the community college and is working closely with an advisor from SCORE at the Small Business Administration.*

References: Several booksellers and businesspeople.

Mind-Mapping

Popularized by Tony Buzan in his 1974 book, *Use Both Sides of Your Brain,* mind-mapping is an organizational technique for those of us who don't think in the Roman Numeral–Capital Letter format that we learned in grade-school outlining. The method, also called patterning and cluster diagraming, is widely used by educators.

"Rather than starting from the top and working down in sentences and lists," says Buzan, "one should start from the centre or main idea and branch out as dictated by the individual ideas and general form of the central theme." The following mind-map shows Sam's plans as he prepares to leave his medical practice and open a bookstore in a small town.

To mind-map your restyling program, take a large piece of paper and in the middle write your main goal, using only one or two words. Draw a circle around your goal. Then on lines that radiate out like the spokes of a wheel, write your subgoals. Now branch out from these spokes and write the activities that will lead to the accomplishment of these goals. You can add new information easily, without having to squeeze it into the proper place on a formal outline. You can branch as often as you wish and even draw lines to show connections.

In most cases each mind-map entry should be only a word or two. Remember, you're not going to hand this in to a teacher; it only has to make sense to you. Don't hesitate to turn your paper around when you mind-map; after all, branches can grow in all directions.

You'll be surprised at how quickly you're able to organize your thoughts through mind-mapping. Most people find it infinitely preferable to outlining when it comes to forming new plans and creating new ideas. Patterns seem to form of their own accord, and you can see connections without worrying, at this point, about prioritizing or ordering.

If you have the luxury of an unused wall in your workroom, put a giant piece of butcher paper on the wall and use various colors of pens or crayons for your mind-map.

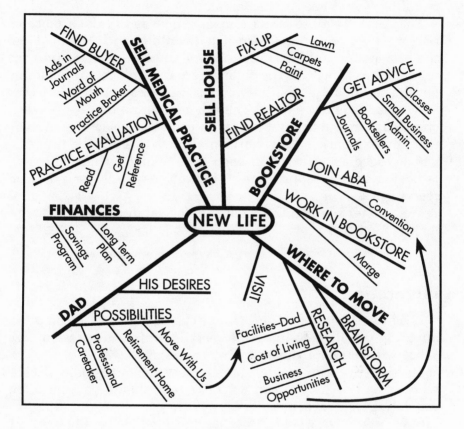

A Master Plan

"Failing to plan often means planning to fail," say Merrill and Donna Douglass, authors of *Manage Your Time, Manage Your Work, Manage Yourself.* For a project as long-term as restyling, you'll need a master plan.

The easiest way to make a master plan is to take a piece of narrow-ruled paper and turn it horizontally with the holes at the bottom. To make a five-year plan, divide the paper into six columns as shown on the following page. In the first column list the secondary goals that you want to accomplish before you leave your primary career. The other columns represent years one, two, three, four, and five, with each line-space the equivalent of two months. Draw horizontal lines to show the times at which you plan to work on each goal. While a chart like this is obviously only approximate, it provides a master plan for restyling.

The master plan on the following page shows Sam's strategy for the next five years.

Integration

Long-term goals are one thing, but to actually accomplish anything you have to integrate restyling into your present life. What will you do about restyling *this Saturday*?

Looking at your master plan and your mind-map, decide which small tasks you can do *this week*. Should you begin by tabulating your expenses, talking with your spouse, taking an interest test? Or would it be better to go to the library and investigate second careers or write for information about places where you might like to live? Maybe you can register for a class at your community college or invite a group of friends over for a brainstorming session.

Enter these small chunks of restyling on your regular monthly or weekly calendar and begin to deal with some of the very small and nonthreatening activities that are the basis of the early stages of restyling. As you begin to accumulate information and acquire relevant material, put it in a special file drawer or box.

ACTIVITY	YEAR ONE	YEAR TWO	YEAR THREE	YEAR FOUR	YEAR FIVE
Dreaming/ Planning	———————————————————————————————→				
Setting Goals	—	- -	- -	- -	- -
Learning Book Business					
Talking with People	———————————————————————————				
Taking Classes	—	——	——	——	——
Conventions		-	-	-	-
Reviewing Finances	—	-	-	-	-
House-Hunting Research	———————————————————————————				
Visiting New Locations	-	-	-	-	-
Present Home					
Fix Up				———————————	
Sell					———
Medical Practice					
Find Buyer				———————————	
Sell					———

Once your restyling plans are written in your regular calendar, once they occupy a physical space in your file cabinet, you'll find that they will take on a life of their own. Gradually, restyling will become less of an "if" and more of a "when."

Resources

Careering and Re-careering for the 1990s: The Complete Guide to Planning Your Future by Ronald L. Krannich (1991, Impact Publications, 10655 Big Oak Circle, Manassas, VA 22111-3040, phone: 703/361-7300). Offering valuable tips and exercises for those who want a full-time second career, this book is a nuts-and-bolts guide not only to making your plans but to implementing them as well.

Getting Unstuck: Breaking Through Your Barriers to Change by Sidney B. Simon (1988, Warner Books, Inc., 666 Fifth Avenue, New York, NY 10103, phone: 800/631-8571). "Stuck," says Simon, "is setting goals and making plans but putting off the first step until tomorrow or next week or next year." He shows how to clarify goals, combat indecisiveness, and start moving.

Use Both Sides of Your Brain by Tony Buzan (1983, E. P. Dutton, 375 Hudson Street, New York, NY 10014, phone: 212/366-2000). The original guide to mind-mapping, this book discusses ways to work more efficiently, effectively, and creatively.

Whatever you can do, or dream you can, begin it.
Boldness has genius, power and magic in it.

GOETHE

8 | *THE MIDLIFE JOURNEY*

Can we all restyle? Why not? Some of us may have to juggle our finances a bit, and others may have to find creative ways to meet the needs of our children. But we all have the right to a glorious adventure in midlife—if we plan for it.

And if we don't? Well, the adventure may not be quite so pleasant. Other people will mark the road map; outside events will control the itinerary.

The restylers profiled in this book are convinced—every one of them—that they have enriched their lives by taking a chance and making a change. "Gene's so rejuvenated," enthuses Pat Estess. "Ever since he left Wall Street, there's this energy in him, this excitement. I like being around him more; he's energized."

Gene plans to continue his work with the Jericho Project, but he also wants to go back to school. "If I can get that master's in public policy," he says, "I'll have more of a background in how to use government for the expansion of Jericho concepts." Like all the restylers my husband and I met, Gene is still restyling; he's still planning for future changes.

As soon as Ken and Shelley Cassie return from Russia, for example, they want to shift the emphasis of their pottery business. They feel that producing and selling custom-designed pottery will allow Ken to experiment with new forms and Shelley to devise new marketing strategies.

And Bruce and Carolyn Bade have ideas for expanding their seminars on recreational vehicles. In addition, says Bruce, "we've had so much fun writing articles for *Trailer Life* that we're thinking of collecting the information and putting it out in book form."

Terrence Grace isn't sure what he'll do after his teaching stint in Honduras is over. He's committed to a one-year stay and then . . . who knows? He may decide to stay longer, or he may take some time out for travel. When, if, he comes back to the United States, he's sure he'll be a different person than he was when he left. "I won't go back to my old lawyer's job," he says with alacrity. "The people were great, the position was good, but it's time to move on."

Jim and Carlene Pasin plan to be moving on within five years. By that time they expect to have turned over their Money Mailer business to their kids, Selena and Tony. By then, says Jim, they'll have found yet another avenue of challenge and enjoyment.

Right now Rich Henke is considering a move out of Los Angeles. "Berkeley would be nice," he muses. "I have a lot of friends there, but gee, there are some good opportunities in Colorado . . ." He's confident that he'll never run out of things to do, places to explore, mountains to climb.

Marian Gibson's eyes take on a determined glint when she talks about a tea room for the elderly. "Temenos House can only help eight families; this would be an opportunity to reach many more," she says. "It's something I think I'm going to have to do, one way or another."

Tom Christensen's travel business is finally beginning to zoom, and he is openly ecstatic. "All those years I have been networking and standing around looking stupid at meetings and conventions and conferences are beginning to pay off," he says with glee. "I have a feeling that one of these days my wife, Sandra, will jump on board. We'll just have to figure out the best way to use her talents." The Christensens have, quite literally, the whole world before them.

David and Laura Rausch are still marking time until their son, Michael, graduates from high school; then they're off to the South Seas. In the meantime, they're enjoying their new home in Seattle and enthusiastically making plans for their new boat. "You have another year or so to talk with us here," says Laura. "Then you'll have to meet us in Tahiti."

Dick and Fran Easton are happily punching away at their computers. One of these days, they're sure, their writing careers will take off, giving them the flexibility and income that they desire. But if that doesn't work out, they'll find something else. "Maybe," muses Fran, "we could sell gourmet brownies. I make a delicious chocolate, caramel, and pecan concoction. I may start looking into business licenses. . . ."

David and Melanie Thimgan continue to enjoy their experiment in small-town living. When Melanie's not at Mother Hubbard's and David isn't working on an architectural project, they're involved with dozens of community projects. "We love Vermont," says David. Then he looks at Melanie and smiles. "Of course Melanie put a brochure about Switzerland on my desk the other day. I suppose one of these days we'll make another move." Having uprooted themselves once, the Thimgans are certainly not afraid to do so again.

Kinney Thiele plans to do just that; she wants to apply for another assignment in the Peace Corps. She'd like to go to southern Africa, possibly Botswana, but Peace Corps administrators may decide to send her to Asia or the South Pacific. "Well," says Kinney, "it would be different." She pauses for a minute and shrugs. "Why not?" she says. "It would be another adventure."

Gary and Dorothy Wood are busily discussing what to do with the condominium they purchased in Cabo San Lucas. "We've one home more than we can afford right now—plus a boat," says Gary. "We have to decide which one to live in, which one to rent, which one to sell." At night before they go to sleep, the Woods analyze the pros and cons of their various options, certain that with the proper planning they can navigate the third quarter of their lives with skill and savvy.

And Bob and Megan Harris are finally planning to settle down, sort of, after years of gypsying. They're going to sell their home in Santa Fe and buy some land in the San Juan Islands, where they dream of starting a co-housing project. This type of living, popular in Denmark, consists of families living in separate units but sharing common facilities such as a dining hall, workshops, playrooms, and laundry facilities. Bob's eyes glow when he speaks of such a project, and he laughs when I tell him it sounds almost like a 1960s commune. "No," he says, "this is the new concept for the nineties."

So is restyling. Those of us who are in or approaching midlife in the 1990s have worked long and hard. Now, we think, we should be able to have some time for ourselves, to follow our own dreams. But unlike the folks of the sixties, we don't want to abandon our responsibilities; and unlike folks many years our senior, we're not ready for the rocking chair. Instead we want a middle road, one that is specially suited to the realities of middle life. Through restyling we can find that road.

Who Did What

Restyling presents different challenges for different people. Some want to retire to part-time work; others dream of full-time leisure. Some plan to use their home as a base for travel; others want to start a new life in a new location. The people profiled in this book have restyled in a variety of ways and had many experiences. This list will help you refer back to the restylers who speak most directly to your own concerns.

RESTYLED TO FULL-TIME WORK

Christensen	104
Estess	138
Gibson	78
Pasin	51

SPOUSES EQUAL PARTNERS IN NEW VENTURE

Bade	33
Cassie	13
Easton	127
Harris	201
Pasin	51
Rausch	113
Thimgan	167
Wood	191

SPOUSE SUPPORTIVE BUT NOT DIRECTLY INVOLVED IN NEW VENTURE

Christensen	104
Estess	138

RESTYLED TO NEW VENTURE WHEN CHILDREN WERE STILL MINORS

Christensen	104
Gibson	78
Harris	201
Henke	64
Rausch	113
Thimgan	167

BOTH SPOUSES LEFT THRIVING CAREERS

Bade	33
Cassie	13
Easton	127
Thimgan	167
Wood	191

SINGLE WOMEN

Gibson	78
Thiele	158

SINGLE MEN

Grace	42
Henke	64

MOVED TO A NEW LOCATION

Bade	33
Grace	42
Harris	201
Pasin	51
Rausch	113
Thimgan	167

NEW LIFESTYLE INVOLVES HELPING OTHERS

Estess	138
Gibson	78
Grace	42
Thiele	158

TRAVEL A SIGNIFICANT PART OF NEW LIFESTYLE

Bade	33
Cassie	13
Christensen	104
Easton	127
Harris	201
Henke	64
Rausch	113
Thiele	158
Wood	191

RESTYLERS WHO SPEAK ABOUT MONEY

All

RESTYLERS WHO SPEAK ABOUT TRANSFERABILITY OF SKILLS

Bade	33
Estess	138
Christensen	104
Gibson	78
Grace	42
Pasin	51
Thiele	158
Thimgan	167
Wood	191

RESTYLERS WHO SPEAK ABOUT MORTALITY

Christensen	104
Easton	127
Gibson	78
Harris	201
Pasin	51
Rausch	113
Thiele	158

CHAPTER NOTES AND SOURCES

Introduction

page 2   The diffuse nature of the word "retirement" makes it tricky for statisticians to track an average or median age of retirement. Is retirement a cessation of paid employment, a move to part-time work, or a sabbatical before re-entering the work force? The 1987–88 study, *Aging America: Trends and Projections,* developed by the Public Policy Institute of the American Association of Retired Persons (AARP), gave 60.6 years as the median retirement age. But, says policy analyst Judith Hushbeck, the 1990 edition omits this as "these kind of statements raise more questions than they answer." But it is true, she continues, that historically the trend has been toward earlier retirement and that "by their early sixties—certainly by age 65—the majority of working Americans leave their career jobs."

Chapter 1: Paving the Road to Midlife

page 7 "WE CANNOT LIVE": Carl Jung, "The Stages of Life," lecture/ essay reprinted in *Modern Man in Search of a Soul*, trans. by W. S. Dell and Cary F. Baynes, Harvest/HBJ, 1933, p. 108.

page 7 A TELEVISION REPORTER: *Newsweek*, April 2, 1990, p. 18.

page 8 TALK SHOW HOST LARRY KING: Cable News Network, November 8, 1989.

What's Midlife All About?

page 8 STATISTICS TELL US: Longevity statistics are 1988 data from the National Center for Health Statistics of the U.S. Census Bureau.

page 8 ERDMAN PALMORE: Erdman Palmore's study is cited by Janet Belsky in her book, *Here Tomorrow*, Johns Hopkins University Press, 1988, p. 6. The original study, "Trends in the Health of the Aged," can be found in the *Gerontologist* 26, (1986): 298–302.

page 10 HANK WALFESH: Hank Walfesh is quoted in Les Honig's article, "Fresh Starts," in *USAIR*, October 1989, p. 72.

page 10 THE STATISTICS: Jacqueline Kelley was interviewed in person on September 21, 1989.

page 11 WHEN GEORGE EASTMAN: This story was related in the *Los Angeles Times*, March 11, 1990.

page 11 ACCORDING TO THE CONFERENCE BOARD: A story on retired folks who return to work appeared in the *San Jose Mercury News* on July 23, 1989. It was reprinted from the *Chicago Tribune*.

page 11 TWENTY YEARS AGO: These statistics were reported in the *Wall Street Journal*, December 8, 1989.

page 11 AND OF THOSE PEOPLE: According to the Bureau of Labor Statistics in 1989, nearly 100,000 people between the age of 45 and 55 say they are retired. But this figure does rely on various definitions of retirement. Many folks who claim to be retired may be working part-time; many others may plan to return to full-time work shortly; and many may be working full-time in a volunteer capacity. There is, once again, no standard definition of the word "retirement."

page 11 "MOST PEOPLE STILL": Carolyn Paul was quoted in *Modern Maturity*, June/July 1985, p. 27.

page 11   "MAINLY YOU HAVE BETTER HEALTH": Ann Smith was quoted in *Fifty Plus,* September 1988, p. 24.

The Four Quarters of Life

page 12   "I RATHER LIKE": Wilma Donahue was interviewed by telephone on February 27, 1990.

page 12   IT'S AN IDEA: Alan Pifer put forth his "third quarter concept" in "Introduction: Squaring the Pyramid" and "The Public Policy Response," chapters in *Our Aging Society: Paradox and Promise,* edited by Alan Pifer and Lydia Bronte, W. W. Norton & Company, 1986, pp. 11–12 and 402–405.

Gee, I Wish I Could But I Can't

page 21   "MOST OF US REACT": Robert Shomer was interviewed in person on March 10–11, 1990.

The Midlife Crisis

page 22   "MIDLIFE CRISIS": Gail Sheehy recognizes the negative connotation of the word "crisis." That is why, she explains, she prefers the word "passage." Nevertheless, in popular parlance as well as throughout her book, the term "midlife crisis" is used.

page 22   DURING THE MIDLIFE PASSAGE: The quoted parts are from *Passages* by Gail Sheehy, Bantam, 1974, pp. 358, 46, 496.

pages   WHEN JAY CARSEY: Jay Carsey's story is related in *Exit*
22–23   *the Rainmaker* by Jonathan Coleman, Atheneum, 1989. The specific parts referred to here are on pp. 202, 122, 316. Carsey's statement that there must be "a lot of people who sit around . . ." is from an article by Charles Trueheart in the *San Francisco Chronicle,* September 17, 1989.

page 24   "IN EVERY CASE": Charles Garfield is quoted in "The Mid-Life Fitness Peak," *Psychology Today,* July/August 1989, p. 32.

page 24   A GROUP OF COLLEGE SOPHOMORES: This experiment is related in *Getting Unstuck: Breaking Through Your Barriers to Change* by Sidney Simon, Warner, 1988, p. 19.

page 25   "IF YOU DO NOT RISK": David Viscott, *Risking,* Pocket Books, 1977, p. 133.

Chapter 2: My-Time: Variations on a Theme

The phrase "My-Time" originated with Marilyn Kennedy of Career Strategies in Wilmette, Illinois.

page 30   "TWO ROADS DIVERGED IN A WOOD": Robert Frost, "The Road Not Taken."

page 30   IN 1973 THE AVERAGE AMERICAN: These statistics and Louis Harris statement are from an article in *Time,* April 24, 1989, p. 58.

page 30   "TIME IS MONEY": Benjamin Franklin, *Advice to a Young Tradesman.*

page 31   AMERICAN ADULTS DON'T CONSIDER: Men's Health/Louis Harris Poll as reported in *Newsweek,* April 2, 1990.

page 31   "SIMPLE 'GIVENS' FROM OUR PAST": Lou Weiss's quote is from an article in the *San Jose Mercury News,* April 19, 1990.

page 31   "MY CLIENTS SAY,": Marilyn Kennedy, Career Strategies, Wilmette, IL, was interviewed by telephone on September 8, 1989.

Downscaling for Freedom

page 32   "HORATIO ALGER LIED": Nancy Mayer, *The Male Mid-Life Crisis: Fresh Starts After Forty,* Doubleday, 1978, p. 65.

page 32   "STRESS USED TO BE NOTICEABLE": Robert Hodges was quoted in "Firms begin to Fight Increase in Worker Stress," by Elizabeth M. Fowler, *The New York Times,* reprinted in *San Jose Mercury News,* September 17, 1989.

page 33   "IT USED TO BE": Bickley Townsend was quoted in "Few Act on their Concerns," by Anita Manning, *USA Today,* June 12, 1990.

Making a Difference

page 41   "ADULT MAN IS SO CONSTITUTED": Erik Erikson, *Insight and Responsibility,* W. W. Norton, 1964, p. 130.

page 42   "GENERATIVITY": Erik Erikson discusses generativity in *A Way of Looking at Things: Selected Papers from 1930 to 1980,* edited by Stephen Schlein, W. W. Norton, 1987, p. 601. This particular paper is "The Human Life Cycle," as published in the *International Encyclopedia of the Social Sciences,* David L. Sills, ed., Vol. 9, pp. 286-92, copyright 1968 by Crowell Collier and Macmillan, Inc.

page 42   JOSEPH KORDICK AND FRANK REILLY: Information about Joseph Kordick and Frank Reilly is from "A New Calling" by Beatrice E. Garcia, *Wall Street Journal,* December 8, 1989.

Pursuing the Always-Wants

page 48   "IT STARTS THE DAY THE POOR KID'S DELIVERED": John Holland was quoted in an article by Maria L. La Ganga in *Los Angeles Times,* reprinted in *San Jose Mercury News* under title "Career dilemma: follow in parents' footsteps?," April 8, 1990.

page 49   A SURVEY BY CHALLENGER, GRAY AND CHRISTMAS: The results of this survey were reported in "Mid-career Changes" by Harriet C. Johnson, *USA Today,* May 10, 1989.

page 49   IT MEANS, SAYS DAVID BIRCH: The full quote by David Birch, according to an article entitled "How America Has Run out of Time," by Nancy Gibbs, *Time,* April 24, 1989, p. 64, is "Running your own business means you are controlling your own destiny."

page 49   ACCORDING TO STUDIES: These studies and Mr. Gray's quote are from "Mid-career Changes" by Harriet C. Johnson, *USA Today,* May 10, 1989.

page 49   ALMOST 25 PERCENT OF NEW BUSINESSES CEASE TO EXIST: This was reported in *Money,* March 1990, p. 76.

page 49   "MY-TIME CAN BE BUSIER THAN BEFORE": Marilyn Kennedy, Career Strategies, Wilmette, IL, was interviewed by telephone on September 8, 1989.

A Thirst for Change

page 50   "IN 1980 . . . WHITE MALE MANAGERS PEAKED": Judith Bardwick was quoted in *US News & World Report,* September 25, 1989, p. 72.

page 50   "OF A HUNDRED PEOPLE WHO ARE HIRED": Judith Bardwick, *The Plateauing Trap,* AMACOM, 1986, pp. 36–37.

page 50   TODAY THERE ARE TEN PEOPLE: Ron Zemke's statement is from Bardwick, pp. 36–37.

page 50   "IN OUR SOCIETY": A. J. Jafee is quoted in *Cashing in on the American Dream,* by Paul Terhorst, Bantam, p. 113.

Profile: Jim and Carlene Pasin

page 51   "CHANGE IS ONE FORM": Linda Ellerbee, *Move On: Adventures in the Real World,* Putnam, 1991, p. 266.

page 57   HE WAS "NO LONGER A 'GOING-TO-BE'": Jacqueline Kelley was interviewed in person on September 21, 1989.

The Years to Come

page 58   THE LIFE EXPECTANCY CHART: Longevity statistics are 1988 data from the National Center for Health Statistics of the U.S. Census Bureau.

Chapter 3: Money Matters

page 61   MORE TIME THINKING ABOUT MONEY OR ABOUT SEX: The results of this poll were reported in "Smart Money" by Donald R. Katz, *Esquire,* March 1986, p. 51.

page 62   "AMAZINGLY, THE PSYCHOLOGICAL AND FINANCIAL ARENAS": Quotes to and references by Kathleen Gurney are from her book, *Your Money Personality: What It Is and How You Can Profit from It,* Doubleday, 1988. See Resources section for information on purchasing this book.

page 62   "IF THE HISTORY OF THE HUMAN RACE": Henry Lindgren, *Great Expectations: The Psychology of Money,* Wm. Kaufmann, Inc., 1980.

page 63   A STUDY BY PSYCHOLOGIST JAMES A. KNIGHT: James Knight, *For the Love of Money,* Lippincott, 1968, p. 83.

Money Mystique

page 63   "IT'S JUST A FIGMENT": Yvonne Emerson and Maria Nemeth, "Love and Lucre," *Moxie,* April, 1990, p. 52 ff.

page 63   "POSITIVE AND NEGATIVE EXPERIENCES": Herb Goldberg and Robert T. Lewis, *Money Madness: The Psychology of Saving, Spending, Loving, and Hating Money,* Morrow, 1978, p. 65.

page 71   GALLUP/KETTERING GLOBAL SURVEY: The results of this survey were reported in "Rich-Poor Gap Dominates the World," *Los Angeles Times,* September 21, 1976, and were cited by Goldberg and Lewis, p. 247.

Rich Is More Important

page 73   EXPERIMENT BY DOOB AND GROSS: A. N. Doob and A. E. Gross, "Status of Frustrator as an Inhibitor of Horn-Honking Responses," *Journal of Social Psychology* 76, (1968): 213–218; cited by Lindgren, pp. 72.

page 73   THE PERCEIVED RELATIONSHIP BETWEEN WEALTH AND WORTH: The discussion on the historical aspects of money is from W. H. Desmond, *Magic, Myth and Money,* Free Press of Glencoe, 1962; cited by Goldberg and Lewis, p. 84.

page 74   IN ORDER TO BELONG TO MENSA: Gurney, p. 35.

page 74   ALBERT EINSTEIN CAME TO THE UNITED STATES: Gurney, p. 12.

page 74   "THE MONEY COMING IN": Thomas Wiseman, *The Money Motive,* Random House, 1974, p. 77.

page 75   "MONEY IS A METAPHOR": Emerson and Nemeth, p. 54.

Purchasing Love

page 75   EXPERIMENT BY URIEL FOA: U. G. Foa, "Interpersonal and Economic Resources," *Science* 171, (1971): 345–351; cited by Lindgren, pp. 79–80.

page 75   STORY OF ANNA GOULD: Lucius Beebe, *The Big Spenders,* Doubleday, 1966, p. viii; cited by Goldberg and Lewis, p. 167.

page 76   "THE MAGNETISM I EXERT IS OF ANOTHER COLOR": J. Paul Getty, *How to Be Rich,* Playboy Press, 1973, p. 9; cited by Goldberg and Lewis, p. 96.

Saving for the What-Ifs

page 76   ADVANTAGES OF BECOMING "INSTANT MILLIONAIRES": Lindgren, p. 77.

Crunching the Numbers

page 86   "I FIGURE $400,000 IS ENOUGH": Paul Terhorst, *Cashing in on the American Dream: How to Retire at 35,* Bantam, 1988, p. 12.

page 90   "IF YOU LEAVE YOUR CAREER": Gary Bowyer was interviewed by telephone on September 14, 1989.

Chapter 4: Family Responsibilities

Joint Expectations

page 103 LABOR FORCE PARTICIPATION RATES: U.S. Bureau of Labor Statistics.

page 104 "STAGGERED RETIREMENT": Kay Wright was quoted by Gail Sato in "Life After Work?," *Moxie*, June 1990, p. 123.

page 104 "THERE'S NO REASON": Robert Shomer was interviewed in person on March 10–11, 1990.

The Nest Stays Full

page 112 MOM WAS ONLY FORTY-SEVEN: Bernice L. Neugarten, "Adaptation and the Life Cycle," *Journal of Geriatric Psychiatry* 4 (1970); cited by Gail Sheehy in *Pathfinders*, Bantam, 1981, p. 278.

page 113 "BOOMERANG KIDS": The increasing number of boomerang kids is discussed by Alison Leigh in " 'Parenthood II': The Nest Won't Stay Empty," *The New York Times*, March 12, 1989.

Profile: David and Laura Rausch

page 113 "MEN FOR THE SAKE OF GETTING A LIVING": Margaret Fuller's quote is from her book *Summer on the Lakes*.

page 113 ONE OUT OF THREE AMERICAN HOUSEHOLDS: *U.S. News and World Report*, January 1, 1990.

pages 120–21 PARENT CARE: Harvey J. Altman, ed., *Alzheimer's Disease: Problems, Prospects, and Perspectives*, Plenum Press, 1987, pp. 285, 329.

Chapter 5: A Sense of Self

page 126 "THE DEFINITION OF 'CAREER' ": Douglas LaBier, *Modern Madness: The Emotional Fallout of Success*, Addison-Wesley, 1986, pp. 25–26.

pages 126–27 "HAVING LIVED OUR LIFE": Allan Fromme, *Life After Work*, AARP, 1985, pp. 15,16; cited by Paul Fremont Brown in *From Here to Retirement*, Word Books, 1988, p. 106.

page 127 ON JULY 20, 1969: Buzz Aldrin recounts this story in his book, *Return to Earth*, Random House, 1973, p. 300.

Personality Factors

page 136 DAVID McCLELLAND IDENTIFIED THREE NEEDS: Leonard H. Chusmir, *Thank God It's Monday,* Plume/NAL, 1990, pp. 39–41, 56–59, 79.

page 136 EDWARD SCISSONS . . . EXPANDED THAT LIST: *U.S. News and World Report,* August 14, 1989, p. 14.

Fly on the Wall

page 148 THE DICTIONARY OF OCCUPATIONAL TITLES: *The Dictionary of Occupational Titles,* U.S. Department of Labor, Fourth Edition, 1977, 1984, p. 1369 ff.

Chapter 6: Discovering Your Dreams

A World of Choices

page 157 "MOST OF US HAVE SECRET DREAMS": Freda Rebelsky was interviewed by telephone on February 22, 1990.

page 157 SOME PEOPLE ARE DOERS: Albert Shapero, "Have You Got What It Takes to Start Your Own Business," *Savvy,* April, 1980; cited by Gail Sheehy in *Pathfinders,* Bantam, 1981, p. 296.

page 158 "DIRECTING THE MOVIES OF YOUR MIND": Adelaide Bry, *Visualization: Directing the Movies of Your Mind,* Barnes and Noble Books, 1979.

Profile: Kinney Thiele

page 158 "I BELIEVE THAT . . . DREAMS": Robert Fulghum, *All I Really Need to Know I Learned in Kindergarten,* Ivy Books/Ballantine, 1988, p. viii.

Greener Pastures

page 166 TEN FACTORS THAT SHOULD BE WEIGHED: Richard Boyer and David Savageau, *Places Rated Almanac,* Prentice Hall, 1989.

page 166 "THE CAPITAL YOU HAVE SITTING IN YOUR EQUITY": John Howells, *Retirement Choices,* Gateway Books, 1987, p. 41.

page 166 THE HOLMES AND RAHE SOCIAL READJUSTMENT RATING SCALE: Thomas H. Holmes and Richard H. Rahe, "The

Social Readjustment: Rating Scale," *Journal of Psychosomatic Research* 11 (1967): 213–18.

Profile: Dave and Melanie Thimgan

page 167 "UNLESS ONE SAYS GOODBYE": Jean Dubuffet's quote appeared in *The New York Times,* obituary, May 15, 1985.

Brainstorming

page 179 TESTS SHOW THAT ADULTS: Michael LeBoeuf, *Imagineering,* Berkley Books, 1980, p. 83.

Chapter 7: Taking Action

page 188 "YOU HAVE BRAINS IN YOUR HEAD": From *Oh, the Places You'll Go!* by Dr. Seuss, Random House, 1990, p. 1. Copyright © 1990 by Theodor S. Geisel and Audrey S. Geisel, Trustees under Trust Agreement dated August 27, 1984. Reprinted by permission of Random House, Inc.

page 188 "BETWEEN WISHING AND HAVING": Leslie Camerson-Bandler, David Gordon, and Michael Lebeau, *Know How: Guided Programs for Inventing Your Own Best Future,* Real People Press, 1985, p. 51.

Profile: Bob and Megan Harris

page 201 BOB'S BOOK: Robert W. Harris, *Gypsying After 40: A Guide to Adventure & Self Discovery,* John Muir Publications, 1987, p. 26.

pages 203–7 FROM THE MANUSCRIPT OF HIS NEXT BOOK: Bob's next book is tentatively titled *From Here to 100: A Guide to the Best Years of Your Life.*

Mind-Mapping

page 214 MIND-MAPPING IS AN ORGANIZATIONAL TECHNIQUE: Tony Buzan, *Use Both Sides of Your Brain,* E. P. Dutton, 1983, pp. 16, 86–115, 145–147, 91.

A Master Plan

page 216 "FAILING TO PLAN": Merrill E. Douglass and Donna N. Douglass, *Manage Your Time, Manage Your Work, Manage Yourself,* AMACOM, 1980, p. 260.

INDEX

19.00